Religion

Cultural Memory
in
the
Present

Mieke Bal and Hent de Vries, Editors

Religion

Edited by
Jacques Derrida and Gianni Vattimo

Stanford University Press
Stanford, California

Stanford University Press
Stanford, California

First published in France as *La Religion: Seminaire de Capri* by
Éditions de Seuil et Éditions Laterza
Originating publishers of the English edition:
Polity Press in association with Blackwell Publishers Ltd.

First published in the U.S.A. by Stanford University Press, 1998

Printed in Great Britain

Cloth ISBN 0–8047–3486–0
Paper ISBN 0–8047–3487–9

LC 98–60374

This book is printed on acid-free paper.

Contents

Circumstances

Gianni Vattimo

A few circumstantial remarks are called for here, not on religion, but on the genesis of this initiative. In 1992, Giuseppe Laterza devised a plan to extend our *Italian Philosophical Yearbook* venture by creating a *European Yearbook*. He entrusted the task to Jacques Derrida and myself, and it merely remained to choose the theme. Religion came to mind and I spoke of this to Maurizio Ferraris. Not long afterwards, in November of the same year, before talking with Thierry Marchaisse of Éditions du Seuil, Maurizio Ferraris and Giuseppe Laterza put the plan to Derrida, asking him also to choose the subject: again, the answer was religion.

This coincidence, which, lying as it does halfway between pre-established harmony and pure chance, is known as the 'spirit of the times', seemed sufficient reason to accept the centrality of that thematic argument. Times have doubtless changed since Hegel wrote that the basic sentiment of his time was expressed in the proposition 'God is dead.' But is 'our' time (which, like that of Hegel, begins with the birth of Christ) really so different? And is the phenomenon, known rightly or wrongly as the 'religious revival' (though more in parliaments, terrorism and the media than in the churches, which continue to empty), really anything other than 'the death of God'? That is the question we asked ourselves, as no doubt everyone else is doing today, and it is the question we put to the friends and colleagues we invited to collaborate with us.

Since the spirit of the times is not the Holy Spirit, it seemed that to write to colleagues requesting essays 'on religion' was a step that was more problematic than ever. It was for this reason that we organized a seminar, held, thanks to the generosity of the Instituto Italiano per gli studi filosofici, at Capri. Our warm thanks go, as ever, to the president of that institute, Gerardo Marotta, and to its secretary, Antonio Gargano. It is this meeting, which took place on 28 February and 1 March 1994, that is occasionally referred to in the essays which follow, particularly Jacques Derrida's.

In conclusion, we would like to thank all the friends who replied to our invitation by coming to Capri and who have submitted the fruits of their reflections to us within the prescribed time limits. Our thanks go most particularly to Hans-Georg Gadamer who, like Plato's Parmenides, was not daunted by the seas of *logoi* which had once again to be crossed.

1

Faith and Knowledge: the Two Sources of 'Religion' at the Limits of Reason Alone

Jacques Derrida

Italics

(1) *How 'to talk religion'? Of religion? Singularly of religion, today? How dare we speak of it in the singular without fear and trembling, this very day? And so briefly and so quickly? Who would be so imprudent as to claim that the issue here is both identifiable and new? Who would be so presumptuous as to rely on a few aphorisms? To give oneself the necessary courage, arrogance or serenity, therefore, perhaps one must pretend for an instant to abstract, to abstract from everything or almost everything, in a certain way. Perhaps one must take one's chance in resorting to the most concrete and most accessible, but also the most barren and desert-like, of all abstractions.*

Should one save oneself by abstraction or save oneself from abstraction? Where is salvation, safety? (In 1807, Hegel writes: 'Who thinks abstractly?': 'Thinking? Abstract? – Sauve qui peut!' *he begins by saying, and precisely in French, in order to translate the cry –* 'Rette sich, wer kann!' *– of that traitor who would flee, in a single movement, thought and abstraction and metaphysics: like the 'plague'.)*

(2) Save, be saved, save oneself. *Pretext for a first question: can a discourse on religion be dissociated from a discourse on salvation: which is to say, on the holy, the sacred, the safe and sound, the unscathed* <indemne>,[1] *the immune (*sacer, sanctus, heilig, *holy, and their alleged equivalents in so many languages)? And salvation, is it necessarily redemption, before or after evil, fault or sin? Now, where* is *evil* <le mal>*? Where is evil* today, *at present? Suppose that there was an exemplary and unprecedented figure of evil, even of that radical evil which seems to mark our time as no other. Is it by identifying this evil that one will accede to what might be the figure or promise of salvation for our time, and thus the singularity of the religious whose return is proclaimed in every newspaper?*

Eventually, we would therefore like to link the question of religion to that of the evil of abstraction. To radical abstraction. Not to the abstract figure of death, of evil or of the sickness of death, but to the forms of evil that are traditionally tied to radical extirpation *and therefore to the deracination of abstraction, passing by way – but only much later – of those sites* of abstraction *that are the machine, technics, technoscience and above all the transcendence of tele-technology. 'Religion and mechane', 'religion and cyberspace', 'religion and the numeric', 'religion and digitality', 'religion and virtual space–time': in order to take the measure of these themes in a short treatise, within the limits assigned us, to conceive a small discursive machine which, however finite and perfectible, would not be too powerless.*

In order to think religion today abstractly, *we will take these powers of abstraction as our point of departure, in order to risk, eventually, the following hypothesis: with respect to all these forces of abstraction and of dissociation (deracination, delocalization, disincarnation, formalization, universalizing schematization, objectification, telecommunication etc.), 'religion'* is at the same time *involved in reacting antagonistically and reaffirmatively outbidding itself.* In this very place, *knowledge and faith, technoscience ('capitalist' and fiduciary)* and *belief, credit, trustworthiness, the act of faith will always have made common cause, bound to one another by the band of their opposition. Whence the aporia – a certain absence of way, path, issue, salvation – and the two sources.*

(3) *To play the card of abstraction, and the aporia of the* no-way-out, *perhaps one must first withdraw to a desert, or even*

isolate oneself on an island. And tell a short story that would not be a myth. Genre: 'Once upon a time', just once, one day, *on an island or in the desert, imagine, in order to 'talk religion', several* men, *philosophers, professors, hermeneuticians, hermits or anchorites, took the time to mimic a small, esoteric and egalitarian, friendly and fraternal community. Perhaps it would be necessary in addition to* situate *such arguments, limit them in time and space, speak of the place and the setting, the moment past,* one day, *date the fugitive and the ephemeral, singularize, act as though one were keeping a diary out of which one were going to tear a few pages. Law of the genre: the ephemeris (and already you are speaking inexhaustibly of the day). Date: 28 February 1994. Place: an island, the isle of Capri. A hotel, a table around which we speak among friends, almost without any* order, *without* agenda, *without order of the day, no watchword* <mot d'ordre> *save for a single word, the clearest and most obscure:* religion. *We believe we can pretend to believe – fiduciary act – that we share in some pre-understanding. We act as though we had some common sense of what 'religion' means through the languages that we believe (how much belief already, to this moment, to this very day!) we know how to speak. We believe in the minimal trustworthiness of this word. Like Heidegger, concerning what he calls the* Faktum *of the vocabulary of being (at the beginning of* Sein und Zeit*), we believe (or believe it is obligatory that) we pre-understand the meaning of this word, if only to be able to question and in order to interrogate ourselves on this subject. Well – we will have to return to this much later – nothing is less pre-assured than such a* Faktum *(in both of these cases, precisely) and the entire question of religion comes down,* perhaps, *to this lack of assurance.*

(4) *At the beginning of a preliminary exchange, around the table, Gianni Vattimo proposes that I improvise a few suggestions. If I may be permitted, I would like to recall them here, in italics, in a sort of schematic and telegraphic preface. Other propositions, doubtless, emerged in a text of different character that I wrote afterwards, cramped by the merciless limits of time and space. An utterly different story, perhaps, but, from near or afar, the memory of words risked in the beginning, that day, will continue to dictate what I write.*

I had at first proposed to bring to the light of day of reflection, misconstruing or denying it as little as possible, an effective and unique situation – that in which we then found ourselves: facts, a common commitment, a date, a place. We had in truth agreed to respond to a double proposition, *at once philosophical and editorial, which in turn immediately raised a* double question: *of language and of nation. Now if, today, the 'question of religion' actually appears in a new and different light, if there is an unprecedented resurgence, both global and planetary, of this ageless thing, then what is at stake is language, certainly – and more precisely the idiom, literality, writing, that forms the element of all revelation and of all* belief, *an element that ultimately is irreducible and untranslatable – but an idiom that above all is inseparable from the social nexus, from the political, familial, ethnic, communitarian nexus, from the nation and from the people: from autochthony, blood and soil, and from the ever more problematic relation to citizenship and to the state. In these times, language and nation form the historical body of all religious passion. Like this meeting of philosophers, the international publication that was proposed to us turns out to be first of all 'Western', and then confided, which is also to say confined, to several European languages, those that 'we' speak here in Capri, on this Italian island: German, Spanish, French, Italian.*

(5) *We are not far from Rome, but are are no longer in Rome. Here we are literally isolated for two days, insulated on the heights of Capri, in the difference between the Roman and the Italic, the latter potentially symbolizing everything that can incline – at a certain remove from the Roman in general. To think 'religion' is to think the 'Roman'. This can be done neither in Rome nor too far from Rome. A chance or necessity for recalling the history of something like 'religion': everything done or said* in its name *ought to keep the critical memory of this appellation. European, it was first of all Latin. Here, then, is a given whose figure at least, as limit, remains contingent and significant at the same time. It demands to be taken into account, reflected, thematized, dated. Difficult to say 'Europe' without connoting: Athens–Jerusalem–Rome–Byzantium, wars of Religion, open war over the appropriation of Jerusalem and of Mount Moriah, over the 'here I am' of Abraham or of Ibrahim before the extreme*

'sacrifice' demanded of him, the absolute offering of the beloved son, the demanded putting-to-death or death given to the unique descendant, repetition suspended on the eve of all Passion. Yesterday (yes, yesterday, truly, just a few days ago), there was the massacre of Hebron at the Tomb of the Patriarchs, a place held in common and symbolic trench of the religions called 'Abrahamic'. We represent and speak four different languages, but our common 'culture', let's be frank, is more manifestly Christian, barely even Judaeo-Christian. No Muslim is among us, alas, even for this preliminary discussion, just at the moment when it is towards Islam, perhaps, that we ought to begin by turning our attention. No representative of other cults either. Not a single woman! We ought to take this into account: speaking on behalf of these mute witnesses without speaking for them, in place of them, and drawing from this all sorts of consequences.

(6) *Why is this phenomenon, so hastily called the 'return of religions', so difficult to think? Why is it so surprising? Why does it particularly astonish those who believed naïvely that an alternative opposed Religion, on the one side, and on the other, Reason, Enlightenment, Science, Criticism (Marxist Criticism, Nietzschean Genealogy, Freudian Psychoanalysis and their heritage), as though the one could not but put an end to the other? On the contrary, it is an entirely different schema that would have to be taken as one's point of departure in order to try to think the 'return of the religious'. Can the latter be reduced to what the* doxa *confusedly calls 'fundamentalism', 'fanaticism' or, in French, 'integrism'? Here perhaps we have one of our preliminary questions, able to measure up to the historical urgency. And among the Abrahamic religions, among the 'fundamentalisms' or the 'integrisms' that are developing universally, for they are at work today in all religions, what, precisely, of Islam? But let us not make use of this name too quickly. Everything that is hastily grouped under the reference to 'Islam'* seems *today to retain some sort of geopolitical or global prerogative, as a result of the nature of its physical violences, of certain of its declared violations of the democratic model and of international law (the 'Rushdie case' and many others – and the 'right to literature'), as a result of both the archaic and modern form of its crimes 'in the name of religion', as a result of its demographic dimensions, of its phallocentric and theologico-*

political figures. Why? Discernment is required: Islam is not Islamism and we should never forget it, but the latter operates in the name of *the former, and thus emerges the grave question of the name.*

(7) *Never treat as an accident the force of the name in what happens, occurs or is said* in the name of *religion, here in the name of Islam. For, directly or not, the theologico-political, like all the concepts plastered over these questions, beginning with that of democracy or of secularization, even of the right to literature, is not merely European, but Graeco-Christian, Graeco-Roman. Here we are confronted by the overwhelming questions of the name and of everything 'done in the name of': questions of the name or noun 'religion', of the names of God, of whether the proper name belongs to the system of language or not, hence, of its untranslatability but also of its iterability (which is to say, of that which makes it a site of repeatability, of idealization and therefore, already, of* techné, *of technoscience, of tele-technoscience in calling at a distance), of its link to the performativity of calling in prayer (which, as Aristotle says, is neither true nor false), of its bond to that which, in all performativity, as in all address and attestation, appeals to the faith of the other and deploys itself therefore in a pledge of faith.*

(8) Light takes place. *And the day. The coincidence of the rays of the sun and topographical inscription will never be separated: phenomenology of religion, religion as phenomenology, enigma of the Orient, of the Levant and of the Mediterranean in the geography of appearing* <paraître>. *Light (*phos*), wherever this* arché *commands or begins discourse and takes the initiative in general (*phos, phainesthai, phantasma, *hence spectre, etc.), as much in the discourse of philosophy as in the discourses of a revelation (*Offenbarung*) or of a revealability (*Offenbarkeit*), of a possibility more originary than manifestation. More originary, which is to say, closer to the source, to the sole and same source. Everywhere light dictates that which even yesterday was naïvely construed to be pure of all religion or even opposed to it and whose future must today be rethought (*Aufklärung, Lumières, *Enlightenment,* Illuminismo*). Let us not forget: even when it did not dispose of any common term to 'designate', as Benveniste*

notes, 'religion itself, the cult, or the priest, or even any of the personal gods', the Indo-European language already concurred in 'the very notion of "god" (deiwos)*, of which the "proper meaning" is "luminous" and "celestial"'.*[2]

(9) *In this same light, and under the same sky, let us this day name* three places: *the island, the Promised Land, the desert. Three aporetical places: with no way out or any assured path, without itinerary or point of arrival, without an exterior with a predictable map and a* calculable *programme. These three places shape our horizon, here and now. (But since thinking and speaking are called for here, they will be difficult within the assigned limits, and a certain absence of horizon. Paradoxically, the absence of horizon conditions the future itself. The emergence of the event ought to puncture every horizon of expectation. Whence the apprehension of an abyss in these places, for example a desert in the desert, there where one neither can nor should see coming what ought or could* – perhaps – *be yet to come. What is still left to come.)*

(10) *Is it a coincidence if we – almost all of us* Mediterranean *by origin and each of us* Mediterranean *by a sort of magnetism – have, despite many differences, all been oriented by a certain phenomenology (again light)? We who today have come together to meet on this island, and who ourselves must have made or accepted this choice, more or less secretly, is it a coincidence if all of us, one day, have been tempted both by a certain dissidence with respect to Husserlian phenomenology and by a hermeneutics whose discipline owes so much to the exegesis of religious texts? Hence the even more pressing obligation: not to forget those, <of either gender> whom this implicit contract or this 'being-together' is obliged to exclude. We should have, we ought to have, begun by allowing them to speak.*

(11) *Let us also remember what, rightly or wrongly, I hold provisionally to be evident: that, whatever our relation to religion may be, and to this or that religion, we are not priests bound by a ministry, nor theologians, nor qualified, competent representatives of religion, nor enemies of religion as such, in the sense that certain so-called Enlightenment philosophers are thought to have*

been. But we also share, it seems to me, something else – let us designate it cautiously – an unreserved taste, if not an unconditional preference, for what, in politics, is called republican democracy as a universalizable model, binding philosophy to the public 'cause', to the res publica, *to 'public-ness', once again to the light of day, once again to the 'lights' of the Enlightenment* <aux Lumières>, *once again to the enlightened virtue of public space, emancipating it from all external power (non-lay, non-secular), for example from religious dogmatism, orthodoxy or authority (that is, from a certain rule of the* doxa *or of belief, which, however, does not mean from all faith). In a less analogical manner (but I shall return to this later) and at least as long and in so far as we continue speaking here together, we shall doubtless attempt to transpose, here and now, the circumspect and suspensive attitude, a certain* epoché *that consists – rightly or wrongly, for the issue is serious – in thinking religion or making it appear 'within the limits of reason alone'.*

(**12**) *Related question: what of this 'Kantian' gesture today? What would a book be like today which, like Kant's, is entitled,* Religion within the Limits of Reason Alone? *This* epoché *also gives its chance to a political event, as I have tried to suggest elsewhere.*[3] *It even belongs to the history of democracy, notably when theological discourse was obliged to assume the forms of the* via negativa *and even there, where it seems to have prescribed reclusive communities, initiatic teachings, hierarchy, esoteric insularity or the desert.*[4]

(**13**) *Before the island – and Capri will never be Patmos – there will have been the Promised Land. How to improvise and allow oneself to be surprised in speaking of it? How not to fear and how not to tremble before the unfathomable immensity of this theme? The figure of the Promised Land – is it not also the essential bond between the promise of place and historicity? By historicity, we could understand today more than one thing. First of all, a sharpened specificity of the concept of religion, the history of its history, and of the genealogies intermingled in its languages and in its name. Distinctions are required: faith has not always been and will not always be identifiable with religion, nor, another point, with theology. All sacredness and all holiness are* *not necessarily, in the strict sense of the term, if there is one, religious. We will have to return to the emergence and the semantics of this noun 'religion', passing by way both of its Roman Occidentality and of the bond it has contracted with the Abrahamic revelations. The latter are not solely events. Such events only happen by taking on the meaning of engaging the historicity of history – and the eventfulness* <événementialité> *of the event as such. As distinct from other experiences of 'faith', of the 'holy', of the 'unscathed' and of the 'safe and sound', of the 'sacred', of the 'divine'; as distinct from other structures that one would be tempted to call by a dubious analogy 'religions', the Testamentary and Koranic revelations are inseparable from a* historicity *of revelation itself. The messianic or eschatological horizon delimits this historicity, to be sure, but only by virtue of having previously inaugurated it.*

(14) *With this emerges another historical dimension, a historicity different from what we evoked a moment ago, unless the two overlap in an infinite mirroring* <en abyme>. *How can this history of historicity be taken into account so as to permit the treatment today of* religion within the limits of reason alone? *How can a history of political and technoscientific reason be inscribed there and thus* brought up to date, *but also a history of radical evil, of its figures that are never simply figures and that – this is the whole evil – are always inventing a new evil? The radical 'perversion of the human heart' of which Kant speaks,*[5] *we now know is* not one, *nor given once and for all, as though it were capable only of inaugurating figures or tropes of itself. Perhaps we could ask ourselves whether this agrees or not with Kant's intention when he recalls that Scripture does indeed 'represent' the historical and temporal character of radical evil even if it is only a 'mode of representation' (*Vorstellungsart*) used by Scripture in function of human 'frailty';*[6] *and this, notwithstanding that Kant struggles to account for the rational origin of an evil that remains inconceivable to reason, by affirming simultaneously that the interpretation of Scripture exceeds the competence of reason and that of all the 'public religions' that ever were, only the Christian religion will have been a 'moral' religion (end of the first* General Remark*). Strange proposition, but which must be taken as seriously as possible in each of its premises.*

(15) *There are in effect for Kant, and he says so explicitly, only* two *families of religion, and in all* two *sources or* two *strata of religion – and hence two genealogies of which it still must be asked why they share the same name whether proper or common <noun>: the* religion of cult alone (des blossen Cultus) *seeks 'favours of God', but at bottom, and in essence, it does not act, teaching only prayer and desire. Man is not obliged to become better, be it through the remission of sins.* Moral (moralische) religion, *by contrast, is interested in the good conduct of life (*die Religion des guten Lebenswandels*); it enjoins him to* action, *it subordinates* knowledge *to it and* dissociates *it from itself, prescribing that man become better by* acting *to this end, in accordance with the following principle: '"It is not essential and hence not necessary for everyone to know what God does or has done for his salvation", but it is essential to know what* man himself must do *in order to become worthy of this assistance.' Kant thus defines a 'reflecting (*reflektierende*) faith', which is to say, a concept whose possibility might well open the space of our discussion. Because it does not depend essentially upon any historical revelation and thus agrees with the rationality of purely practical reason,* reflecting faith *favours* good will beyond all knowledge. *It is thus opposed to 'dogmatic (*dogmatische*) faith'. If it breaks with this 'dogmatic faith', it is in so far as the latter claims to know and thereby ignores the difference between faith and knowledge*

Now the principle of such an opposition – and this is why I emphasize it – could not be simply definitional, taxonomic or theoretical; it serves not simply to classify heterogeneous religions under the same name; it could also define, even for us today, a place of conflict, if not of war, in the Kantian sense. Even today, albeit provisionally, it could help us structure a problematic.

Are we ready to measure without flinching the implications and consequences of the Kantian thesis? The latter seems strong, simple and dizzying: the Christian religion would be the only truly 'moral' religion; a mission would thus be reserved exclusively for it and for it alone: that of liberating a 'reflecting faith'. It necessarily follows therefore that pure morality and Christianity are indissociable in their essence and in their concept. If there is no Christianity without pure morality, it is because Christian revelation teaches us something essential about the very idea of morality. From this it follows that the idea of a morality that is pure but non-Christian would be absurd; it would exceed both understanding and reason, it would be a contradiction in terms. The unconditional universality of the categorical imperative is evangelical. The moral law inscribes itself at the bottom of our hearts like a memory of the Passion. When it addresses us, it either speaks the idiom of the Christian – or is silent.

This thesis of Kant (which we would like later to relate to what we will call 'globalatinization' *<mondialatinisation>)*[7] *– is it not also, at the core of its content, Nietzsche's thesis at the same time that he is conducting an inexpiable war against Kant? Perhaps Nietzsche would have said 'Judaeo-Christian', but the place occupied by Saint Paul among his privileged targets clearly demonstrates that it was Christianity, a certain internalizing movement within Christianity, that was his primary enemy and that bore for him the gravest responsibility. The Jews and European Judaism even constituted in his eyes a desperate attempt to resist, in so far as there was any resistance, a last-ditch protest from within, directed against a certain Christianity.*

This thesis doubtless tells us something about the history of the world – nothing less. Let us indicate, rather schematically, at least two of its possible consequences, and two paradoxes among many others:

1. *In the definition of 'reflecting faith' and of what binds the idea of pure morality indissolubly to Christian revelation, Kant recurs to the logic of a simple* principle, *that which we cited a moment ago verbatim: in order to conduct oneself in a moral manner, one must act as though God did not exist or no longer concerned himself with our salvation. This shows who is moral and who is therefore Christian, assuming that a Christian owes it to himself to be moral: no longer turn towards God at the moment of acting in good faith; act as though God had abandoned us. In enabling us to think (but also to suspend in theory) the existence of God, the freedom or the immortality of the soul, the union of virtue and of happiness, the concept of 'postulate' of practical reason guarantees this radical dissociation and assumes ultimately rational and philosophical responsibility, the consequence* here in this world, in experience, *of this*

abandonment. Is this not another way of saying that Christianity can only answer to its moral calling and morality, to its Christian calling if it endures in this world, in phenomenal history, the death of God, well beyond the figures of the Passion? That Christianity is the death of God thus announced and recalled by Kant to the modernity of the Enlightenment? Judaism and Islam would thus be perhaps the last two monotheisms to revolt against everything that, in the Christianizing of our world, signifies the death of God, death in God, two non-pagan monotheisms that do not accept death any more than multiplicity in God (the Passion, the Trinity etc.), two monotheisms still alien enough at the heart of Graeco-Christian, Pagano-Christian Europe, alienating themselves from a Europe that signifies the death of God, by recalling at all costs *that 'monotheism' signifies no less faith in the One, and in the living One, than belief in a single God.*

2 *With regard to this logic, to its formal rigour and to its possibilities, does not Heidegger move in a different direction? He insists, indeed, in* Sein und Zeit *upon the character of originary conscience (*Gewissen*), being-responsible-guilty-indebted (*Schuldigsein*) or attestation (*Bezeugung*) as both* pre-moral *(or pre-ethical, if 'ethical' still refers to that meaning of* ethos *considered by Heidegger to be derivative, inadequate and of recent origin) and* pre-religious. *He would thus appear to go back before and beyond that which joins morality to religion, meaning here, to Christianity. This would in principle allow for the repetition of the Nietzschean genealogy of morals, but dechristianizing it where necessary and extirpating whatever Christian vestiges it still might contain. A strategy all the more involuted and necessary for a Heidegger who seems unable to stop either settling accounts with Christianity or distancing himself from it – with all the more violence in so far as it is already too late, perhaps, for him to deny certain proto-Christian motifs in the ontological repetition and existential analytics.*

What are we calling here a 'logic', its 'formal rigour' and its 'possibilities'? The law itself, a necessity that, it is clear, undoubtedly programmes an infinite spiral of outbidding, a maddening instability among these 'positions'. The latter can be occupied successively or simultaneously by the same 'subjects'. From one religion to the other, the 'fundamentalisms' and the 'integrisms' hyperbolize today this outbidding. They exacerbate it at a moment when – we shall return to this later – globalatinization (this strange alliance of Christianity, as the experience of the death of God, and tele-technoscientific capitalism) is at the same time hegemonic and finite, ultra-powerful and in the process of exhausting itself. Simply, those who are involved in this outbidding can pursue it from all angles, adopting all 'positions', either simultaneously or successively, to the uttermost limit.

Is this not the madness, the absolute anachrony of our time, the disjunction of all self-contemporaneity, the veiled and cloudy day of every today?

(16) *This definition of* reflecting faith *appears in the first of the four* Parerga *added at the end of each section of* Religion within the Limits of Reason Alone. *These* Parerga *are not integral parts of the book; they 'do not belong within' 'religion in the limits of pure reason', they 'border upon' it. I stress this for reasons that are in part theo-topological, even theo-architectonic: these* Parerga *situate perhaps the fringe where we might be able, today, to inscribe our reflections. All the more since the first* Parergon, *added in the second edition, thereby defines the secondary task (*parergon*) which, concerning what is morally indisputable, would consist in surmounting all the difficulties connected to transcendent questions. When translated into the element of religion, moral ideas pervert the purity of their transcendence. They can do this in two times two ways, and the resulting square could today frame, providing that the appropriate transpositions are respected, a programme of analysis of the forms of evil perpetrated at the four corners of the world 'in the name of religion'. We will have to limit ourselves to an indication of the titles of this programme and, first, of the criteria (nature/superna-rural, internal/external, theoretical elucidation/practical action, constative/performative): (a) the allegedly* internal *experience (of the effects of grace): the* fanaticism *or* enthusiasm *of the illuminated (*Schwärmerei*); (b) the allegedly* external *experience (of the miraculous):* superstition (Aberglaube)*; (c) the alleged elucidations of the* understanding *in the consideration of the supernatural* *(secrets,* Geheimnisse*): illuminatism, the frenzy of the initiates; (d) the risky attempt of acting upon the supernatural (means of obtaining grace): thaumaturgy.*

When Marx holds the critique of religion to be the premise of all ideology-critique, when he holds religion to be the ideology par excellence, even for the matrix of all ideology and of the very movement of fetishization, does his position not fall, whether he would have wanted it or not, within the parergonal framework *of this kind of rational criticism? Or rather, more plausible but also more difficult to demonstrate, does he not already deconstruct the fundamentally Christian axiomatics of Kant? This could be one of our questions, the most obscure one no doubt, because it is not at all certain that the very principles of the Marxist critique do not still appeal to a heterogeneity between faith and knowledge, between practical justice and cognition. This heterogeneity, by the way, may ultimately not be irreducible to the inspiration or to the spirit of* Religion within the Limits of Reason Alone. *All the more since these figures of evil discredit,* as much *as they accredit, the 'credit' which is the act of faith. They exclude as much as they explain, they demand perhaps more than ever this recourse to religion, to the principle of faith, even if it is only that of a radically fiduciary form of the 'reflecting faith' already mentioned. And it is this mechanics, this machine-like return of religion, that I would here like to question.*

(17) *How then to think – within the limits of reason alone – a religion which, without again becoming 'natural religion', would today be effectively universal? And which, for that matter, would no longer be restricted to a paradigm that was Christian or even Abrahamic? What would be the project of such a 'book'? For with* Religion within the Limits of Reason Alone, *there is a World involved that is also an Old–New Book or Testament. Does this project retain a meaning or a chance? A geopolitical chance or meaning? Or does the idea itself remain, in its origin and in its end, Christian? And would this necessarily be a limit, a limit like any other? A Christian – but also a Jew or a Muslim – would be someone who would harbour doubts about this limit, about the* existence *of this limit or about its* reducibility *to any other limit, to the current figure of limitation.*

(18) *Keeping these questions in mind, we might be able to gauge two temptations. In their schematic principle, one would be 'Hegelian': ontotheology which determines absolute knowledge as the truth of religion, in the course of the final movement described in the conclusions of* The Phenomenology of Spirit *or of* Faith and Knowledge, *which announces in effect a 'religion of modern times' (*Religion der neuen Zeit*) founded on the sentiment that 'God himself is dead.' 'Infinite pain' is still only a 'moment' (*rein als Moment*), and the* moral sacrifice *of empirical existence only dates the absolute Passion or the speculative Good Friday (*spekulativer Karfreitag*). Dogmatic philosophies and natural religions should disappear and, out of the greatest 'asperity', the harshest impiety, out of kenosis and the void of the most serious privation of God (*Gottlosigkeit*), ought to resuscitate the most serene liberty in its highest totality. Distinct from faith, from prayer or from sacrifice, ontotheology destroys religion, but, yet another paradox, it is also perhaps what informs, on the contrary, the theological and ecclesiastical, even religious, development of faith. The other* temptation *(perhaps there are still good reasons for keeping this word) would be 'Heideggerian': beyond such ontotheology, where the latter ignores both prayer and sacrifice. It would accordingly be necessary that a 'revealability' (*Offenbarkeit*) be allowed to reveal itself, with a light that would manifest (itself) more originarily than all revelation (*Offenbarung*). Moreover, the distinction would have to made between* theo-*logy (the discourse on God, faith or revelation) and* theio-*logy (discourse on being-divine, on the essence and the divinity of the divine). The experience of the sacred, the holy or the saved (*heilig*) would have to be reawakened* unscathed. *We would have to devote all our attention to this chain, taking as our point of departure this last word (*heilig*), this German word whose semantic history seems to resist the rigorous dissociation that Levinas wishes to maintain between a natural sacredness that would be 'pagan', even Graeco-Christian, and the holiness* <saintété>[8] *of (Jewish) law, before or under the Roman religion. As for the 'Roman',[9] does not Heidegger proceed, from* Sein und Zeit *on, with an ontologico-existential repetition and rehearsal of Christian motifs that at the same time are hollowed out and reduced to their originary possibility? A pre-Roman possibility, precisely? Did he not confide to Löwith, several years earlier, in 1921, that in order to assume the spiritual* *heritage that constitutes the facticity of his 'I am', he ought to have said: 'I am a "Christian theologian"'? Which does not mean 'Roman'. To this we shall return.*

(19) *In its most abstract form, then, the aporia within which we are struggling would perhaps be the following: is revealability (*Offenbarkeit*) more originary than revelation (*Offenbarung*), and hence independent of all religion? Independent in the structures of its experience and in the analytics relating to them? Is this not the place in which 'reflecting faith' at least originates, if not this faith itself? Or rather, inversely, would the event of revelation have consisted in revealing revealability itself, and the origin of light, the originary light, the very invisibility of visibility? This is perhaps what the believer or the theologian might say here, in particular the Christian of originary Christendom, of that* Urchristentum *in the Lutheran tradition to which Heidegger acknowledges owing so much.*

(20) *Nocturnal light, therefore, more and more obscure. Let us step up the pace in order to finish: in view of a* third place *that could well have been* more than *archi-originary, the most anarchic and anarchivable place possible, not the island nor the Promised Land, but a certain desert, that which makes possible, opens, hollows or infinitizes the other. Ecstasy or existence of the most extreme abstraction. That which would orient here 'in' this desert, without pathway and without interior, would still be the possibility of a* religio *and of a* relegere, *to be sure, but before the 'link' of* religare, *problematic etymology and doubtless reconstructed, before the link between men as such or between man and the divinity of the god it would also be like the condition of the 'link' reduced to its minimal semantic determination: the holding-back* <halte> *of scruple (*religio*), the restraint of shame, a certain* Verhaltenheit *as well, of which Heidegger speaks in the* Beiträge zur Philosophie, *the respect, the responsibility of repetition in the wager* <gage> *of decision or of affirmation (*re-legere*) which links up with itself in order to link up with the other. Even if it is called the social nexus, link to the other in general, this fiduciary 'link' would precede all determinate community, all positive religion, every onto-anthropo-theological horizon. It would link pure singularities prior to any social or political determination,* *prior to all intersubjectivity, prior even to the opposition between the sacred (or the holy) and the profane. This can therefore resemble a desertification, the risk of which remains undeniable, but it can – on the contrary – also* render possible *precisely what it appears to threaten. The abstraction of the desert can thereby open the way to everything from which it withdraws. Whence the ambiguity or the duplicity of the religious trait or retreat, of its abstraction or of its subtraction. This deserted re-treat thus makes way for the repetition of that which will have* given way *precisely for that in whose name one would protest against it, against that which only resembles the void and the indeterminacy of mere abstraction.*

Since everything has to be said in two *words, let us give* two names *to the duplicity of these origins. For here origin is duplicity itself, the one and the other. Let us name these two sources, these two fountains or these two tracks that are still invisible in the desert. Let us lend them two names that are still 'historical', there where a certain concept of history itself becomes inappropriate. To do this, let us refer* – provisionally, *I emphasize this, and for pedagogical or rhetorical reasons – first to the 'messianic', and second to the* chora, *as I have tried to do more minutely, more patiently and, I hope, more rigorously elsewhere.*[10]

(21) First name*: the* messianic, *or messianicity without messianism. This would be the opening to the future or to the coming of the other as the advent of justice, but without horizon of expectation and without prophetic prefiguration. The coming of the other can only emerge as a singular event when no anticipation* sees it coming, *when the other and death – and radical evil – can come as a surprise at any moment. Possibilities that both open and can always interrupt history, or at least the* ordinary course *of history. But this ordinary course is that of which philosophers, historians and often also the classical theoreticians of the revolution speak. Interrupting or tearing history itself apart, doing it by deciding, in a decision that can consist in letting the other come and that can take the apparently passive form of the* other's decision*: even there where it appears in itself, in me, the decision is moreover always that of the other, which does not exonerate me of responsibility. The messianic exposes itself to absolute surprise and, even if it always takes the phenomenal form of peace or of*

justice, it ought, exposing itself so abstractly, be prepared (waiting without awaiting itself*) for the best as for the worst, the one never coming without opening the possibility of the other. At issue there is a 'general structure of experience'. This messianic dimension does not depend upon any messianism, it follows no determinate revelation, it belongs properly to no Abrahamic religion (even if I am obliged here, 'among ourselves', for essential reasons of language and of place, of culture, of a provisional rhetoric and a historical strategy of which I will speak later, to continue giving it names marked by the Abrahamic religions).*

(22) *An invincible desire for justice is linked to this expectation. By definition, the latter is not and ought not to be certain of anything, either through knowledge, consciousness, conscience, foreseeability or any kind of programme as such. This abstract messianicity belongs from the very beginning to the experience of faith, of believing, of a credit that is irreducible to knowledge and of a trust that 'founds' all relation to the other in testimony. This justice, which I distinguish from right, alone allows the hope, beyond all 'messianisms', of a universalizable culture of singularities, a culture in which the abstract possibility of the impossible translation could nevertheless be announced. This justice inscribes itself in advance in the promise, in the act of faith or in the appeal to faith that inhabits every act of language and every address to the other. The universalizable culture of this faith, and not of another or before all others, alone permits a 'rational' and universal discourse on the subject of 'religion'. This messianicity, stripped of everything, as it should, this faith without dogma which makes its way through the risks of absolute night, cannot be contained in any traditional opposition, for example that between reason and mysticism. It is announced wherever, reflecting without flinching, a purely rational analysis brings the following paradox to light: that the foundation of law – law of the law, institution of the institution, origin of the constitution – is a 'performative' event that cannot belong to the set that it founds, inaugurates or justifies. Such an event is unjustifiable within the logic of what it will have opened. It is the decision of the other in the undecidable. Henceforth reason ought to recognize there what Montaigne and Pascal call an undeniable 'mystical foundation of authority'. The* mystical *thus understood allies belief or credit, the*

fiduciary or the trustworthy, the secret (which here signifies 'mystical') to foundation, to knowledge, we will later say also, to science as 'doing', as theory, practice and theoretical practice – which is to say, to a faith, to performativity and to technoscientific or tele-technological performance. Wherever this foundation founds in foundering, wherever it steals away under the ground of what it founds, at the very instant when, losing itself thus in the desert, it loses the very trace of itself and the memory of a secret, 'religion' can only begin and begin again: quasi-automatically, mechanically, machine-like, spontaneously. Spontaneously, *which is to say, as the word indicates, both as the origin of what flows from the source,* sponte sua, *and with the automaticity of the machine. For the best and for the worst, without the slightest assurance or anthropo-theological horizon. Without this desert in the desert, there would be neither act of faith, nor promise, nor future, nor expectancy without expectation of death and of the other, nor relation to the singularity of the other. The chance of this desert in the desert (as of that which* resembles to a fault, *but without reducing itself to, that* via negativa *which makes its way from a Graeco-Judaeo-Christian tradition) is that in uprooting the tradition that bears it, in atheologizing it, this abstraction, without denying faith, liberates a universal rationality and the political democracy that cannot be dissociated from it.*

(23) *The* second name *(or first name prior to all naming), would be* chora, *such as Plato designates it in the* Timaeus[11] *without being able to reappropriate it in a consistent self-interpretation. From the open interior of a corpus, of a system, of a language or a culture,* chora *would situate the abstract spacing,* place itself, *the place of absolute exteriority, but also the place of a bifurcation between two approaches to the desert. Bifurcation between a tradition of the* 'via negativa' *which, in spite of or within its Christian act of birth, accords its possibility to a Greek – Platonic or Plotinian – tradition that persists until Heidegger and beyond: the thought of that which is beyond being (*epekeina tes ousias*). This Graeco-Abrahamic hybridization remains anthropo-theological. In the figures of it known to us, in its culture and in its history, its 'idiom' is not universalizable. It speaks solely at the borders or in view of the Middle-Eastern desert, at the source of monotheistic revelations and of Greece. It is there that we can try*

to determine the place where, on this island today, 'we' persist and insist. If we insist, and we must for some time still, upon the names that are given us as our heritage, it is because, in respect of this borderline place, a new war of religions is redeploying as never before to this day, in an event that is at the same time both interior and exterior. *It inscribes its seismic turbulence directly upon the fiduciary globality of the technoscientific, of the economic, of the political and of the juridical. It brings into play the latter's concepts of the political and of international right, of nationality, of the subjectivity of citizenry, of the sovereignty of states. These hegemonical concepts tend to reign over a world, but only from their finitude: the growing tension of their power is not incompatible, far from it, with their precariousness any more than with their perfectibility. The one can never do anything without recalling itself to the other.*

(24) *The surge* <déferlement> *of 'Islam' will be neither understood nor answered as long as the exterior and interior of this borderline place have not been called into question; as long as one settles for an internal explanation (interior to the history of faith, of religion, of languages or cultures as such), as long as one does not define the passageway between this interior and all the apparently exterior dimensions (technoscientific, tele-biotechnological, which is to say also political and socioeconomic etc.).*

For, in addition to investigating the ontotheologico-political tradition that links Greek philosophy to the Abrahamic revelations, perhaps we must also submit to the ordeal of that which resists such interrogation, which will have always resisted, from within or as though from an exteriority that works and resists inside. Chora, *the 'ordeal of* chora'[12] *would be, at least according to the interpretation I believed justified in attempting, the name for place, a place name, and a rather singular one at that, for that spacing which, not allowing itself to be dominated by any theological, ontological or anthropological instance, without age, without history and more 'ancient' than all oppositions (for example, that of sensible/intelligible), does not even announce itself as 'beyond being' in accordance with a path of negation, a* via negativa. *As a result,* chora *remains absolutely impassible and heterogeneous to all the processes of historical revelation or of anthropo-theological experience, which at the very least suppose its abstraction. It will never have entered religion and will never permit itself to be sacralized, sanctified, humanized, theologized, cultivated, historicized. Radically heterogeneous to the safe and sound, to the holy and the sacred, it never admits of any* indemnification. *This cannot even be formulated in the present, for* chora *never presents itself as such. It is neither Being, nor the Good, nor God, nor Man, nor History. It will always resist them, will have always been (and no future anterior, even, will have been able to reappropriate, inflect or reflect a* chora *without faith or law) the very place of an infinite resistance, of an infinitely impassible persistence* <restance>*: an utterly faceless other.*

(25) Chora *is nothing (no being, nothing present), but not the Nothing which in the anxiety of* Dasein *would still open the question of being. This Greek noun says in our memory that which is not reappropriable, even by our memory, even by our 'Greek' memory; it says the immemoriality of a desert in the desert of which it is neither a threshold nor a mourning. The question remains open, and with it that of knowing whether this desert can be thought and left to announce itself 'before' the desert that we know (that of the revelations and the retreats, of the lives and deaths of God, of all the figures of kenosis or of transcendence, of* religio *or of historical 'religions'); or whether, 'on the contrary', it is 'from' this last desert that we can glimpse that which precedes the first* <l'avant-premier>, *what I call the desert in the desert. The indecisive oscillation, that reticence (*epoché *or* Verhaltenheit*) already alluded to above (between revelation and revealability,* Offenbarung *and* Offenbarkeit, *between event and possibility or virtuality of the event), must it not be respected for itself? Respect for this singular indecision or for this hyperbolic outbidding between two originarities, the order of the 'revealed' and the order of the 'revealable', is this not at once the chance of every responsible decision and of another 'reflecting faith', of a new 'tolerance'?*

(26) *Let us suppose it agreed upon, among ourselves, that all of us here are for 'tolerance', even if we have not been assigned the mission of promoting it, practising it or founding it. We would be here to try to think what 'tolerance' could henceforth be. I immediately place quotation-marks around this word in order to*

abstract and extract it from its origins. And thereby to announce, through it, through the density of its history, a possibility that would not be solely Christian. For the concept of tolerance, stricto sensu, *belongs first of all to a sort of Christian domesticity. It is* literally, *I mean behind this name, a secret of the Christian community. It was printed, emitted, transmitted and circulated in the name of the Christian faith and would hardly be without relation to the rise, it too Christian, of what Kant calls 'reflecting faith' – and of* pure morality *as that which is distinctively Christian. The lesson of tolerance was first of all an exemplary lesson that the Christian deemed himself alone capable of giving to the world, even if he often had to learn it himself. In this respect, the French Enlightenment,* les Lumières, *was no less essentially Christian than the* Aufklärung. *When it treats of tolerance, Voltaire's* Philosophical Dictionary *reserves a dual privilege for the Christian religion. On the one hand it is exemplarily tolerant, to be sure, it teaches tolerance better than any other religion, before every other religion. In short, a little in the manner of Kant, believe it or not, Voltaire seems to think that Christianity is the sole 'moral' religion, since it is the first to feel itself obliged and capable of setting an example. Whence the ingenuity, and at times the inanity of those who sloganize Voltaire and rally behind his flag in the combat for critical modernity – and, far more seriously, for its future. For, on the other hand, the Voltairian lesson was addressed above all to Christians, 'the most intolerant of all men'.*[13] *When Voltaire accuses the Christian religion and the Church, he invokes the lesson of originary Christianity, 'the times of the first Christians', Jesus and the Apostles, betrayed by 'the Catholic, Apostolic and Roman religion'. The latter is 'in all its ceremonies and in all its dogmas, the opposite of the religion of Jesus'.*[14]

Another 'tolerance' would be in accord with the experience of the 'desert in the desert', it would respect the distance of infinite alterity as singularity. And this respect would still be religio, religio *as scruple or reticence, distance, dissociation, disjunction, coming from the threshold of all religion in the* link of repetition to itself, *the threshold of every social or communitarian link.*[15]

Before and after the logos *which was in the beginning, before and after the Holy Sacrament, before and after the Holy Scriptures.*

Post-scriptum

Crypts . . .

(27) [. . .] **Religion?** Here and now, this very day, if one were still supposed to *speak* of it, of religion, perhaps one could attempt to think it in *itself* or to devote oneself to this task. No doubt, but to try above all to *say* it and to *utter a verdict* concerning it, with the necessary rigour, which is to say, with the reticence, modesty, respect or fervour, in a word the scruple (*religio*) demanded at the very least by that which is or claims to be, in its essence, a religion. As its name indicates, it would be necessary, therefore, one would be tempted to conclude, to speak of this essence with a sort of *religio*-sity. In order not to introduce anything alien, leaving it thus intact, safe, *unscathed*. Unscathed in the experience of the unscathed that it will have wanted to be. Is not the unscathed <*l'indemne*>[16] the very matter – the thing itself – of religion?

But no, on the contrary, someone will say. One would not be speaking *of* it if one were to speak *in its name*, if one were to settle for *reflecting* religion as in a mirror, specularly, religiously. Moreover, someone else might say, or is it the same one, to break with it, even to suspend for an instant one's religious affiliation, has this not been the very resource, since time immemorial, of the most authentic faith or of the most originary sacredness? One must in any case take into account, if possible in an areligious, or even irreligious manner, what religion at present might *be*, as well as what is *said* and *done*, what *is happening* at this very moment, in the world, in history, *in its name*. Wherever religion can no longer reflect or at times assume or bear its name. And one should not say lightly, as though in passing, 'this very day', 'at this very moment' and 'in the world', 'in history', while forgetting what happens *there*, returning to or surprising *us*, still under the name of religion, even in the name of religion. What *happens to us there* concerns precisely the experience and radical interpretation of everything that these words are felt to mean: the unity of a 'world' and of a 'being-in-the-world', the concept of world or of history in its Western tradition (Christian or Graeco-Christian, extending to Kant, Hegel, Husserl, Heidegger), and no less that of *day* as well as that of the *present*. (Much later we will have to get around to scrutinizing these two motifs, each as enigmatic as the other: *presence* unscathed by the present, on the one hand, *and believing* unscathed by belief, on the other; or yet again: the sacrosanct, the safe and sound on the one side, *and* faith, trustworthiness or credit on the other.) Like others before, the new 'wars of religion' are unleashed over the human earth (which is not the world) and struggle even today to control the sky *with finger and eye*: digital systems and virtually immediate panoptical visualization, 'air space', telecommunications satellites, information highways, concentration of capitalistic-mediatic power – in three words, *digital culture, jet* and *TV* without which there could be no religious manifestation today, for example no voyage or discourse of the Pope, no organized emanation <*rayonnement*> of Jewish, Christian or Muslim cults, whether 'fundamentalist'[17] or not. Given this, the cyberspatialized or cyberspaced wars of religion have no stakes other than this determination of the 'world', of 'history', of the 'day' and of the 'present'. The stakes certainly can remain implicit, insufficiently thematized, poorly articulated. By repressing them, on the other hand, many others can also be dissimulated or displaced. Which is to say, as is always the case with the topics of repression, inscribed in other places or other systems; this never occurs without symptoms and fantasies, without spectres (*phantasmata*) to be investigated. In both cases and according to both logics, we ought to take into account every *declared* stake in its greatest radicality as well as asking ourselves what the depths of such radicality might virtually encrypt, down to its very roots. The *declared* stakes already appear to be without limit: what is the 'world', the 'day', the 'present' (hence, all of history, the earth, the humanity of man, the rights of man, the rights of man and of woman, the political and cultural organization of society, the difference between man, god and animal, the phenomenality of the day, the value or 'indemnity' of life, the right to life, the treatment of death etc.)? What is the present, which is to say: what is history? time? being? being in its purity <*dans sa propriété*> (that is, unscathed, safe, sacred, holy, *heilig*)? What of holiness or of sacredness? Are they the same thing? What of the divinity of God? How many meanings can one give to *theion*? Is this a good way to pose the question?

(28) **Religion?** *In the singular?* Perhaps, *may-be* (this should always remain possible) there is *something else*, of course, and other interests (economic, politico-military etc.) behind the new 'wars of religion', behind what presents itself under the name of religion, beyond what defends or attacks in its name, kills, kills itself or kills one another and for that invokes declared stakes, or in other words, names *indemnity* in the light of day. But inversely, if what is thus *happening to us*, as we said, often (but not always) assumes the figures of evil and of the worst in the unprecedented forms of an *atrocious* 'war of religions', the latter in turn does not always speak its name. Because it is not certain that in addition to or in face of the most spectacular and most barbarous crimes of certain 'fundamentalisms' (of the present or of the past), *other* over-armed forces are not *also* leading 'wars of religion', albeit unavowed. Wars or military 'interventions', led by the Judaeo-Christian West in the name of the best causes (of international law, democracy, the sovereignty of peoples, of nations or of states, even of humanitarian imperatives), are they not also, from a certain side, wars of religion? The hypothesis would not necessarily be defamatory, nor even very original, except in the eyes of those who hasten to believe that all these just causes are not only secular but *pure* of all religiosity. To determine a war of religion *as such*, one would have to be certain that one can delimit the religious. One would have to be certain that one can distinguish all the predicates of the religious (and, as we shall see, this is not easy: there are at least *two* families, two strata or sources that overlap, mingle, contaminate each another without ever merging; and just in case things are still too simple, one of the two is precisely the drive to remain unscathed, on the part of that which is allergic to contamination, *save by itself, auto-immunely*). One would have to dissociate the essential traits of the religious as such from those that establish, for example, the concepts of ethics, of the juridical, of the political or of the economic. And yet, nothing is more problematic than such a dissociation. The fundamental concepts that often permit us to isolate or to *pretend* to isolate the *political* – restricting ourselves to this particular circumscription – remain religious or in any case theologico-political. A single example. In one of the most rigorous attempts to isolate in its purity the sphere of the political (notably by separating it from the economic and the religious), in order to

identify the political and the political enemy in wars of religion, such as the Crusades, Carl Schmitt was obliged to acknowledge that the ostensibly purely political categories to which he resorted were the product of a secularization or of a theologico-political heritage. And when he denounced the process of 'depoliticization' or of neutralization of the political that was underway, it was explicitly with respect to a European legal tradition that in his eyes doubtless remained indissociable from 'our' thought of the political.[18] Even supposing that one accepts such premises, the unprecedented forms of today's wars of religion could also imply radical challenges to our project of delimiting the political. They would then constitute a response to everything that our idea of democracy, for example, with all its associated juridical, ethical and political concepts, including those of the sovereign state, of the citizen-subject, of public and private space etc., still entails that is religious, inherited in truth from a determinate religious stratum.

Henceforth, despite the ethical and political urgencies that do not permit **the response** to be put off, reflection upon the Latin noun 'religion' will no longer be held for an academic exercise, a philological embellishment or an etymological luxury: in short, for an alibi destined to suspend judgement or decision, at best for another *epoché*.

(29) Religion, in the *singular*? Response: 'Religion is **the response**.' Is it not there, perhaps, that we must seek the beginning of a response? Assuming, that is, that one knows what *responding* means, and also *responsibility*. Assuming, that is, that one knows it – and believes in it. No response, indeed, without a principle of responsibility: one must respond to the other, before the other and for oneself. And no responsibility without a *given word*, a sworn faith <*foi jurée*>, without a pledge, without an oath, without some *sacrament* or *ius iurandum*. Before even envisaging the semantic history of testimony, of oaths, of the given word (a genealogy and interpretation that are indispensable to whomever hopes to think religion under its proper or secularized forms), before even recalling that some sort of 'I promise the truth' is always at work, and some sort of 'I make this commitment before the other from the moment that I address him, even and perhaps above all to commit perjury', we must formally take note of the fact that **we are already speaking Latin**. We make a point of this in order to recall that the world today speaks Latin (most often via Anglo-American) when it authorizes itself in the *name* of *religion*. Presupposed at the origin of all address, coming from the other *to whom it is also addressed*, the wager <*gageure*> of a sworn promise, taking immediately God as its witness, cannot not but have already, if one can put it this way, engendered God quasi-mechanically. *A priori* ineluctable, a descent of God *ex machina* would stage a transcendental addressing machine. One would thus have begun by posing, retrospectively, the absolute right of anteriority, the absolute 'birthright' <*le droit d'aînesse absolu*> of a One who is not born. For in taking God as witness, even when he is not named in the most 'secular' <*laïque*> pledge of commitment, the oath cannot *not* produce, invoke or convoke him as already there, and therefore as unengendered and unengenderable, prior to being itself: unproducible. And absent in place. Production and reproduction of the unproducible absent in place. Everything begins with the presence of *that* absence. The 'deaths of God', before Christianity, in it and beyond it, are only figures and episodes. The unengenderable thus re-engendered is the empty place. Without God, no absolute witness. No absolute witness to be taken as witness in testifying. But with God, a God that is present, the existence of a third (*terstis, testis*) that is absolute, all attestation becomes superfluous, insignificant or secondary. Testimony, which is to say, testament as well. In the irrepressible invoking of a witness, God would remain then one *name of the witness*, he would be *called* as witness, thus *named*, even if sometimes the named of this name remains unpronounceable, indeterminable, in short: unnameable in his very name; and even if he ought to remain absent, non-existent, and above all, in every sense of the word, unproducible. God: the witness as 'nameable–unnameable', present–absent witness of every oath or of every possible pledge. As long as one supposes, *concesso non dato*, that religion has the slightest relation to what we thus call God, it would pertain not only to the general history of nomination, but, more strictly here, under its name of *religio*, to a history of the *sacramentum* and of the *testimonium*. It would *be* this history, it would merge with it. On the boat that brought us from Naples to Capri, I told myself that I would begin by recalling this sort of too luminous evidence, but I did not dare. I also told myself, silently, that one would blind oneself to the phenomenon called 'of religion' or of the 'return of the religious' *today* if one continued to oppose so naïvely Reason *and* Religion, Critique or Science *and* Religion, technoscientific Modernity *and* Religion. Supposing that what was at stake was to understand, would one understand anything about 'what's-going-on-today-in-the-world-with-religion' (and why 'in the world'? What is the 'world'? What does such a presupposition involve? etc.) if one continues to believe in this opposition, even in this incompatibility, which is to say, if one remains within a *certain* tradition of the Enlightenment, one of the many Enlightenments of the past three centuries (not of an *Aufklärung*, whose critical force is profoundly rooted in the Reformation), but yes, this light of Lights, of the *Lumières*, which traverses like a single ray a *certain* critical and anti-religious vigilance, anti-Judaeo-Christiano-Islamic, a *certain* filiation 'Voltaire–Feuerbach–Marx–Nietzsche–Freud–(and even)–Heidegger'? Beyond this opposition and its determinate heritage (no less represented on the other side, that of religious authority), perhaps we might be able to try to 'understand' how the imperturbable and interminable development of critical and technoscientific reason, far from opposing religion, bears, supports and supposes it. It would be necessary to demonstrate, which would not be simple, that religion and reason have the same source. (We associate here reason with philosophy and with science as technoscience, as critical history of the production of knowledge, of knowledge *as* production, know-how and intervention at a distance, tele-technoscience that is always high-performance and performative by essence etc.) Religion and reason develop in tandem, drawing from this common resource: the testimonial pledge of every performative, committing it to respond as much *before* the other as *for* the high-performance performativity of technoscience. The same unique source divides itself mechanically, automatically, and sets itself reactively in opposition to itself: whence the two sources in one. This reactivity is a process of *sacrificial indemnification*, it strives to restore the unscathed (*heilig*) that it itself threatens. And it is also the possibility of the two, of $n+1$, the same possibility as that of the *testimonial deus ex machina*. As for the *response*, it is *either or*. *Either* it addresses the absolute other as such, with an address that is understood, heard, respected faithfully and responsibly; *or* it retorts, retaliates, compensates and *indemnifies itself* in the war of resentment and of reactivity. One of the two responses ought always to be able to contaminate the other. It will never be proven whether it is the one or the other, never in an act of determining, theoretical or cognitive judgement. This might be the place and the responsibility of what is called belief, trustworthiness or fidelity, the fiduciary, 'trust' <*la 'fiance'*> in general, the tribunal <*instance*> of faith.

(30) But **we are already speaking Latin.** For the Capri meeting, the 'theme' I believed myself constrained to propose, religion, was named in Latin, let us never forget it. Does not 'the question of *religio*', however, quite simply merge, one could say, with the question of Latin? By which should be understood, beyond a 'question of language and of culture', the strange phenomenon of Latinity and of its globalization. We are not speaking here of universality, even of an idea of universality, only of a process of universalization that is finite but enigmatic. It is rarely investigated in its geopolitical and ethico-juridical scope, precisely where such a power finds itself overtaken, deployed, its *paradoxical* heritage revived by the global and still irresistible hegemony of a 'language', which is to say, also of a culture that in part is not Latin but Anglo-American. For everything that touches religion in particular, for everything that speaks 'religion', for whoever speaks religiously or about religion, Anglo-American remains Latin. *Religion* circulates in the world, one might say, like an *English word <comme un mot anglais>* that has been to Rome and taken a detour to the United States. Well beyond its strictly capitalist or politico-military figures, a hyper-imperialist appropriation has been underway now for centuries. It imposes itself in a particularly palpable manner within the conceptual apparatus of international law and of global political rhetoric. Wherever this apparatus dominates, it articulates itself through a discourse on religion. From here on, the word 'religion' is calmly (and violently) applied to things which have always been and remain foreign to what this word names and arrests in its history. The same remark could apply to many other words, for the entire 'religious vocabulary' beginning with 'cult', 'faith', 'belief', 'sacred', 'holy', 'saved', 'unscathed' (*heilig*). But by ineluctable contagion, no semantic cell can remain alien, I dare not say 'safe and sound', 'unscathed', in this apparently borderless process. *Globalatiniza-*

tion (essentially Christian, to be sure), this word names a unique event to which a meta-language seems incapable of acceding, although such a language remains, all the same, of the greatest necessity here. For at the same time that we no longer perceive its limits, we know that such globalization is finite and only projected. What is involved here is a Latinization and, rather than globality, a globalization that is running out of breath <*essoufflée*>, however irresistible and imperial it still may be. What are we to think of this running out of breath? Whether it holds a future or is held in store for it, we do not know and by definition cannot know. But at the bottom of such non-knowing, this expiring breath is blasting the ether of the world. Some breathe there better than others, some are stifled. The war of religions deploys itself there in its element, but also under a protective stratum that threatens to burst. The co-extensiveness of the two questions (religion and worldwide Latinization) marks the dimensions of what henceforth cannot be reduced to a question of language, culture, semantics, nor even, without doubt, to one of anthropology or of history. **And what if *religio* remained untranslatable?** No *religio* without *sacramentum*, without alliance and promise of testifying truthfully to the truth, which is to say, to speak the truth: that is to say, to begin with, no religion without the promise of keeping one's promise to tell the truth – and to have already told it! – in the very act of promising. To have already told it, *veritas*, in Latin, and thus to consider it told. The event to come has already taken place. The promise promises *itself*, it is *already* promised, that is the sworn faith, the given word, and hence the response. *Religio* would begin there.

(31) **And if *religio* remained untranslatable?** And if this question, and *a fortiori* the response to which it appeals, were to inscribe us already in an idiom whose translation remains problematic? What does it mean to respond? It is to swear – the faith: *respondere, antworten, answer, swear (swaran)*: 'to be compared with the got. *swaran* [from which come *schwören*, *beschwören*, 'swear', 'conjure', 'adjure', etc.], "to swear, to pronounce solemn formulas": this is almost literally *respondere*.'[19]

'Almost literally . . .' he says. As always, recourse to knowledge is temptation itself. Knowing is *temptation*, albeit in a somewhat more singular sense than believed when referring habitually

(habitually, at least) to the Evil Genius or to some original sin. The temptation of knowing, the temptation of knowledge, is to believe not only that one knows what one knows (which wouldn't be too serious), but also that one knows what knowledge is, that is, free, structurally, of belief or of **faith** – of the fiduciary or of trustworthiness. The temptation to believe in knowledge, here for example in the precious authority of Benveniste, can hardly be separated from a certain fear and trembling. Before what? Before a scholarship that is recognized, no doubt, and legitimate and respectable, but also before the confidence with which, authorizing himself without trembling through this authority, Benveniste (for example) proceeds with the cutting edge of assured distinction. For example, between the *proper* meaning and its other, the *literal* sense and its other, as though precisely *that itself* which is here in question (for example the response, responsibility or religion etc.) did not arise, in a quasi-automatic, machine-like or mechanical manner, out of the hesitation, indecision and margins between the two ostensibly assured terms. *Scruple*, hesitation, indecision, reticence (hence modesty *<pudeur>*, respect, *restraint* before that which should remain sacred, holy or safe: unscathed, immune) – this too is what is meant by *religio*. It is even the meaning that Benveniste believes obliged to retain with reference to the 'proper and constant usages' of the word during the classical period.[20] Let us nevertheless cite this page of Benveniste while emphasizing the words 'proper', 'literally', an 'almost literally' that is almost mind-boggling, and finally what is said to have 'disappeared' and the 'essential' that 'remains'. The places to which we call attention situate in our eyes chasms over which a great scholar walks with tranquil step, as though he knew what he was talking about, while at the same time acknowledging that at bottom he really doesn't know very much. And all this *goes on*, as we can see, in the enigmatic Latin derivation, in the 'prehistory of Greek and Latin'. All that *goes on* in what can no longer be isolated as a *religious vocabulary*, which is to say, in a relationship of right to religion, in the experience of the promise or of the indemnificatory offering, of a word committing a future to the present but concerning an event that is past: 'I promise you that it happened.' What happened? Who, to be precise? A son, yours. How beautiful to have an example. Religion, nothing less:

Together with *spondeo*, we must consider *re-spondeo*. The *proper* meaning of *respondeo* and the relation with *spondeo* emerge *literally* from a dialogue of Plautus (*Captiui*, 899). The parasite Ergasilus brings Hegion good news: his son, long disappeared, is about to return. Hegion *promises* Ergasilus to feed him all his days, *if what he says is true*. And the latter *commits himself* in turn:

898 [. . .] sponden tu istud? – Spondeo.
899 At ego tuum tibi aduenisse filium respondeo.

'Is this a *promise*? – It's a *promise*. – And I, for my part, promise you that your son has arrived.'

This dialogue is constructed according to a legal formula: a *sponsio* by the one, a *re-sponsio* by the other, forms of a security that are henceforth reciprocal: 'I guarantee you, in return, that your son has really arrived.'

This exchange of guarantees (cf. our expression *answer for . . .*) gives rise to the meaning, already well established in Latin, 'respond'. *Respondeo, responsum*, is said of the interpreters of the gods, of priests, notably of the haruspices, *giving a promise in return for the offering*, depositing a security in return for a gift; it is the 'response' of an oracle, of a priest. This explains a legal usage of the verb: *respondere de iure*, 'to give a legal consultation'. The jurist, with his competence, guarantees the value of the opinion he gives.

Let us note a symmetrical Germanic expression: old engl. *and-swaru* 'response' (engl. answer), compared to the got. *swaran* 'to swear, pronounce solemn words': it is *almost literally respondere*.

Thus we can determine precisely, in the prehistory of Greek and of Latin, the meaning of a term that is of the *greatest importance in religious vocabulary*, and the value that is derived from the root **spend-* with respect to other verbs that indicate offering in general.

In Latin, *an important part of the initial distinction has disappeared, but the essential remains* and this is what determines the juridical notion of *sponsio* on the one hand, and on the other, the link with the Greek concept of *spondé*.[21]

(32) But religion does not follow the movement of **faith** any more necessarily than the latter rushes towards faith in God. For if the concept of 'religion' implies an institution that is separable, identifiable, circumscribable, tied through its letter to the Roman *ius*, its essential relation both to faith and to God is anything but self-evident. When we speak, **we Europeans**, so ordinarily and so confusedly today about a 'return of the religious', what do we

thereby name? To what do we refer? The 'religious', the religiosity that is vaguely associated with the experience of the sacredness of the divine, of the holy, of the saved or of the unscathed (*heilig*) – is it religion? In what and to what extent does a 'sworn faith', a belief have to be *committed* or *engaged*? Inversely, not every sworn faith, given word, trustworthiness, trust or confidence in general is necessarily inscribed in a 'religion', even if the latter does mark the convergence of two experiences that are generally held to be equally religious:

1 the experience of *belief*, on the one hand (believing or credit, the fiduciary or the trustworthy in the act of faith, fidelity, the appeal to blind confidence, the testimonial that is always beyond proof, demonstrative reason, intuition); and
2 the experience of the unscathed, of *sacredness* or of *holiness*, on the other?

These two veins (or two strata or two sources) of the religious should be distinguished from one another. They can doubtless be associated with each other and certain of their possible co-implications analysed, but they should never be confused or reduced to one another as is almost always done. In principle, it is possible to sanctify, to sacralize the unscathed or to maintain oneself *in the presence* of the sacrosanct in various ways without bringing into play an act of belief, if at least belief, faith or fidelity signifies here acquiescing to the testimony of the other – of the *utterly other* who is inaccessible in its absolute source. And there where every other is utterly other *<où tout autre est tout autre>*. Conversely, if it carries beyond the presence of what would offer itself to be seen, touched, proven, the acquiescence of trust still does not in itself necessarily involve the sacred. (In this context two points deserve consideration: first, the distinction proposed by Levinas between the sacred and the holy; we shall do that elsewhere; secondly, the necessity for these two heterogeneous sources of religion to mingle their waters, if one can put it that way, without ever, it seems to us, amounting simply to the same.)

(33) We met, thus, at Capri, **we Europeans**, assigned to languages (Italian, Spanish, German, French) in which the same word, *religion*, should mean, or so we thought, the same thing. As

for the trustworthiness of this word, we shared our presupposition with Benveniste. The latter seems in effect to believe himself capable of recognizing and isolating, in the article on *sponsio* that we evoked a moment ago, what he refers to as 'religious vocabulary'. But everything remains problematic in this respect. How can discourses, or rather, as was just suggested, 'discursive practices', be articulated and made to cooperate in attempting to take the measure of the question, 'What is religion?'

'What is . . .?', which is to say, *on the one hand*, what is it in its *essence*? And *on the other*, what *is* it (present indicative) at present? What is it doing, what is being done with it at present, today, today in the world? So many ways of insinuating, in each of these words – *being, essence, present, world* – a response into the question. So many ways of imposing the answer. Of pre-imposing it or of prescribing it *as* religion. There we might have, perhaps, a pre-definition: however little may be known of religion *in the singular*, we do know that it is always a response and responsibility that is prescribed, not chosen freely in an act of pure and abstractly autonomous will. There is no doubt that it implies freedom, will and responsibility, but let us try to think this: will and freedom *without autonomy*. Whether it is a question of sacredness, sacrificiality or of faith, the other makes the law, the law is other: to give ourselves back, and up, to the other. To every other and to the utterly other.

The said 'discursive practices' would respond to several types of programme:

1 Assuring oneself of a provenance by **etymologies**. The best illustration would be given by the divergence concerning the *two possible etymological sources* of the word *religio*: (a) *relegere*, from *legere* ('harvest, gather'): Ciceronian tradition continued by W. Otto, J.-B. Hollmann, Benveniste; (b) *religare*, from *ligare* ('to tie, bind'). This tradition would go from Lactantius and Tertullian to Kobbert, Ernout-Meillet, Pauly-Wissowa. In addition to the fact that etymology never provides a law and only provides material for thinking on the condition that it allows itself to be thought as well, we shall attempt later to define the implication or tendency *<charge> common to the two sources* of meaning thus distinguished. Beyond a case of simple synonyms, the two

semantic sources perhaps overlap. They would even repeat one another not far from what in truth would be the origin of repetition, which is to say, the division of the same.

2 The search for historico-semantical **filiations** or **genealogies** would determine an immense field, with which the meaning of the word is put to the test of historical transformations and of institutional structures: history and anthropology of religions, in the style of Nietzsche, for example, as well as in that of Benveniste when he holds 'Indo-European institutions' as 'witnesses' to the history of meaning or of an etymology – which in itself, however, proves nothing about the effective use of a word.

3 An analysis above all concerned with **pragmatic** and functional effects, more structural and also more political, would not hesitate to investigate the usages or applications of the lexical resources, where, in the face of new regularities, of unusual recurrences, of unprecedented contexts, discourse liberates words and meaning from all archaic memory and from all supposed origins.

These three biases seem, from different points of view, legitimate. But even if they respond, as I believe they do, to irrefutable imperatives, my provisional hypothesis (which I advance all the more prudently and timidly for not being able to justify it sufficiently in the limited space and time available) is that here, in Capri, the last type ought to dominate. It should not exclude the others – that would lead to too many absurdities – but it should privilege the signs of what in the world, *today*, singularizes the use of the word 'religion' as well as experience of 'religion' associated with the word, there where no memory and no history could suffice to announce or gather it, at least not at first sight. I would have had therefore to invent an operation, a discursive machine, if one prefers, whose economy not only does justice, in the space and time available, to these three demands, to each of the imperatives that we feel, at least, to be irrefutable, but which would also organize the hierarchy and the urgencies. At a certain speed, at a rhythm given within the narrow limits <available>.

(34) **Etymologies, filiations, genealogies, pragmatics.** We will not be able to undertake here all the analyses required by

distinctions that are indispensable but rarely respected or practised. There are many of them (religion/faith, belief; religion/piety; religion/cult; religion/theology; religion/theiology; religion/ontotheology; or yet again, religious/divine – mortal or immortal; religious/sacred–saved–holy–unscathed–immune – *heilig*). But among them, before or after them, we will put to the test the quasi-transcendental privilege we believe ourselves obliged to grant the distinction between, *on the one hand*, the experience of belief (trust, trustworthiness, confidence, faith, the credit accorded the *good faith of the utterly other* in the experience of witnessing) and, *on the other*, the experience of sacredness, even of holiness, of the unscathed that is safe and sound (*heilig*, holy). These comprise two distinct sources or foci. 'Religion' figures their *ellipse* because it both comprehends the two foci but also sometimes shrouds their irreducible duality in silence, in a manner precisely that is secret and *reticent*.

In any case, the history of the word 'religion' should in principle forbid every non-Christian from using the name 'religion', in order to recognize in it what 'we' would designate, identify and isolate there. Why add here this qualification of 'non-Christian'? In other words, why should the concept of religion be solely Christian? Why, in any case, does the question deserve to be posed and the hypothesis taken seriously? Benveniste also recalls that there is no 'common' Indo-European term for what we call 'religion'. The Indo-Europeans did not conceive 'as a separate institution' what Benveniste, for his part, calls 'the omnipresent reality that is religion'. Even today, wherever such a 'separate institution' is not recognized, the word 'religion' is inadequate. There has not always been, therefore, nor is there always and everywhere, nor will there always and everywhere ('with humans' or elsewhere) be *something*, a thing that is *one and identifiable*, identical with itself, which, whether religious or irreligious, all agree to call 'religion'. And yet, one tells oneself, **one still must respond**. Within the Latin sphere, the origin of *religio* was the theme of challenges that in truth were interminable. Between two readings or two lessons, therefore, two provenances: on the one hand, supported by texts of Cicero, *relegere*, what would seem to be the avowed formal and semantic filiation: bringing together in order to return and begin again; whence *religio*, scrupulous attention, respect, patience, even modesty, shame or piety – and, on the other hand (Lactantius and Tertullian) *religare*, etymology 'invented by Christians', as Benveniste says,[22] and linking religion to the *link*, precisely, to obligation, ligament, and hence to obligation, to debt etc., between men or between man and God. At issue would still be, in an entirely different place, on an entirely different theme, a division of the source and of the meaning (and we are not yet done with this dualization). This debate on the *two sources*, etymological but also 'religious', of the word *religio* is without doubt fascinating and passionate (it is related to the Passion itself, in so far as one of the two disputed sources has been claimed to be Christian). But whatever its interest or necessity might be, such a divergence is for us limited in scope. In the first place, because nothing gets decided at the source, as we have just suggested.[23] Secondly, because the two competing etymologies can be retraced to the same, and in a certain manner to the possibility of repetition, which produces the same as much as it confirms it. In both cases (*re-legere* or *re-ligare*), what is at issue is indeed a persistent bond that bonds itself first and foremost to itself. What is at issue is indeed a reunion *<rassemblement>*, a re-assembling, a re-collecting. A resistance or a reaction to disjunction. To ab-solute alterity. 'Recollecting', *recollecter*, is moreover the translation proposed by Benveniste,[24] who glosses it thus: 'return for a new choice, return to revise a previous operation', whence the sense of 'scruple', but also of choice, of reading and of election, of intelligence, since there can be no selectivity without the bonds of collectivity and recollection. Finally, it is in the bond to the self, marked by the enigmatic 're-', that one should perhaps try to reconstrue the passage between these different meanings (*re-legere, re-ligare, re-spondeo*, in which Benveniste analyses what he also calls, elsewhere, the 'relation' to *spondeo*). All the categories of which we could make use to translate the common meaning of the 're-' would be inadequate, and first of all because they can only *re*-introduce into the definition what has to be defined, as though it already had been defined. For example, in pretending to know what is the 'proper meaning', as Benveniste says, of words such as repetition, resumption, renewal, reflection, re-election, recollection – in short, religion, 'scruple', response and responsibility.

Whatever side one takes in this debate, it is to the ellipse of these double Latin foci that the entire modern (geo-theologico-political) problematic of the 'return of the religious' refers. Whoever would not acknowledge either the legitimacy of this double foci or the Christian prevalence that has imposed itself globally within the said Latinity would have to refuse the very premises of such a debate.[25] And with them, any attempt to *think* a situation in which, as in times past, there will perhaps no longer exist, just as once it did not yet exist, any 'common Indo-European term for "religion"'.[26]

(35) But, **one still must respond**. And without waiting. Without waiting too long. **In the beginning**, Maurizio Ferraris at the Hotel Lutétia. 'I need,' he tells me, 'we need a theme for this meeting in Capri.' In a whisper, yet without whispering, almost without hesitating, mechine-like, I respond, 'Religion.' Why? From where did this come to me, and yes, mechanically? Once the theme was agreed upon, discussions were improvised – between two walks at night towards Faraglione, which can be seen in the distance, between Vesuvius and Capri. (Jensen refers to it, Faraglione, and Gradiva returns perhaps, the ghost of light, the shadowless shadow of noon, *das Mittagsgespenst*, more beautiful than all the great ghosts of the island, better 'habituated' than they, as she puts it, 'to being dead', and for a long time.) I had thus subsequently to justify an answer to the question, why I had named, all of a sudden, machine-like, 'religion'? And this justification would have become, today, my response to the question of *religion*. Of religion today. For, of course, it would have been madness itself to have proposed to treat religion *itself*, in general or in its essence; rather the troubled question, the common concern is: 'What is going on today with it, with what is designated thus? What is going on there? What is happening and so badly? What is happening under this old name? What in the world is suddenly emerging or re-emerging under this appellation?' Of course, this form of question cannot be separated from the more fundamental one (on the essence, the concept and the history of religion *itself*, and of what is called 'religion'). But its approach, first of all, should have been, according to me, more direct, global, massive and immediate, spontaneous, without defence, almost in the style of a philosopher obliged to issue a brief press release. The response that I gave almost without hesitation to Ferraris must have come back to

me from afar, resonating from an alchemist's cavern, in whose depths the word was a precipitate. 'Religion', a word dictated by who knows what or whom: by everyone perhaps, by the reading of the nightly news televised on an international network, by the everyman we believe we see, by the state of the world, by the whole of what is as it goes (God, its synonym in short, or History as such, and so on). Today once again, today finally, today otherwise, the great question would still be religion and what some hastily call its 'return'. To say things in this way and to believe that one knows of what one speaks, would be to begin by no longer understanding anything at all: as though religion, the question of religion was *what succeeds in returning*, that which all of a sudden would come as a surprise to what one believes one knows: man, the earth, the world, history falling thus under the rubric of anthropology, of history or of every other form of human science or of philosophy, even of the 'philosophy of religion'. First error to avoid. It is typical and examples of it could be multiplied. If there is a question of religion, it ought no longer to be a 'question-of-religion'. Nor simply a response to this question. We shall see why and wherein the question of religion is first of all the question of the question. Of the origins and the borders of the question – as of the response. 'The thing' tends thus to drop out of sight as soon as one believes oneself able to master it under the title of a discipline, a knowledge or a philosophy. And yet, despite the impossibility of the task, a demand is addressed to us: it should be delivered <*tenir*>, done, or left to 'deliver itself' <*se tenir*> – this discourse, in a few traits, in a limited number of words. Economy dictated by publishing exigencies. But why, always the question of number, were there ten commandments, subsequently multiplied by so and so many? Where here would be the just ellipsis we are enjoined to say in keeping it silent. Where the reticence? And what if the ellipsis, the silent figure and the 'keeping quiet' of reticence were precisely, we will come to that later, religion? We are asked, in the collective name of several *European* publishers, to state a position in a few pages on religion, and that does not appear monstrous today, when a serious treatise on religion would demand the construction of new Libraries of France and of the universe, even if, not *believing that one is thinking* anything new, one would content oneself with remembering, archiving, classifying, taking note in a memoir, of what one *believes* one already *knows*.

Faith and knowledge: between believing one knows and knowing one believes, the alternative is not a game. Let us choose, then, I told myself, a quasi-aphoristic form as one chooses a machine, the least pernicious machine to treat of *religion* in a certain number of pages: 25 or a few more, we were given; and, let us say, arbitrarily, to de-cipher or anagrammatize the 25, 52 very unequal sequences, as many *crypts* dispersed in a non-identified field, a field that is none the less already approaching, like a desert about which one isn't sure if it is sterile or not, or like a field of ruins and of mines and of wells and of caves and of cenotaphs and of scattered seedings; but a non-identified field, not even like a world (the Christian history of this word, 'world', already puts us on guard; the world is not the universe, nor the cosmos, nor the earth).

(36) **In the beginning**, the title will have been my first aphorism. It condenses two traditional titles, entering into a contract with them. We are committed to deforming them, dragging them elsewhere while developing if not their negative or their unconscious, at least the logic of what they might have let speak about religion independently of the meanings they wanted to say. In Capri, at the beginning of the session, improvising, I spoke of light and in the name of the island (of the necessity of dating, that is, of signing a finite meeting in its time and in its space, from the singularity of a place, of a Latin place: Capri, which is not Delos, nor Patmos – nor Athens, nor Jerusalem, nor Rome). I had insisted on the light, the relation of all religion to fire and to light. There is the light of revelation and the light of the Enlightenment. Light, *phos*, revelation, orient and origin of *our* religions, photographic instantaneity. Question, demand: in view of the Enlightenment of today and of tomorrow, in the light of other Enlightenments (*Aufklärung, Lumières, illuminismo*) how **to think religion** in the daylight of today without breaking with the philosophical tradition? In our 'modernity', the said tradition demarcates itself in an exemplary manner – it will have to be shown why – in basically Latin titles that name religion. First of all in a book by Kant, in the epoch and in the spirit of the *Aufklärung*, if not of the *Lumières*: *Religion within the Limits of Reason Alone* (1793) was

also a book on radical evil. (What of reason and of radical evil today? And if the 'return of the religious' was not without relation to the return – modern or postmodern, for once – of certain phenomena, at least, of radical evil? Does radical evil destroy or institute the possibility of religion?) Then, the book of Bergson, that great Judaeo-Christian, *The Two Sources of Morality and of Religion* (1932), between the two world wars and on the eve of events of which one knows that one does not yet know how to think them, and to which no religion, no religious institution in the world remained foreign or survived *unscathed, immune, safe and sound.* In both cases, was the issue not, as today, that of thinking religion, the possibility of religion, and hence of its interminable and ineluctable return?

(37) **'To think religion?'** you say. As though such a project would not dissolve the very question in advance. To hold that religion is properly *thinkable*, and even if thinking is neither seeing, nor knowing, nor conceiving, is still to hold it in advance in respect; thus, over short or long, the affair is decided. Already in speaking of these notes as of a machine, I have once again been overcome by a desire for economy, for concision: by the desire to draw, in order to be quick, the famous conclusion of the *Two Sources* . . . towards another place, another discourse, other argumentative stakes. The latter could always be – I do not exclude it – a hijacked translation, or a rather free formalization. The book's concluding words are memorable: '**the effort required to accomplish, down to our refractory planet, the essential function of the universe, which is a machine for the making of gods**'. What would happen if Bergson were made to say something entirely different from what he believed he wanted to say but what perhaps was surreptitiously dictated to him? What would happen if he had, as though despite himself, left a place or a passage for a sort of symptomatic *retraction*, following the very movement of hesitation, indecision and of scruple, of that turning back (*retractare*, says Cicero to define the *religious* act or being) in which perhaps the *double source* – the double stratum or the double root – of *religio* consists? Were such the case, then that hypothesis would receive perhaps a doubly *mechanical* form. 'Mechanical' would have to be understood here in a meaning that is rather 'mystical'. Mystical or secret because contradictory and

distracting, both inaccessible, disconcerting and familiar, *unheimlich*, uncanny to the very extent that this machinality, this ineluctable automatization produces and re-produces what *at the same time detaches from and reattaches to* the family (*heimisch*, homely), to the familiar, to the domestic, to the proper, to the *oikos* of the ecological and of the economic, to the *ethos*, to the place of dwelling. This quasi-spontaneous automaticity, as irreflective as a reflex, repeats again and again the double movement of abstraction and attraction that *at the same time detaches and reattaches to* the country, the idiom, the literal or to everything confusedly collected today under the terms 'identity' or 'identitarian'; in two words, that which at the same time ex-propriates and re-appropriates, de-racinates and re-enracinates, *ex-appropriates* according to a logic that we will later have to formalize, that of auto-immune auto-indemnification.

Before speaking so calmly of the 'return of the religious' today, two things have to be explained in one. Each time what is involved is a machine, a tele-machine:

1 The said 'return of the religious', which is to say the spread of a complex and overdetermined phenomenon, is not a simple *return*, for its globality and its figures (tele-techno-media-scientific, capitalistic and politico-economic) remain original and unprecedented. And it is not a *simple* return *of the religious*, for it comports, as one of its two tendencies, a radical destruction of the religious (*stricto sensu*, the Roman and the statist, like everything that incarnates the European political or juridical order against which all non-Christian 'fundamentalisms' or 'integrisms' are waging war, to be sure, but also certain forms of Protestant or even Catholic orthodoxy). It must be said as well that in face of them, another self-destructive affirmation of religion, I would dare to call it auto-immune, could well be at work in all the projects known as 'pacifist' and economic, 'catholic' or not, which appeal to universal fraternization, to the reconciliation of 'men, sons of the same God', and above all when these brothers belong to the monotheistic tradition of the Abrahamic religions. It will always be difficult extricating this pacifying movement from a *double horizon* (the one hiding or dividing the other):

(a) The *kenotic* horizon of the death of God and the anthropological re-immanentization (the rights of man and of *human* life above all obligation towards absolute and transcendent truth of commitment before the divine order: an Abraham who would henceforth refuse to sacrifice his son and would no longer envisage what was always madness). When one hears the official representatives of the religious hierarchy, beginning with the most mediatic and most Latinoglobal and cederomized of all, the Pope, speak of this sort of ecumenical reconciliation, one also hears (not only, to be sure, but also) the announcement or reminder of a certain 'death of God'. Sometimes one even has the impression that he speaks only of that – which speaks through his mouth. And that another death of God comes to haunt the Passion that animates him. But what's the difference, one will say. Indeed.

(b) This declaration of peace can also, pursuing war by other means, dissimulate a *pacifying* gesture, in the most European-colonial sense possible. Inasmuch as it comes from Rome, as is often the case, it would try first, and first in Europe, upon Europe, to impose surreptitiously a discourse, a culture, a politics and a right, to impose them on all the other monotheist religions, including the non-Catholic Christian religions. Beyond Europe, through the same schemes and the same juridico-theologico-political culture, the aim would be to impose, in the name of peace, a globalatinization. The latter becomes henceforth European-Anglo-*American* in its idiom, as we said above. The task seems all the more urgent and problematic (incalculable calculation of religion for our times) as the demographic disproportion will not cease henceforth to threaten external hegemony, leaving the latter no stratagems other than internalization. The field of this war or of this pacification is henceforth without limit: all the religions, their centres of authority, the religious cultures, states, nations or ethnic groups that they represent have unequal access, to be sure, but often one that is immediate and potentially without limit, to the same world market. They are at the same time producers, actors and sought-after consumers, at times exploiters, at times victims. <At stake in the struggle> is thus the access to world (transnational or trans-state) networks of telecommunication and of tele-technoscience. Henceforth religion 'in the singular' accompanies and even precedes the critical and tele-technoscientific reason, it watches over it as its shadow. It is its wake, the shadow of light itself, the pledge of faith, the guarantee of trustworthiness, the fiduciary experience presupposed by all production of shared knowledge, the testimonial performativity engaged in all technoscientific performance as in the entire capitalistic economy indissociable from it.

2 The same movement that renders indissociable religion and tele-technoscientific reason in its most critical aspect reacts inevitably *to itself*. It secretes its own antidote but also its own power of auto-immunity. We are here in a space where all self-protection of the unscathed, of the safe and sound, of the sacred (*heilig*, holy) must protect itself against its own protection, its own police, its own power of rejection, in short against its own, which is to say, against its own immunity. It is this terrifying but fatal logic of the *auto-immunity of the unscathed*[27] that will always associate Science and Religion.

On the one hand, the 'lights' and Enlightenment of tele-technoscientific critique and reason can only suppose trustworthiness. They are obliged to put into play an irreducible 'faith', that of a 'social bond' or of a 'sworn faith', of a testimony ('I promise to tell you the truth beyond all proof and all theoretical demonstration, believe me, etc.'), that is, of a performative of promising at work even in lying or perjury and without which no address to the other would be possible. Without the performative experience of this elementary act of faith, there would neither be 'social bond' nor address of the other, nor any performativity in general: neither convention, nor institution, nor constitution, nor sovereign state, nor law, nor above all, here, that structural performativity of the productive performance that binds from its very inception the knowledge of the scientific community to doing, and science to technics. If we regularly speak here of technoscience, it is not in order to cede to a contemporary stereotype, but in order to recall that, more clearly than ever before, we now know that the scientific act is, through and through, a practical intervention and a technical performativity in the very energy of its essence. And for this very reason it plays with place, putting distances and speeds to work. It delocalizes, removes or brings close, actualizes or virtualizes, accelerates or decelerates. But wherever this tele-technoscientific critique develops, it brings into play and confirms the fiduciary credit of an elementary faith which is, at least in its essence or calling, religious (the elementary condition, the milieu of the religious if not religion itself). We speak of trust and of credit or of trustworthiness in order to underscore that this elementary act of faith also underlies the essentially economic and capitalistic rationality of the tele-technoscientific. No calculation, no assurance will ever be able to reduce its ultimate necessity, that of the testimonial signature (whose theory is not necessarily a theory of the subject, of the person or of the ego, conscious or unconscious). To take note of this is to give oneself the means of understanding why, in principle, today, there is no incompatibility, in the said 'return of the religious', between the 'fundamentalisms', the 'integrisms' or their 'politics' and, on the other hand, rationality, which is to say, the tele-techno-capitalistico-scientific fiduciarity, in all of its mediatic and globalizing dimensions. This rationality of the said 'fundamentalisms' can also be hypercritical[28] and not recoil before what can sometimes resemble a deconstructive radicalization of the critical gesture. As for the phenomena of ignorance, of irrationality or of 'obscurantism' that are so often emphasized and denounced, so easily and with good reason, they are often residues, surface effects, the reactive slag of immunitary, indemnificatory or auto-immunitary reactivity. They mask a deep structure or rather (but also at the same time) a fear of self, a reaction against that with which it is partially linked: the dislocation, expropriation, delocalization, deracination, disidiomatization and dispossession (in all their dimensions, particularly sexual – *phallic*) that the tele-techno-scientific machine does not fail to produce. The reactivity of resentment opposes this movement to itself by dividing it. It *indemnifies* itself thus in a movement that is at once immunitary and auto-immune. The reaction to the machine is as automatic (and thus machinal) as life itself. Such an internal splitting, which opens distance, is also peculiar or 'proper' to religion, appropriating religion for the 'proper' (inasmuch as it is also the *unscathed*: *heilig,* holy, sacred, saved, immune and so on), appropriating religious indemnification to all forms of property, from the linguistic idiom in its 'letter', to blood and soil, to the family and to the nation. This internal and immediate reactivity, at once immunitary and auto-immune, can alone account for what will be called the religious resurgence in its double and contradictory phenomenon. The word *resurgence* <*déferlement*> imposes itself upon us to suggest the redoubling of a wave that appropriates even that to which, enfolding itself, it seems to be opposed – and simultaneously gets carried away itself, sometimes in terror and terrorism, taking with it precisely that which protects it, its own 'antibodies'. Allying itself with the enemy, hospitable to the antigens, bearing away the other with itself, this resurgence grows and *swells* with the power of the adversary. From the shores of whatever island, one doesn't know, here is the resurgence we believe we see coming, without doubt, in its spontaneous swelling, irresistibly automatic. But we believe we see it coming without any horizon. We are no longer certain that we see and that there is a future where we see it coming. The future tolerates neither foresight nor providence. It is therefore in it, rather, caught and surprised by this resurgence, that 'we' in truth are carried away – and it is this that we would like to *think*, if this word can still be used here.

Religion today allies itself with tele-technoscience, to which it reacts with all its forces. It *is, on the one hand*, globalization; it produces, weds, exploits the capital and knowledge of tele-mediatization: neither the trips and global spectacularizing of the Pope, nor the interstate dimensions of the 'Rushdie affair', nor planetary terrorism would otherwise be possible, at this rhythm – and we could multiply such indications *ad infinitum*. But, *on the other hand*, it reacts immediately, *simultaneously*, declaring war against that which gives it this new power only at the cost of dislodging it from all its proper places, *in truth from place itself*, from the *taking-place* of its truth. It conducts a terrible war against that which protects it only by threatening it, according to this double and contradictory structure: immunitary and auto-immunitary. The relation between these two motions or these two sources is ineluctable, and therefore automatic and mechanical, between one which has the form of the machine (mechanization, automatization, machination or *mechane*), and the other, that of living spontaneity, of the *unscathed* property of life, that is to say, of another (claimed) self-determination. But the auto-immunitary haunts the community and its system of immunitary survival like the hyperbole of its own possibility. Nothing in *common*, nothing immune, safe and sound, *heilig* and holy, nothing unscathed in the most autonomous living present without a risk of auto-immunity. As always, the risk charges itself twice, the same finite risk. Two times rather than one: with a menace and with a chance. In two words, it must take charge of – one could also say: take in trust – the *possibility* of that **radical evil** without which good would be for nothing.[29]

. . . and pomegranates

(*Having posed these premises or general definitions, and given the diminishing space available, we shall cast the fifteen final propositions in a form that is even more granulated, grainy, disseminated, aphoristic, discontinuous, juxtapositional, dogmatic, indicative or virtual, economic; in a word, more than ever telegraphic.*)

(38) Of a discourse to come – on the to-come and repetition. Axiom: no to-come without heritage and the possibility of *repeating*. No to-come without some sort of *iterability*, at least in the form of a covenant with oneself and *confirmation* of the originary *yes*. No to-come without some sort of messianic memory and promise, of a messianicity older than all religion, more originary than all messianism. No discourse or address of the other without the possibility of an elementary promise. Perjury and broken promises require the *same* possibility. No promise, therefore, without the promise of a confirmation of the *yes*. This *yes* will have implied and will always imply the trustworthiness and fidelity of a faith. No faith, therefore, nor future without everything technical, automatic, machine-like supposed by iterability. In this sense, the technical is the possibility of faith, indeed its very chance. A chance that entails the greatest risk, even the menace of **radical evil**. Otherwise, that of which it is the chance

would not be faith but rather programme or proof, predictability or providence, pure knowledge and pure know-how, which is to say annulment of the future. Instead of opposing them, as is almost always done, they ought to be thought *together*, as *one and the same possibility*: the machine-like and faith, and the same holds for the machinal and all the values entailed in the sacrosanct (*heilig*, holy, safe and sound, unscathed, intact, immune, free, vital, fecund, fertile, strong, and above all, as we will soon see, 'swollen') – more precisely in the sacrosanctity of the **phallic** effect.

(39) This double value, is it not, for example, that signified by a phallus in its differentiality, or rather by the **phallic**, *the effect of the phallus*, which is not necessarily the property of man? Is it not the phenomenon, the *phainesthai*, the day of the *phallus*? – but also, by virtue of the law of iterability or of duplication that can *detach* it from its pure and proper presence, is it not also its *phantasma*, in Greek, its ghost, its spectre, its double or its fetish? Is it not the *colossal automaticity* of the erection (the maximum of life to be kept unscathed, indemnified, immune and safe, sacrosanct), but also and precisely by virtue of its reflex-character, that which is most mechanical, most separable from the life it represents? The phallic – is it not also, as distinct from the penis and once detached from the body, the marionette that is erected, exhibited, fetishized and paraded in processions? Is this not where one grasps, virtuality of virtuality, the power or potency of a logic powerful enough to account for (*logon didonai*) – counting on and calculating the incalculable – everything that binds the tele-technoscientific machine, this enemy of life in the service of life, to the very source and resource of the religious: to faith in the most living as dead and automatically *sur-viving*, resuscitated in its spectral *phantasma*, the holy, safe and sound, unscathed, immune, sacred – in a word, everything that translates *heilig*? Matrix, once again, of a cult or of a culture of the generalized fetish, of an unlimited fetishism, of a fetishizing adoration of the Thing itself. One could, without being arbitrary, read, select, connect everything in the semantic genealogy of the unscathed – 'saintly, sacred, safe and sound, *heilig, holy*' – that speaks of force, life-force, fertility, growth, augmentation, and above all *swelling*, in the spontaneity of erection or of pregnancy[30]. To be

brief, it does not suffice to recall here all the phallic cults and their well-known phenomena at the core of so many religions. The three 'great monotheisms' have inscribed covenants or founding promises in an *ordeal of the unscathed* that is always a circumcision, be it 'exterior or interior', literal or, as was said before Saint Paul, in Judaism itself, 'circumcision of the heart'. And this would perhaps be the place to enquire why, in the most lethal explosions of a violence that is inevitably ethnico-religious – why, on all sides, women in particular are singled out as victims (not 'only' of murders, but also of the rapes and mutilations that precede and accompany them).

(40) The religion of the living – is this not a tautology? Absolute imperative, holy law, law of salvation: saving the living intact, the unscathed, the safe and sound (*heilig*) that has the right to absolute respect, restraint, modesty. Whence the necessity of an enormous task: reconstituting the chain of analogous motifs in the sacrosanctifying attitude or intentionality, in relation to that which is, should remain or should be allowed to be what it is (*heilig*, living, strong and fertile, erect and fecund: safe, whole, unscathed, immune, sacred, holy and so on). Salvation and health. Such an intentional attitude bears several names of the same family: respect, modesty, restraint, inhibition, *Achtung* (Kant), *Scheu, Verhaltenheit, Gelassenheit* (Heidegger), restraint or *holding-back* <*halte*> in general.[31] The poles, themes, causes are not the same (the law, sacredness, holiness, the god to come and so on), but the movements appear quite analogous in the way they relate to them, *suspending* themselves, and *in truth interrupting themselves.* All of them involve or mark a restraint <*halte*>. Perhaps they constitute a sort of universal, not 'religion' as such, but a universal structure of religiosity. For if they are not in themselves properly religious, they always open the possibility of the religious without ever being able to limit or restrain it. This possibility remains divided. On the one hand, to be sure, it is respectful or inhibited abstention before what remains sacred mystery, and what ought to remain intact or inaccessible, like the mystical immunity of a secret. But in thus holding back, the same halting also opens an access without mediation or representation, hence not without an intuitive violence, to that which remains unscathed. That is another dimension of the mystical. Such a universal allows or

promises perhaps the global translation of *religio*, that is: scruple, respect, restraint, *Verhaltenheit*, reserve, *Scheu*, shame, discretion, *Gelassenheit*, etc. – all stop short of that which must or should remain safe and sound, intact, unscathed, before what must be allowed to be what it ought to be, sometimes even at the cost of sacrificing itself and in prayer: the other. Such a universal, such an 'existential' universality, could have provided at least the mediation of a *scheme* to the globalatinization of *religio*. Or in any case, to its possibility.

What would then be required is, in the same movement, to account for a double postulation: *on the one hand*, the absolute respect of life, the 'Thou shalt not kill' (at least thy neighbour, if not the living in general), the 'fundamentalist' prohibition of abortion, of artificial insemination, of performative intervention in the genetic potential, even to the ends of gene therapy etc.; *and on the other* (without even speaking of wars of religion, of their terrorism and their killings) the no less universal sacrificial vocation. It was not so long ago that this still involved, here and there, human sacrifice, even in the 'great monotheisms'. It always involves sacrifice of the living, more than ever in large-scale breeding and slaughtering, in the fishing or hunting industries, in animal experimentation. Be it said in passing that certain ecologists and certain vegetarians – at least to the extent that they believe themselves to have remained pure of (unscathed by) all carnivorousness, even symbolic[32] – would be the only 'religious' persons of the time to respect one of these two pure sources of religion and indeed to bear responsibility for what could well be the future of a religion. What are the *mechanics* of this double postulation (respect of life and sacrificiality)? I refer to it as *mechanics* because it reproduces, with the regularity of a technique, the instance of the non-living or, if you prefer, of the dead in the living. It was also the automation according to the phallic effect of which we spoke above. It was the marionette, the dead machine yet more than living, the spectral fantasy of the dead as the principle of life and of sur-vival <*sur-vie*>. This mechanical principle is apparently very simple: life has absolute value only if it is worth *more than* life. And hence only in so far as it mourns, becoming itself in the labour of infinite mourning, in the indemnification of a spectrality without limit. It is sacred, holy, infinitely respectable only in the name of what is worth more than it and what is not restricted to the naturalness of the bio-zoological (sacrificeable) – although true sacrifice ought to sacrifice not only 'natural' life, called 'animal' or 'biological', but also that which is worth more than so-called natural life. Thus, respect of life in the discourses of religion as such concerns 'human life' only in so far as it bears witness, in some manner, to the infinite transcendence of that which is worth more than it (divinity, the sacrosanctness of the law).[33] The price of human life, which is to say, of anthropo-theological life, the price of what ought to remain safe (*heilig*, sacred, safe and sound, unscathed, immune), as the absolute price, the price of what ought to inspire respect, modesty, reticence, this price is priceless. It corresponds to what Kant calls the dignity (*Würdigkeit*) of the end in itself, of the rational finite being, of absolute value beyond all comparative market-price (*Marktpreis*). This dignity of life can only subsist beyond the present living being. Whence, transcendence, fetishism and spectrality; whence, the religiosity of religion. This excess above and beyond the living, whose life only has absolute value by being worth more than life, more than itself – this, in short, is what opens the space of death that is linked to the automaton (exemplarily 'phallic'), to technics, the machine, the prosthesis: in a word, to the dimensions of auto-immune and self-sacrificial supplementarity, to this death-drive that is silently at work in every community, every *auto-co-immunity*, constituting it as such in its iterability, its heritage, its spectral tradition. Community as *com-mon auto-immunity*: no community <is possible> that would not cultivate its own auto-immunity, a principle of sacrificial self-destruction ruining the principle of self-protection (that of maintaining its self-integrity intact), and this in view of some sort of invisible and spectral sur-vival. This self-contesting attestation keeps the auto-immune community alive, which is to say, open to something other and more than itself: the other, the future, death, freedom, the coming or the love of the other, the space and time of a spectralizing messianicity beyond all messianism. It is there that the possibility of religion persists: the *religious* bond (scrupulous, respectful, modest, reticent, inhibited) between the value of life, its absolute 'dignity', and the theological machine, the 'machine for making gods'.[34]

(**41**) Religion, as a response that is both ambiguous and ambivalent <*à double détente et à double entente*>, is thus an ellipsis:

the ellipsis of **sacrifice.** Is a religion imaginable without sacrifice and without prayer? The sign through which Heidegger believes ontotheology can be recognized is when the relation to the absolute Being or to the supreme Cause has freed itself of both, thereby losing access to sacrificial offering no less than to prayer. But there as well, two sources: the divided law, the *double bind*, also the dual foci, the ellipsis or originary duplicity of religion, consists therein, that the law of the unscathed, the salvation of the safe, the humble respect of that which is sacrosanct (*heilig*, holy) *both requires and excludes* sacrifice, which is to say, the indemnification of the unscathed, the price of immunity. Hence: auto-immunization and the sacrifice of sacrifice. The latter always represents the same movement, the price to pay for not injuring or wronging the absolute other. **Violence** of sacrifice in the name of non-violence. Absolute respect enjoins first and foremost sacrifice of self, of one's most precious interest. If Kant speaks of the 'holiness' of the moral law, it is while explicitly holding a discourse on 'sacrifice', which is to say, on another instantiation of religion 'within the limits of reason *alone*': the Christian religion as the only 'moral' religion. Self-sacrifice thus sacrifices the most proper in the service of the most proper. As though *pure* reason, in a process of auto-immune indemnification, could only oppose religion as such to *a* religion or *pure* faith to this or that belief.

(42) In our 'wars of religion', **violence** has two ages. The one, already discussed above, appears 'contemporary', in sync or in step with the hypersophistication of military tele-technology – of 'digital' and cyberspaced culture. The other is a 'new archaic violence', if one can put it that way. It counters the first and everything it represents. Revenge. Resorting, in fact, to the same resources of mediatic power, it *reverts* (according to the return, the resource, the repristination and the law of internal and auto-immune reactivity we are trying to formalize here) as closely as possible to the body proper and to the premachinal living being. In any case, to its desire and to its phantasm. Revenge is taken against the decorporalizing and expropriating machine by resorting – reverting – to bare hands, to the sexual organs or to primitive tools, often to weapons other than firearms <*l'arme blanche*'>. What is referred to as 'killings' and 'atrocities' – words

never used in 'clean' or 'proper' wars, where, precisely, the dead are no longer counted (guided or 'intelligent' missiles directed at entire cities, for instance) – is here supplanted by tortures, beheadings and mutilations of all sorts. What is involved is always avowed vengeance, often declared as **sexual** revenge: rapes, mutilated genitals or severed hands, corpses exhibited, heads paraded, as not so long ago in France, impaled on the end of stakes (phallic processions of 'natural religions'). This is the case, for example, but it is only an example, in Algeria today, in the name of Islam, invoked by both belligerent parties, each in its own way. These are also symptoms of a reactive and negative recourse, the vengeance of the body proper against an expropriatory and delocalizing tele-technoscience, identified with the globality of the market, with military-capitalistic hegemony, with the globalatinization of the European democratic model, in its double form: secular and religious. Whence – another figure of double origin – the foreseeable alliance of the worst effects of fanaticism, dogmatism or irrationalist obscurantism with hypercritical acumen and incisive analysis of the hegemonies and the models of the adversary (globalatinization, religion that does not speak its name, ethnocentrism putting on, as always, a show of 'universalism', market-driven science and technology, democratic rhetoric, 'humanitarian' strategy or 'keeping the peace' by means of peacekeeping forces, while never counting the dead of Rwanda, for instance, in the same manner as those of the United States of America or of Europe). This archaic and ostensibly more savage radicalization of 'religious' violence claims, in the name of 'religion', to allow the living community to rediscover its roots, its place, its body and its idiom intact (unscathed, safe, pure, proper). It spreads death and unleashes self-destruction in a desperate (auto-immune) gesture that attacks the blood of its own body: as though thereby to eradicate uprootedness and reappropriate the sacredness of life safe and sound. Double root, double uprootedness, double eradication.

(43) Double rape. A *new cruelty* would thus ally, in wars that are also wars of religion, the most advanced technoscientific calculability with a reactive savagery that would like to attack the body proper directly, the **sexual** thing, that can be raped, mutilated or simply denied, desexualized – yet another form of the

same violence. Is it possible to speak today of this double rape, to speak of it in a way that wouldn't be too foolish, uninformed or inane, while 'ignoring' 'psychoanalysis'? To ignore psychoanalysis can be done in a thousand ways, sometimes through extensive psychoanalytic knowledge that remains culturally disassociated. Psychoanalysis is ignored when it is not integrated into the most powerful discourses today on right, morality, politics, but also on science, philosophy, theology etc. There are a thousand ways of avoiding such consistent integration, even in the institutional milieu of psychoanalysis. No doubt, 'psychoanalysis' (we have to proceed more and more quickly) is receding in the West; it never broke out, never really crossed the borders of a part of 'old Europe'. This 'fact' is a legitimate part of the configuration of phenomena, signs, symptoms that we are questioning here under the title of 'religion'. How can one invoke a new Enlightenment in order to account for this 'return of the religious' without bringing into play at least some sort of logic of the unconscious? Without bringing it to bear on the question of radical evil and working out the reaction to radical evil that is at the centre of Freudian thought? This question can no longer be separated from many others: the repetition-compulsion, the 'death-drive', the difference between 'material truth' and 'historical truth' that imposes itself upon Freud with respect to 'religion', precisely, and that works itself out above all in closest proximity to an interminable **Jewish question**. It is true that psychoanalytic knowledge can in turn uproot and reawaken faith by opening itself to a new space of testimoniality, to a new instance of attestation, to a new experience of the symptom and of truth. This new space would have to be also, although not exclusively, legal and political. We shall have to return to this.

(44) We are constantly trying to think the interconnectedness, albeit otherwise, of knowledge *and* faith, technoscience *and* religious belief, calculation *and* the sacrosanct. In the process we have not ceased to encounter the alliance, holy or not, of the calculable and the incalculable. As well as that of the innumerable and of number, of the binary and of the digital. Demographic calculation, for instance, today concerns *one* of the aspects, at least, of the 'religious question' in its geopolitical dimension. As to the future of a religion, the question of number concerns as much the quantity of 'populations' as the living indemnity of 'peoples'. This does not merely signify that the religious factor has to be taken into account, but that the manner in which the faithful are counted must be changed in an age of globalization. Whether it is 'exemplary' or not, the **Jewish question** continues to be a rather good example (sample, particular case) for future elaboration of this demographic-religious problematic. In truth, this question of *numbers* obsesses, as is well known, the Holy Scriptures and the monotheisms. When they feel themselves threatened by an **expropriative and delocalizing** tele-technoscience, 'peoples' also fear new forms of invasion. They are terrified by alien 'populations', whose growth as well as presence, indirect or virtual – but as such, all the more oppressive – becomes incalculable. New ways of counting, therefore. There is more than one way of interpreting the unheard-of survival of the small 'Jewish people' and the global extension of its religion, single source of the two monotheisms which share in a certain domination of the world and of which, in dignity at least, it is the equal. There are a thousand ways of interpreting its resistance to attempts at extermination as well as to a demographic disproportion, the like of which is not known. But what will come of this survival the day (already arrived, perhaps) when globalization will be saturated? Then, 'globalization', a term so frequently encountered in American discourse,[35] will perhaps no longer allow the surface of the human earth to be segmented into micro-climates, those historical, cultural, political micro-zones, little Europe and the Middle East, in which the Jewish people has had such great difficulty surviving and bearing witness to its faith. 'I understand Judaism as the possibility of giving the Bible a context, of keeping this book readable', says Levinas. Does not the globalization of demographic reality and calculation render the probability of such a 'context' weaker than ever and as threatening for survival as the worst, the radical evil of the 'final solution'? 'God is the future' says Levinas also – while Heidegger sees the 'last god' announcing himself in the very absence of future: 'The last god: his occurring (*Wesung*) is found in the hint (*im Wink*), in the onset of an arrival still outstanding (*dem Anfall und Ausbleib der Ankunft*), as well as in the flight of the gods that are past and of their hidden metamorphosis.'[36]

This question is perhaps the most grave and most urgent for the state and the nations of Israel, but it concerns also all the Jews, and doubtless also, if less obviously, all the Christians in the world. Not at all Muslims today. And to this day, this is a fundamental difference between the three original 'great monotheisms'.

(45) Is there not always another *place* of dispersion? Where the source today divides itself again, like *the same* dissociating itself between faith and knowledge? The original reactivity to an **expropriative and delocalizing** tele-technoscience must respond to at least two figures. The latter are superimposed upon one another, they relay or replace each other, producing in truth at the very place of the emplacement nothing but indemnifying and auto-immune supplementarity:

1 Violent sundering *<arrachement>*, to be sure, from the radicality of roots (*Entwürzelung*, Heidegger would say; we cited him above) and from all forms of originary *physis*, from all the supposed resources of a force held to be authentically generative, sacred, unscathed, 'safe and sound' (*heilig*): ethnic identity, descent, family, nation, blood and soil, proper name, proper idiom, proper culture and memory.
2 But also, more than ever, the counter-fetishism of the same desire inverted, the animist relation to the tele-technoscientific machine, which then becomes a machine of evil, and of radical evil, but a machine to be manipulated as much as to be exorcised. Because this evil is to be domesticated and because one increasingly *uses* artifacts and prostheses of which one is totally ignorant, in a growing disproportion between knowledge and know-how, the space of such technical experience tends to become more animistic, magical, mystical. The spectral aspect of this experience persists and then tends to become – in proportion to this disproportion, one might say – increasingly **primitive and archaic**. So much so that its rejection, no less than its apparent appropriation, can assume the form of a religiosity that is both structural and invasive. A certain ecologist spirit can participate in this. (But a distinction must be drawn here between a vague ecologist ideology and ecological discourses and

politics that are often both competent and rigorous.) Never in the history of humanity, it would seem, has the disproportion between scientific incompetence and manipulatory competence been as serious. It is not even measurable any longer with respect to machines that are used everyday, with a mastery that is taken for granted and whose proximity is ever closer, more interior, more domestic. To be sure, in the recent past every soldier did not *know* how his firearm functioned although he *knew* very well how to use it. Yesterday, all the drivers of automobiles or travellers in a train did not always know very well how 'it works'. But their relative incompetence stands in no common (quantitative) measure nor in any (qualitative) analogy with that which today characterizes the relationship of the major part of humanity to the machines by which they live or with which they strive to live in daily familiarity. Who is capable of explaining scientifically to children how telephones function today (by undersea cables or by satellite), and the same is true of television, fax, computer, electronic mail, CD-ROMS, magnetic cards, jet planes, the distribution of nuclear energy, scanners, echography etc.?

(46) The same religiosity is obliged to ally the reactivity of the **primitive and archaic** return, as we have already said, *both* to obscurantist dogmatism *and* to hypercritical vigilance. The machines it combats by striving to appropriate them are also machines for destroying historical tradition. They can displace the traditional structures of national citizenship, they tend to efface both the borders of the state and the distinctive properties of languages. As a result, the religious reaction (rejection and assimilation, introjection and incorporation, impossible indemnification and mourning) normally follows two avenues that compete with each other and are apparently antithetical. Both of them, however, can as easily oppose or support a 'democratic' tradition: *either* the fervent return to national citizenship (patriotism of the home in all its forms, affection for the nation-state, awakening of nationalism or of ethnocentrism, most often allied with Churches or religious authorities) *or*, on the contrary, a protest that is universal, cosmopolitan or ecumenical: 'Ecologists, humanists, believers of all countries, unite in an International of anti-tele-technolog-

ism!' What is involved here, moreover, is an International that – and it is the singularity of our time – can only develop through the networks it combats, using the means of the adversary. At the same speed against an adversary that in truth is the same. The same <but> double, which is to say, what is called the contemporary in the blatant anachrony of its dislocation. Auto-immune indemnification. This is why these 'contemporary' movements are obliged to search for their salvation (the safe and sound as the sacrosanct), as well as their health in the paradox of a new alliance between the tele-technoscientific and the **two** sources of religion (the unscathed, *heilig, holy*, on the one hand, and faith or belief, the fiduciary on the other). The 'humanitarian' would provide a good example of this. 'Peacekeeping forces' as well.

(47) Of what should one take particular note in trying to formalize, in a concise manner, the axiom of the **two** sources around each of the two 'logics' if you like, or each of the two distinct 'resources' of what in the West goes by the Latinate name, 'religion'? Let us remember the hypothesis of these two sources: on the one hand, the fiduciar-*ity* of confidence, trustworthiness <*fiabilité*> or of trust <*fiance*> (belief, faith, credit and so on), and on the other, the unscathed-*ness* of the unscathed (the safe and sound, the immune, the holy, the sacred, *heilig*). Perhaps what in the first place ought be stressed is this: each of these axioms, as such, already reflects and presupposes the other. An *axiom* always affirms, as its name indicates, a value, a price; it confirms or promises an evaluation that should remain intact and entail, like every value, an act of faith. Secondly, both of these two axioms renders possible, but not necessary, something like a religion, which is to say, an instituted apparatus consisting of dogmas or of articles of faith that are both determinate and inseparable from a given historical *socius* (Church, clergy, socially legitimated authority, people, shared idiom, community of the faithful committed to the same faith and sanctioning the same history). But the gap between the opening of this *possibility (as a universal structure)* and the *determinate necessity* of this or that religion will always remain irreducible; and sometimes <it operates> within each religion, between on the one hand that which keeps it closest to its 'pure' and proper possibility, and on the other, its own historically determined necessities or authorities. Thus, one

can always criticize, reject or combat this or that form of sacredness or of belief, even of religious authority, in the name of the most originary possibility. The latter can be *universal* (faith or trustworthiness, 'good faith' as the condition of testimony, of the social bond and even of the most radical questioning) or already *particular*, for example belief in a specific originary event of revelation, of promise or of injunction, as in the reference to the Tables of the Law, to early Christianity, to some fundamental word or scripture, more archaic and more pure than all clerical or theological discourse. But it seems impossible to deny the *possibility* in whose name – thanks to which – the derived *necessity* (the authority or determinate belief) would be put in question, suspended, rejected or criticized, even deconstructed. One can *not* deny it, which means that the most one can do is to deny it. Any discourse that would be opposed to it would, in effect, always succumb to the figure or the logic of denial *<dénégation>*. Such would be the place where, before and after all the Enlightenments in the world, reason, critique, science, tele-technoscience, philosophy, **thought** in general, retain the *same* resource as religion in general.

(**48**) This last proposition, in particular in so far as it concerns **thought**, calls for several essential qualifications. It is impossible here to devote to it the necessary elaborations or to multiply, which would be easy, references to all those who, before and after all the Enlightenments in the world, believed in the independence of critical reason, of knowledge, technics, philosophy and thought with respect to religion and even to all faith. Why then privilege the example of Heidegger? Because of its extreme character and of what it tells us, in these times, about a certain 'extremity'. Without doubt, as we recalled it above, Heidegger wrote in a letter to Löwith in 1921: 'I am a "Christian theologian".'[37] This declaration would merit extended interpretation and certainly does not amount to a simple declaration of faith. But it neither contradicts, annuls nor excludes this other certainty: Heidegger not only declared, very early and on several occasions, that philosophy was in its very principle 'atheistic', that the idea of philosophy is 'madness' for faith (which at the least supposes the converse), and the idea of a Christian philosophy as absurd as a 'squared circle'. He not only excluded the very possibility of a philosophy of religion. He not only proposed a radical separation between philosophy and theology, the positive study of faith, if not between thought and theiology,[38] the discourse on the divinity of the divine. He not only attempted a 'destruction' of all forms of the ontotheological etc. He also wrote, in 1953: 'Belief [or faith] has no place in thought (*Der Glaube hat im Denken keinen Platz*).'[39] The context of this firm declaration is, to be sure, rather particular. The word *Glaube* seems to concern *first of all* a form of belief: credulity or the blind acceptance of authority. Heidegger was concerned with translating a *Spruch* (a saying, a sentence, decree, decision, poem, in any case a saying that cannot be reduced to its statement, whether theoretical, scientific or even philosophical, and that is tied in a singular and performative way to language). In a passage that concerns presence (*Anwesen, Präsenz*) and presence in the representation of representing (*in der Repräsentation des Vorstellens*), Heidegger writes: 'We can not scientifically prove (*beweisen*) the translation nor ought we simply by virtue of any authority put our trust in it [accredit it, believe it] (*glauben*). The reach of proof [inferred as 'scientific'] is too short. Belief has no place in thinking (*Der Glaube hat im Denken keinen Platz*).' Heidegger thus dismisses, back to back, scientific proof (which might suggest that to the same extent he accredits non-scientific testimony) and belief, here credulous and orthodox confidence that, closing its eyes, acquiesces and dogmatically sanctions authority (*Autorität*). Certainly, and who would contradict this? But Heidegger still extends with force and radicality the assertion that belief *in general* has no place in the experience or the act of thinking *in general*. And there we would have difficulty following him. First along his own path. Even if one succeeds in averting, in as rigorous a manner as possible, the risk of confusing modalities, levels, contexts, it still seems difficult to dissociate faith in general (*Glaube*) from what Heidegger himself, under the name of *Zusage* ('accord, acquiescing, trust or confidence'), designates as that which is most irreducible, indeed most originary in thought, prior even to that questioning said by him to constitute the piety (*Frömmigkeit*) of thinking. It is well known that without calling this last affirmation into question, he subsequently explained that it is the *Zusage* that constitutes the most proper movement of thinking, and that without it (although Heidegger does not state it in this form) the question itself would not emerge.[40] This recall to a sort of faith, this recall to the trust of the *Zusage*, 'before' all questioning, thus 'before' all knowledge, all philosophy etc., finds a particularly striking formulation relatively late (1957). It is formulated in the form – rare for Heidegger, whence the interest often attached to it – not of self-criticism or remorse but of a return to a formulation that demands to be nuanced, refined, let us say, to be re-engaged differently. But this gesture is less novel and singular than it might seem. Perhaps we will try to show elsewhere (it would require more time and space) that it accords with everything which, beginning with the existential analytics of the thought of being and of the truth of being, reaffirms continuously what we will call (in Latin, alas, and in a manner too Roman for Heidegger) a certain *testimonial sacredness* or, we would even go so far as to say, a sworn word *<foi jurée>*. This reaffirmation continues throughout Heidegger's entire work. It resides in the decisive and largely underestimated motif of attestation (*Bezeugung*) in *Sein und Zeit* as well as in all the other motifs that are inseparable from and dependent upon it, which is to say, *all* the existentials and, specifically, that of conscience (*Gewissen*), originary responsibility or guilt (*Schuldigsein*) and *Entschlossenheit* (resolute determination). We cannot address here the immense question of the ontological repetition, in all these concepts, of a so markedly Christian tradition. Let us therefore limit ourselves to situating a principle of reading. Like the experience of authentic attestation (*Bezeugung*) and like everything that depends upon it, the point of departure of *Sein und Zeit* resides in a situation that cannot be radically alien to what is called *faith*. Not religion, to be sure, nor theology, but that which in faith acquiesces before or beyond all questioning, in the already common experience of a language and of a 'we'. The reader of *Sein und Zeit* and the signatory who takes him as witness are already situated in this element of faith from the moment that Heidegger says 'we' to justify the choice of the 'exemplary' being that is *Dasein*, the questioning being that must be interrogated as an exemplary witness. And what renders possible, for this 'we', the positing and elaboration of the question of being, the unfolding and determining of its 'formal structure' (*das Gefragte, das Erfragte, das Befragte*), *prior to all questioning* – is it not what Heidegger then calls a *Faktum*, that is, the vague and ordinary pre-comprehension of the meaning of being, and first of all of the words 'is' or 'be' in language or in a language (§ 2)? This *Faktum* is not an empirical fact. Each time Heidegger employs this word, we are necessarily led back to a zone where acquiescence is *de rigueur*. Whether this is formulated or not, it remains a requirement prior to and in view of every possible question, and hence prior to all philosophy, all theology, all science, all critique, all reason etc. This zone is that of a faith incessantly reaffirmed throughout an open chain of concepts, beginning with those that we have already cited (*Bezeugung, Zusage*, etc.), but it also communicates with everything in Heidegger's way of thinking that marks the reserved holding-back of restraint (*Verhaltenheit*) or the sojourn (*Aufenthalt*) in modesty (*Scheu*) in the vicinity of the unscathed, the sacred, the safe and sound (*das Heilige*), the passage or the coming of the last god that man is doubtless not yet ready to receive.[41] That the movement proper to this faith does not constitute a religion is all too evident. Is it, however, untouched <*indemne*> by all religiosity? Perhaps. But by all 'belief', by that 'belief' that would have 'no place in thinking'? This seems less certain. Since the major question remains, in our eyes, albeit in a form that is still quite new: 'What does it mean to believe?', we will ask (elsewhere) how and why Heidegger can at the same time affirm one of the possibilities of the 'religious', of which we have just schematically recalled the signs (*Faktum, Bezeugung, Zusage, Verhaltenheit, Heilige*, etc.) and reject so energetically 'belief' or 'faith' (*Glaube*).[42] Our hypothesis again refers back to the two sources or two strata of religion which we distinguished above: the experience of sacredness and the experience of belief. More receptive to the first (in its Graeco-Hölderlinian or even archeo-Christian tradition), Heidegger was probably more resistant to the second, which he constantly reduced to figures he never ceased to put into question, not to say 'destroy' or denounce: dogmatic or credulous belief in authority, to be sure, but also belief according to the religions of the Book and ontotheology, and above all, that which in the belief in the other could appear to him (wrongly, we would say) to appeal necessarily to the egological subjectivity of an *alter ego*. We are speaking here of the belief that is demanded, required, of the faithful belief in what, having come from the utterly other <*de l'autre tout autre*>, there where its originary presentation in person would forever be impossible (**witnessing** or given word in the most elementary and irreducible sense, promise of truth up to and including perjury), would constitute the condition of *Mitsein*, of the relation to or address of the other in general.

(49) Beyond the culture, semantics or history of law – moreover intertwined – which determine this word or this concept, the experience of **witnessing** situates a convergence of *these* two sources: the *unscathed* (the safe, the sacred or the saintly) and the *fiduciary* (trustworthiness, fidelity, credit, belief or faith, 'good faith' implied in the worst 'bad faith'). We speak of *these* two sources there, in one place of their convergence, for the figure of the two sources, as we have verified, proliferates, can no longer be counted, and therein lies perhaps another reason of our questioning. In testimony, truth is promised beyond all proof, all perception, all intuitive demonstration. Even if I lie or perjure myself (and always and especially when I do), I promise truth and ask the other to believe the other that I am, there where I am the only one able to bear witness and where the order of proof or of intuition will never be reducible to or homogeneous with the elementary trust <*fiduciarité*>, the 'good faith' that is promised or demanded. The latter, to be sure, is never pure of all iterability nor of all technics, and hence of all **calculability**. For it also promises its repetition from the very first instant. It is involved <*engagé*> in every address of the other. From the first instant it is co-extensive with this other and thus conditions every 'social bond', every questioning, all knowledge, performativity and every tele-technoscientific performance, including those of its forms that are the most synthetic, artificial, prosthetic, calculable. The act of faith demanded in bearing witness exceeds, through its structure, all intuition and all proof, all knowledge ('I swear that I am telling the truth, not necessarily the "objective truth", but the truth of what I believe to be the truth, I am telling you this truth, believe me, believe what I believe, there, where you will never be able to see nor know the irreplaceable yet universalizable, exemplary place from which I speak to you; perhaps my testimony is false, but I am sincere and in good faith, it is not false <as> testimony'). What therefore does the promise of this axiomatic (quasi-transcendental) performative do that conditions and foreshadows 'sincere' declarations no less than lies and perjuries, and thus all address of the other? It amounts to saying: 'Believe what I say as

one believes in a miracle.' Even the slightest testimony concerning the most plausible, ordinary or everyday thing cannot do otherwise: it must still appeal to faith as would a miracle. It offers itself like the miracle itself in a space that leaves no room for disenchantment. The experience of disenchantment, however indubitable it is, is only one modality of this 'miraculous' experience, the reactive and passing effect, in each of its historical determinations, of the testimonially miraculous. That one should be called upon to believe in testimony as in a miracle or an 'extraordinary story' – this is what inscribes itself without hesitation in the very concept of bearing witness. And one should not be amazed to see examples of 'miracles' invading all the problematics of testimony, whether they are classical or not, critical or not. *Pure* attestation, if there is such a thing, pertains to the experience of faith and of the miracle. Implied in every 'social bond', however ordinary, it also renders itself indispensable to Science no less than to Philosophy and to Religion. This source can collect or scatter itself, rejoin or disjoin itself. Either at the same time or successively. It can appear contemporaneous with itself where testimonial trust in the pledge <*gage*> of the other unites belief in the other with the sacralization of a presence–absence or with a sanctification of the law, as law of the other. It can divide itself in various ways. First of all, in the alternative between sacredness without belief (index of this algebra: 'Heidegger') and faith in a holiness without sacredness, in a desacralizing truth, even making of a certain disenchantment the condition of authentic holiness (index: 'Levinas' – notably the author of *From the Sacred to the Holy*). As a follow-up, it can dissociate itself when what constitutes the said 'social bond' in belief is also an interruption. There is no opposition, fundamentally, between 'social bond' and 'social unravelling'. A certain interruptive unravelling is the condition of the 'social bond', the very respiration of all 'community'. This is not even the knot of a reciprocal condition, but rather the possibility that every knot can come undone, be cut or interrupted. This is where the *socius* or the relation to the other would disclose itself to be the secret of testimonial experience – and hence, of a certain faith. If belief is the ether of the address and relation to the utterly other, it is <to be found> in the experience itself of non-relationship or of absolute *interruption* (indices: 'Blanchot', 'Levinas' . . .). Here as well, the hypersanctification of this non-relation or of this transcendence would come about by way of desacralization rather than through secularization or laicization, concepts that are too Christian; perhaps even by way of a certain 'atheism', in any case by way of a radical experience of the resources of 'negative theology' – and going beyond even this tradition. Here we would have to separate – thanks to another vocabulary, for example Hebraic (the holiness of *kidouch*) – the sacred and the holy, and no longer settle for the Latinate distinction, recalled by Benveniste, between the natural sacredness in things and the holiness of institutions or of the law.[43] This interruptive dis-junction enjoins a sort of incommensurable equality within absolute dissymmetry. The law of this untimeliness interrupts and makes history, it undoes all contemporaneity and opens the very space of faith. It designates disenchantment as the *very resource of the religious*. The first and the last. Nothing seems therefore more uncertain, more difficult to sustain, nothing seems here or there more imprudent than a self-assured discourse on the age of disenchantment, the era of secularization, the time of laicization etc.

(50) **Calculability**: question, apparently arithmetic, of two, or rather of n + One, through and beyond the demography of which we spoke above. Why should there always have to be *more than one* source? There would not have to be two sources of religion. There would be faith and religion, faith or religion, because *there are at least two*. Because there are, for the best and for the worst, division and iterability of the source. This supplement introduces the incalculable at the heart of the calculable. (Levinas: 'It is this being-two <*être à deux*> that is human, that is spiritual.') But the more than One <*plus d'Un*>[44] is at once more than two. There is no alliance of two, unless it is to signify in effect the pure madness of pure faith. The worst violence. The more than One is this n + One which introduces the order of faith or of trust in the address of the other, but also the mechanical, machine-like division (testimonial affirmation and reactivity, 'yes, yes', etc., answering machine and the possibility of **radical evil**: perjury, lies, remote-control murder, ordered at a distance even when it rapes and kills with bare hands).

(51) The possibility of **radical evil** both destroys and institutes the religious. Ontotheology does the same when it suspends

sacrifice and prayer, the truth of this prayer that maintains itself, recalling Aristotle one more time, beyond the true and the false, beyond their opposition, in any case, according to a certain concept of truth or of judgement. Like benediction, prayer pertains to the originary regime of testimonial faith or of martyrdom that we are trying to think here in its most 'critical' force. Ontotheology en**crypts** faith and destines it to the condition of a sort of Spanish Marrano who would have lost – in truth, dispersed, multiplied – everything up to and including the memory of his unique secret. Emblem of a still life: an opened pomegranate, one Passover evening, on a tray.

(52) At the bottom without bottom of this **crypt**, the One + *n* incalculably engenders all these supplements. *It makes violence of itself, does violence to itself and keeps itself from the other.* The auto-immunity of religion can only indemnify itself without assignable end. On the bottom without bottom of an always virgin impassibility, *chora* of tomorrow in languages we no longer know or do not yet speak. This place is unique, it is the One without name. It *makes way, perhaps*, but without the slightest generosity, neither divine nor human. The dispersion of ashes is not even promised there, nor death given.

(This, perhaps, is what I would have liked to say of a certain Mount Moriah – while going to Capri, last year, close by the Vesuvius of Gradiva. Today I remember what I had just finished reading in Genet at Chatila, *of which so many of the premises deserve to be remembered here, in so many languages, the actors and the victims, and the eves and the consequence, all the landscapes and all the spectres: 'One of the questions I will not avoid is that of religion.'*[45] Laguna, 26 April 1995.)

Translated by Samuel Weber

Notes

1 *Translator's note*: the use of angle brackets < > indicates interpolations of the translator. Such brackets contain either a few words from the original or short emendations. Parentheses and square brackets reproduce those in the French text. All footnotes stem from the author except where otherwise indicated (as here).

2 Emile Benveniste, *Indo-European Language and Society*, trans. Elizabeth Palmer (Faber and Faber, London, 1973), pp. 445–6. We shall often cite Benveniste in order to leave him a responsibility – that of speaking for example with assurance of 'proper meaning', precisely in the case of the sun or of light, but also with regard to everything else. This assurance seems greatly exaggerated and more than problematic. (*Translator's note*: the published English translation has been modified throughout in the interest of greater literalness.)

3 Cf. 'Sauf le nom', in Jacques Derrida, *On the Name*, ed. Tom Dutoit, trans. David Wood, John P. Leavey Jr and Ian McLeod, (Stanford, Stanford University Press, 1995), notably p. 80 ff.

4 In 'How to avoid speaking: denials', in *Languages of the Unsayable: the Play of Negativity in Literature and Literary Theory*, ed. by Sanford Budick and Wolfgang Iser (New York, Columbia University Press, 1989), pp. 3–70, I treat in a more precise manner, in an analogous context, the themes of hierarchy and of 'topolitology'.

5 I. Kant, *Religion Within the Limits of Reason Alone*, Book I, section 3.

6 Ibid., Book I, section 4.

7 *Translator's note*: It should be noted that the French neologism created by Derrida – '*mondialatinisation*' – emphasizes the notion of 'world', whereas the English word used in this translation: 'globalatinization' – stresses that of 'globality'. Since 'globe' suggests 'earth' rather than 'world', the use of 'globalatinization' here tends to efface an important distinction made throughout this chapter. The interest of this problem, however, is that it may not 'simply' be one of translation. For if, as Derrida argues in this chapter, the major idiom and vehicle of the process of *mondialatinisation* today is precisely Anglo-American, then the very fact that the notion of 'globality' comes to supplant that of 'world' in the most common usage of this language must itself be highly significant. This difficulty of translation, in short, adds a new question to those raised in this chapter: what happens to the notion of 'world', and to its distinction from 'earth' and 'globe', if the predominant language of 'mondialatinization' tends to speak not of 'world' but of 'globality'?

8 The Latin (even Roman) word used by Levinas, for example in *Du sacré au saint* [*From the Sacred to the Holy*] (Paris, Éditions de Minuit, 1977) is, to be sure, only the translation of a Hebrew word (*kidouch*).

9 Cf., for example, M. Heidegger, *Andenken* (1943): 'Poets, when they are in their being, are prophetic. But they are not "prophets" in the Judaeo-Christian sense of the word. The "prophets" of these religions do not restrict themselves to the anticipatory-founding

word of the Sacred (*das voraufgründende Wort des Heiligen*). They immediately announce the god upon whom one can subsequently count as upon the certain guarantee of salvation in superterrestrial beatitude. The poetry of Hölderlin should not be disfigured with the "religious" element of "religion", which remains the business of the Roman way of interpreting (*eine Sache der römischen Deutung*) the relations between humans and gods.' The poet is not a Seer (*Seher*) nor a divine (*Wahrsager*). 'The Sacred (*das Heilige*) that is uttered in poetic prediction only opens the time of an apparition of the gods and indicates the region where it resides (*die Ortschaft des Wohnens*) on this earth of man required by the destiny of history . . . His dream [the poet's] is divine, but it does not dream a god.' (*Gesamtausgabe*, vol. IV, p. 114.)

More than twenty years later, in 1962, this protest is renewed against Rome, against the essentially Roman figure of religion. It brings together into a single configuration modern humanism, technics, politics and law. In the course of his trip to Greece, after visiting the orthodox monastery of Kaisariani, above Athens, Heidegger notes: 'What the little church possesses that is Christian remains in harmony with ancient Greece, a pervasive spirit that does not bow before the theocratic thought seeped in canon law (*dem kirchenstaatlich-juristischen Denken*) of the Roman Church and its theology. On the site where today there is the convent, there was formerly a "pagan" sanctuary (*ein "heidnisches" Heiligtum*) dedicated to Artemis' (*Aufenthalte, Séjours*, Paris, ed. du Rocher, 1989, French translation F. Vezin slightly modified, p. 71).

Prior to this, when his journey brings him close to the island of Corfu – yet another island – Heidegger recalls that *another island*, Sicily, appeared to Goethe to be closer to Greece; and the same recollection associates in two phrases the 'traits of a romanized, Italian (*römisch-italienischen*) Greece', seen in the 'light of modern humanism', and the coming of the 'machine age' (ibid., p. 19). And since the island also figures our gathering-place <*lieu d'insistance*>, let us not forget that for Heidegger, this Greek voyage remains above all a 'sojourn' (*Aufenthalt*), a modest (*Scheu*) stopover <*halte*> in the vicinity of Delos, the visible or manifest, a meditation of unveiling via its name. Delos is also the 'saintly' or 'sacred' island (*die heilige Insel*) (ibid., p. 50).

10 See 'Khora', in Derrida, *On the Name*, and *Specters of Marx*, trans. Peggy Kamuf (New York and London, Routledge, 1994) and 'Force of law', in D. Cornell et al. (eds), *Deconstruction and the Possibility of Justice* (New York and London, Routledge, 1992), pp. 3–67.

11 I must refer here to the reading of this text, in particular to the

'political' reading of it, that I propose in 'How to avoid speaking: denials', 'Khora' and 'Sauf le nom'.

12 See 'Sauf le nom', p. 76. *Translator's note*: In the published English version, *'l'épreuve de Khôra'* is translated more idiomatically as 'the test of Chora'.

13 Even if Voltaire responds to the question, 'What is tolerance?' by stating that 'It is the prerogative of humanity', the example of excellence here, the most elevated inspiration of this 'humanity' remains Christian: 'Of all the religions, Christianity is without doubt that which ought to inspire the greatest tolerance, even if until now Christians have been the most intolerant of men' (*Philosophical Dictionary*, article 'Tolerance').

The word 'tolerance' thus conceals a story: it tells above all an intra-Christian history and experience. It delivers the message that Christians address to other Christians. Christians ('the most intolerant') are reminded, by a co-religionist and in a mode that is essentially co-religionist, of the word of Jesus and of the authentic Christianity at its origins. If one were not fearful of shocking too many people all at once, one could say that by their vehement anti-Christianity, by their opposition above all to the Roman Church, as much as by their declared preference, sometimes nostalgic, for primitive Christianity, Voltaire and Heidegger belong to the same tradition: proto-Catholic.

14 Voltaire, 'Tolerance', *Philosophical Dictionary*.

15 As I have tried to do elsewhere (*Specters of Marx*, p. 23 ff.), I propose to think the condition of justice in relation to a certain sundering <*déliaison*>, in relation to the always-safe, always-to-be-saved possibility of this secret of disassociation, rather than through the bringing-together (*Versammlung*) towards which Heidegger retraces it, in his concern, doubtless legitimate in part, to extract *Dike* from the authority of *Ius*, which is to say, from its more recent ethico-juridical representations.

16 *Indemnis*: that which has not suffered damage or prejudice, *damnum*; this latter word will have given in French '*dam*' ('*au grand dam*': to the detriment or displeasure of . . .) and comes from *dap-no-m*, tied to *daps*, *dapis*, that is, to the sacrifice offered the Gods as ritual compensation. In this latter case, one could speak of *indemnification* and we will use this word here or there to designate both the process of compensation and the restitution, sometimes sacrificial, that *re*constitutes purity intact, renders integrity safe and sound, restores cleanliness <*propreté*> *and property unimpaired. This is indeed what the word 'unscathed'* <*indemne*> says: the pure, non-contaminated, untouched, the sacred and holy before all profanation,

all wound, all offence, all lesion. It has often been chosen to translate *heilig* ('sacred, safe and sound, intact') in Heidegger. Since the word *heilig* will be at the centre of these reflections, we therefore had to elucidate here and now the use that we shall be making of the words 'unscathed', 'indemnity', 'indemnification'. In what follows, we shall associate them regularly with the words 'immune', 'immunity', 'immunization', and above all, 'auto-immunity'.

17 There is insufficient space to multiply in this regard the images or the indications, one could say the icons of our time: the *organization, conception* (generative forces, structures and capital) as well as the *audiovisual representation* of cultic or socio-religious phenomena. In a digitalized 'cyberspace', prosthesis upon prosthesis, a heavenly glance, monstrous, bestial or divine, something like an eye of CNN, watches permanently: over Jerusalem and its three monotheisms, over the multiplicity, the unprecedented speed and scope of the moves of a Pope versed in televisual rhetoric (of which the last encyclical, *Evangelium vitae*, against abortion and euthanasia, for the sacredness or holiness of a life that is safe and sound – unscathed, *heilig*, holy – for its reproduction in conjugal love – sole immunity admitted, with priestly celibacy, against human immuno-deficiency virus (HIV) – is immediately transmitted, massively 'marketed' and available on CD-ROM; everything down to the signs of presence in the mystery of the Eucharist is 'cederomized'; over airborn pilgrimages to Mecca; over so many miracles transmitted live (most frequently, healings, which is to say, returns to the unscathed, *heilig*, holy, indemnifications) followed by commercials, before thousands in an American television studio; over the international and televisual diplomacy of the Dalai Lama etc.

So remarkably adapted to the scale and the evolutions of global demography, so well adjusted to the technoscientific, economic and mediatic powers of our time, the power of all these phenomena to bear witness finds itself formidably intensified, at the same time as it is collected in a digitalized space by supersonic airplanes or by audiovisual antennae. The ether of religion will always have been hospitable to a certain spectral virtuality. Today, like the sublimity of the starry heavens at the bottom of our hearts, the 'cederomized' 'cyberspaced' religion also entails the accelerated and hypercapitalized relaunching of founding spectres. On CD-ROM, heavenly trajectories of satellites, jet, TV, e-mail or Internet networks. Actually or virtually universalizable, ultra-internationalizable, incarnated by new 'corporations' that are increasingly independent of the powers of states (democratic or not, it makes little difference at bottom, all of that has to be reconsidered, like the 'globalatinity' of international law in its current state, which is to say, on the threshold of a process of accelerated and unpredictable transformation).

18 Without even speaking of other difficulties and of other possible objections to the Schmittian theory of the political, and thus also of the religious. I take the liberty of referring here to *Politiques de l'amitié*, (Paris, Galilée, 1994, English trans. *Politics of Friendship*, London, Verso Books, forthcoming).

19 Benveniste, *Indo-European Language*, p. 475, article 'Libation, 1: sponsio'.

20 Ibid., p. 521. For example, 'This is where the expression *religio est*, "to have scruples", comes from . . . This usage is constant during the classical period. . . . In sum, *religio* is a hesitation that holds back, a scruple that prevents, and not a sentiment that guides an action or that incites one to practice a cult. It seems to us that this meaning, demonstrated by ancient usage beyond the slightest ambiguity, imposes a single interpretation for *religio*: that which Cicero gives in attaching *religio* to *legere*.'

21 Ibid., pp. 475–6. Only the foreign words and the expression 'answer for' are emphasized by Benveniste.

22 Ibid., p. 516 ff. The Indo-European vocabulary does not dispose of any 'common term' for 'religion' and it is in 'the nature itself of this notion not to lend itself to a single and constant appellation'. Correlatively, we would have considerable difficulty in discovering, as such, what one would retrospectively be tempted to identify under this name, which is to say, an institutional reality resembling what we call 'religion'. We would in any case have difficulty in finding anything of that order in the form of a socially separable entity. Moreover, when Benveniste proposes to study solely *two terms*, Greek and Latin, which, he says, 'can pass for *equivalents* of "religion"', we ought for our part to underscore two significant traits, two paradoxes as well, even two logical scandals:

    1 Benveniste presupposes thus an assured meaning of the word 'religion', since he authorizes himself to identify its 'equivalents'. However, it seems to me that he at no point thematizes or problematizes this pre-comprehension or this presupposition. Nothing permits one to authorize the hypothesis that in his eyes the 'Christian' meaning provides here the guiding reference, since, as he himself says, 'the interpretation by *religare* ("bond, obligation") . . . invented by Christians [is] historically false.'
    2 On the other hand, when, after the Greek word *threskeia* ('cult and piety, ritual observance', and much later 'religion'), Benveniste retains – and this is the other term of the pair – the word *religio*, it is only as an 'equivalent' (which could hardly mean identical) to

'religion'. We find ourselves confronted by a paradoxical situation that describes very well, at an interval of one page, the double and disconcerting use that Benveniste makes, deliberately or not, of the word 'equivalent' – which we emphasize thus:

(a) 'We shall retain solely two terms [*threskeia* and *religio*] which, one in Greek and the other in Latin, can pass for equivalents of "religion"' (p. 517). Here, then, are two words that can pass, in short, for equivalents of one of them, which itself, on the following page, is said not to have any equivalent in the world, not at least in 'Western languages', which would render it 'infinitely more important in all respects'!

(b) 'We now come to the second term, infinitely more important in all respects: it is the Latin *religio*, which remains, in all Western languages, the sole and constant word, for which no *equivalent* or substitute has ever been able to impose itself' (p. 518; emphasis added). It is a 'proper meaning' (attested to by Cicero), and it is the 'proper and constant usages' (pp. 519, 521) that Benveniste intends to identify for this word which is in short an equivalent (among others, but without equivalent!) for that which cannot be designed in short by anything but itself, which is to say, by an equivalent without equivalent.

At bottom, is this not the least deficient definition of religion? In any case, what Benveniste's formal or logical inconsistency designates is perhaps the most faithful reflection, even the most theatrical symptom of what actually occurred in the 'history of humanity', and what we here call the 'globalatinization' of 'religion'.

23 See Section 33, points 1 and 2, pp. 34–5.

24 Benveniste, *Indo-European Language*, p. 521.

25 Something that Heidegger doubtless would have done, given that in his eyes the claimed 'return of the religious' would signify nothing but the persistence of a Roman determination of 'religion'. The latter would go together with a dominant juridical system and concept of the state that themselves would be inseparable from the 'machine age'. (See Section 18, note 9, pp. 67–8).

26 Benveniste, *Indo-European Language*, p. 516.

27 The 'immune' (*immunis*) is freed or exempted from the charges, the service, the taxes, the obligations (*munus*, root of the common of community). This freedom or this exemption was subsequently transported into the domains of constitutional or international law (parliamentary or diplomatic immunity), but it also belongs to the history of the Christian Church and to canon law; the immunity of temples also involved the inviolability of the asylum that could be found there (Voltaire indignantly attacked this 'immunity of temples'

as a 'revolting example' of 'contempt for the laws' and of 'ecclesiastical ambition'); Urban VIII created a congregation of ecclesiastical immunity: against taxes and military service, against common justice (privilege designated as that of the *for*) and against police searches, etc. It is especially in the domain of biology that the lexical resources of immunity have developed their authority. The immunitary reaction protects the 'indemn-ity' of the body proper in producing antibodies against foreign antigens. As for the process of auto-immunization, which interests us particularly here, it consists for a living organism, as is well known and in short, of protecting itself against its self-protection by destroying its own immune system. As the phenomenon of these antibodies is extended to a broader zone of pathology and as one resorts increasingly to the positive virtues of immuno-depressants destined to limit the mechanisms of rejection and to facilitate the tolerance of certain organ transplants, we feel ourselves authorized to speak of a sort of general logic of auto-immunization. It seems indispensable to us today for thinking the relations between faith and knowledge, religion and science, as well as the duplicity of sources in general.

28 This is testified to by certain phenomena, at least, of 'fundamentalism' or of 'integrism', in particular in 'Islamism', which represents today the most powerful example of such fundamentalisms as measured by the scale of global demography. The most evident characteristics are too well known to dwell on (fanaticism, obscurantism, lethal violence, terrorism, oppression of women, etc.). But it is often forgotten that, notably in its ties to the Arab world, and through all the forms of brutal immunitary and indemnificatory reactivity against a techno-economical modernity to which a long history prevents it from adapting, this 'Islamism' also develops a radical critique of what ties democracy *today, in its limits, in its concept and its effective power*, to the market and to the tele-technoscientific reason that dominates it.

29 *Translator's note*: '*sans lequel on ne saurait bien faire*': in addition to the ambiguity of the more literal meaning of this phrase, (a) 'without which nothing good could be done', and (b) 'without which nothing could be done well', the French expression here recalls the colloquial idiom 'ça commence à bien faire: y en a marre,' which adds the ironic connotation of 'that's enough!' to the dialectic of good and evil.

30 Let us worry <*Egrenons*> the premisses here of a work to come. Let them be drawn first, and once again, from that rich chapter of Benveniste's *Indo-European Language and Society*, addressing the Sacred and the Holy after having opportunely recalled several

'methodological difficulties'. It is true that to us these 'difficulties' seem even more serious and more fundamental than to Benveniste – even if he is willing to acknowledge the risk of 'seeing the object of study dissolve bit by bit' (p. 445). Maintaining the cult of 'original meaning' (religion itself, and the 'sacred'), Benveniste identifies, through the enormously complex network of idioms, filiations and etymologies studied, the recurrent and insistent theme of the 'fertility' of the 'strong', of the 'powerful', in particular in the figure or the imaginal scheme of *swelling*.

We may be permitted the following long citation, while referring the reader to the article itself for the rest: 'The adjective *sura* does not signify merely "strong"; it is also a qualification of a number of gods, of several heroes including Zarathustra, and of certain notions such as "dawn". Here, comparison with related forms of the same root can lead us to the original meaning. The Vedic verb *su- sva* signifies "to swell, grow", implying "force" and "prosperity"; whence *sura-*, "strong, valiant". The same conceptional relation joins in Greek the present *kueîn*, "to be pregnant, carry in the womb", the noun *kûma*, "swelling (of waves), flood", on the one hand, and *kûros*, "force, sovereignty", *kúrios*, "sovereign", on the other. This juxtaposition brings out the initial identity of the meaning of "swell" and, in each of the three languages, a specific evolution ... In Indo-Iranian no less than in Greek the meaning evolves from "swelling" to "strength" or "prosperity" ... Between gr. *kuéo*, "to be pregnant", and *kúrios*, "sovereign", between Av. *sura*, "strong", and *spénta*, relations are thus restored which, little by little, make more precise the singular origin of the notion of "sacred" ... The holy and sacred character is thus defined through a notion of exuberant and fecund force, capable of bringing to life, of causing the productions of nature to burst forth' (pp. 448–9).

One could also inscribe under the title of the 'two sources' the remarkable fact, often emphasized by Benveniste, that 'almost everywhere' there corresponds to the 'notion of the "sacred" not one but two distinct terms'. Benveniste analyses them, notably in German (the Gothic *weihs*, 'consecrated', and the Runic *hailag*, ger. *heilig*) in Latin *sacer* and *sanctus*, in Greek *hágios* and *hierós*. At the origin of the German *heilig*, the Gothic adjective *hails* translates the idea of 'soundness, health, physical integrity', translation of the Greek *hygies, hygiainon*, 'in good health'. The corresponding verbal forms signify 'render or become healthy, heal'. (On might situate here – although Benveniste does not – the necessity for every religion or all sacralization also to involve healing – *heilen* – health, hail or promise of a cure – *cura, Sorge* – horizon of redemption, of the restoration of the unscathed, of indemnification). The same for the English, 'holy', neighbour of 'whole' ('entire, intact', therefore 'safe, saved, unscathed in its integrity, immune'). The Gothic *hails*, 'in good health, in possession of physical integrity', carries with it a wish, as does the Greek *khaîre*, 'hail!'. Benveniste underscores its 'religious value' 'Whoever possesses "hail" <*le "salut"*>, that is, whose physical integrity is intact, is also capable of conferring "hail". "To be intact" is the luck that one wishes, predicts or expects. It is natural to have seen in such perfect "integrity" a divine grace, a sacred meaning. By its very nature, divinity possesses the gift of integrity, of being hail, of luck, and can impart it to human beings ... In the course of history the primitive Gothic term *weihs* was replaced by *hails, hailigs*' (pp. 451–2).

31 Elsewhere, in a seminar, I attempt to reflect in a more sustained manner on this value of the hold and on its lexical ramifications, in particular surrounding the use of *halten* by Heidegger. In addition to *Aufenthalt* (stopover, ethos, often involving the *heilig*), *Verhaltenheit* (modesty or respect, scruple, reserve or silent discretion that suspends itself in and as reticence) would be only one example, albeit a major one for what concerns us here and taking into account the role played by this concept in the *Beiträge zur Philosophie* with respect to the 'last god', or the 'other god', the god who comes or the god who passes. I refer here, in particular regarding this last theme, to the recent study by Jean-François Courtine, 'Les traces et le passage de Dieu dans les *Beiträge zur Philosophie* de Martin Heidegger' ('The traces and passing of God in Heidegger's *Contributions to Philosophy*'), in *Archivio di filosofia*, 1994, nos 1–3. When he refers to Heidegger's insistence on modern nihilism as 'uprooting' (*Entwürzelung*), Courtine rightly associates it with what is said of – and always implicitly against – the *Gestell* and all 'technical-instrumental manipulation of beings' (*Machenschaft*), with which he even associates 'a critique of the idea of creation directed primarily against Christianity' (p. 528). This seems to go in the direction of the hypothesis developed above: Heidegger directs suspicion at the same time against 'religion' (especially Christian–Roman), against belief, and against that in technics which menaces the safe and sound, the unscathed or the immune, the sacrosanct (*heilig*). The interest of his 'position' consists, simplifying considerably, in the way it tends to take its distance <*se déprendre*> from *both* religion and technics, or rather from what is called *Gestell* and *Machenschaft*, as though they were the same. The *same*, yes, as what we are trying to say here as well, modestly and in our fashion. And the *same* neither excludes nor effaces any of the differential folds. But once this *same possibility*

is recognized or thought, it is not certain that it calls only for a Heideggerian 'response', nor that the latter is alien or exterior to this *same possibility*, be it the logic of the unscathed, or the auto-immune indemnification that we are trying to approach here. We shall return to this later in this text and elsewhere.

32 That is, of what in Western cultures remains sacrificial, up to and including its industrial, sacrificial and 'carno-phallogo-centric' implementation. On this latter concept, I take the liberty of referring to '"Eating Well", or the calculation of the subject', in Jacques Derrida, *Points ... Interviews, 1974–94*, ed. Elisabeth Weber, trans. Peggy Kamuf et al. (Stanford, Stanford University Press, 1995), pp. 255–87.

33 Concerning the association and disassociation of these two values (*sacer* and *sanctus*), we refer below to Benveniste and to Levinas.

34 *Translator's note*: Henri Bergson, *The Two Sources of Morality and Religion*, trans. R. Ashley Audra and Cloudesley Brereton, with the assistance of W. Horsfall Carter (Notre Dame, University of Notre Dame Press, 1986), p. 317.

35 *Translator's note*: Although Derrida uses the English word '*globalisation*' here, elsewhere he consistently uses the French term, '*mondialisation*' and the neologism, '*mondialatinisation*', which have been translated throughout as 'globalization' and 'globalatinization'.

36 *Beiträge zur Philosophie*, p. 256. French translation and cited by J.-F. Courtine, 'Les traces et le passage de Dieu', p. 533. On a certain question of the future, Judaism and Jewishness, I permit myself to refer to 'Archive fever: A Freudian Impression', trans. Eric Prenowitz, *diacritics*, 25 (Summer, 1995), pp. 9–63.

37 This letter to Löwith, dated 19 August 1921, was recently cited in French by J. Barash, *Heidegger et son siècle* (Paris, PUF, 1995), p. 80, n. 3, and by Françoise Dastur, in 'Heidegger et la théologie', *Revue philosophique de Louvain*, May–August 1994, nos 2–3, p. 229. Together with that of Jean-François Courtine cited above, the latter study is one of the most illuminating and richest, it seems to me, that have been published on this subject in recent years.

38 I take the liberty, in regard to these questions, of referring once again to 'How to avoid speaking'. As to the divinity of the divine, the *theion*, which would thus be the theme of a theiology, distinct both from theology and from religion, the multiplicity of its meanings should not be overlooked. Already in Plato, and more specifically in the *Timaeus*, where there are no less than four concepts of the divine (see on this point the remarkable work of Serge Margel, *Le Tombeau du dieu artisan*, Paris, Éditions de Minuit, 1995). It is true that this multiplicity does not prevent but on the contrary commands one to return to the unitary pre-comprehension, to the horizon of meaning

as it is called, of the same word. Even if, in the final accounting, this horizon itself must be abandoned.

39 'The Anaximander fragment', in Martin Heidegger, *Early Greek Thinking*, trans. David Farrell Krell and Frank A. Capuzzi (San Francisco, Harper, 1984), p. 57; 'Der Spruch des Anaximander', *Holzwege*, Klostermann, 1950, p. 343.

40 On these issues – and since I am unable to develop them here – I take the liberty of referring to *Of Spirit: Heidegger and the Question*, trans. Geoffrey Bennington and Rachel Bowlby (Chicago and London, University of Chicago Press, 1989), p. 129 ff. Cf. also Dastur, 'Heidegger et la théologie', p. 233, n. 21.

41 On all these themes, the corpus that would have to be invoked is immense and we are incapable of doing justice to it here. It is above all determined by the discourse of a conversation between the Poet (to whom is assigned the task of saying, and hence of saving the unscathed, *das Heilige*) and the Thinker, who searches for the signs of the god. On the *Beiträge*, particularly rich in this respect, I refer once again to the study of Jean-François Courtine and to all the texts that it evokes and interprets.

42 Samuel Weber has reminded me, and I thank him for doing so, of the very dense and difficult pages devoted by Heidegger to 'The Thought of the Eternal Return as Belief (*als ein Glaube*)' in his *Nietzsche* (Neske, 1961, vol. I, p. 382; English trans. David Farrell Krell, San Francisco, Harper, 1991, pp. 121–32). In re-reading these passages it strikes me as impossible in a footnote to do justice to their richness. complexity and strategy. I will try to return to this elsewhere. While waiting, however, just these two points: (1) Such a reading would suppose a patient and thoughtful sojourn with the holding (*Halt, Haltung, Sichhalten*) discussed above (n. 31, p. 75–6) throughout Heidegger's way of thinking. (2) This 'holding' is an essential determination of belief, at least as Heidegger interprets it in his reading of Nietzsche and notably of the question posed in *The Will to Power*: 'What is a *belief*? How is it born?' All belief is a *holding-for-true* (*Jeder Glaube ist ein* Für-Wahr-halten).' No doubt that Heidegger remains very careful and suspensive in his interpretation of this 'concept of belief' (*Glaubensbegriff*) in Nietzsche, which is to say of the latter's 'concept of truth and of "holding-himself (*Sichhalten*) in truth and for truth"'. He even declares that he abandons the task, as well as that of representing the Nietzschean grasp of the difference between religion and philosophy. Nevertheless, he multiplies preliminary indications in referring to sentences dating from the period of *Zarathustra*. These indications reveal that in his eyes, if belief is constituted by 'holding-for-true' and by

'holding-oneself in truth', and if truth signifies for Nietzsche the 'relation to the entity in its totality', then belief, which consists in 'taking for true something represented (*ein Vorgestelltes als Wahres nehmen*)', remains therefore metaphysical in some way, and therefore unequal to what in thought should exceed both the order of representation and the totality of the entity. This would be consistent with the affirmation cited above: '*Der Glaube hat im Denken keinen Platz.*' Of the Nietzschean definition of belief (*Für-Wahr-halten*), Heidegger declares first that he retains only one thing, but 'the most important', which is to say, 'holding to what is true and maintaining oneself in it' (*das Sichhalten an das Wahre and im Wahren*). And a little further on he adds: 'If maintaining-oneself in the true constitutes a modality of human life, then no decision concerning the essence of belief and Nietzsche's concept of belief in particular can be made before his conception of truth as such and its relation to "life" has been elucidated, which is to say, for Nietzsche: its relation to the entity in its totality (*zum Seienden im Ganzen*). Without having acquired a sufficient notion of the Nietzschean conception of belief, we would not attempt to say what the word "religion" signifies for him . . .' (p. 386; trans. p. 124).

43 Benveniste, *Indo-European Language*, particularly pp. 449, 453–6, 468.

44 *Translator's note*: '*Plus d'un*' can also mean 'one no more'. See: *Specters of Marx*, passim.

45 J. Genet, *Genet à Chatila* (Paris, Solin, 1992), p. 103.

2

The Trace of the Trace

Gianni Vattimo

It is often said that religious experience is an experience of leave-taking. But if this is true, the journey undertaken is most likely one of return. Perhaps not by its essential nature, but *de facto*, given the conditions of existence in modernity (the Christian West, secularized modernity, a *fin-de-siècle* state of anxiety over the impending threat of new and apocalyptic dangers), religion comes to be experienced as a return. In religion, something that we had thought irrevocably forgotten is made present again, a dormant trace is reawakened, a wound re-opened, the repressed returns and what we took to be an *Überwindung* (overcoming, realization and thus a setting aside) is no more than a *Verwindung*, a long convalescence that has once again to come to terms with the indelible trace of its sickness. If it is a matter of return, could this re-presentation[1] of religion be accidental to its proper essence – as if by some individual, social or historical accident we had simply forgotten it, distanced ourselves from it (perhaps culpably) and now, thanks to some other chance circumstance, the forgetfulness were suddenly dispelled? But a mechanism of this kind (such that there is an essential truth, in this case of religion, that stands unmoving somewhere, while individuals and generations come and go around it with a wholly external and irrelevant movement) has already become unworkable for us in philosophy. If we declare a thesis true, must we also say that all the greater or lesser thinkers of the past who did not recognize it were stupid and carelessly unthinking? And if not, does this mean that there is a history of the truth (a history of Being) that is not inessential to its 'content'? Such considerations discourage one from regarding the re-presentation and return of religion in our experience as something purely incidental that may be set aside in order to focus solely on the contents that are conveyed in this way. Rather, there is a legitimate suspicion that the return may be an (or the) essential aspect of religious experience itself

We therefore want to follow this trace of the trace, to take as constitutive for a renewed reflection on religion the very fact of its return, its re-presentation, its calling to us with a voice that we are sure we have heard before. If we accept that it is not an external aspect accidental to religious experience, then the actual forms taken by this return in our highly specific historical conditions will themselves be considered essential. But where should one look in order to assess the actual ways in which the return of the religious occurs in the present day? It seems that there are two principal types that are not immediately connected to one another, at least not at first glance. On the one hand, the robust presence in our popular culture of the return of the religious (as a need, in the new vitality of churches and sects, and in the search for different doctrines and practices, the 'fashion' for Eastern religions and so forth) is motivated above all by the sense of impending global threats that appear quite new and without precedent in the history of humanity. It began immediately after the Second World War with the fear of possible atomic war, and now that the new state of international relations makes this threat seem less imminent, there is a growing fear of an uncontrolled proliferation of these same weapons, and more generally an anxiety in the face of the risks to the ecology of the planet, not to mention those associated with the new possibilities of genetic engineering. A no less widespread fear, at least among advanced societies, is that of losing the meaning of existence, of that true and profound boredom which seems inevitably to accompany consumerism. It is above all the radicality of these risks, which seem to threaten the existence of the species and its very 'essence' (it is possible now to modify the genetic code), that evokes and renders contemporary once again that 'too extreme a hypothesis' which for Nietzsche was God. Even that form of the return of the religious expressed in the often violent search for and affirmation of local, ethnic and tribal identities may in the majority of cases be traced back to a rejection of modernization as destructive of the authentic roots of existence.

In contrast to the predominantly 'fundamentalist' inspiration of the new religiousness inspired by the apocalyptic fears present in our society, from the perspective of philosophy and explicit reflection the return of the religious seems to take place in ways that are quite different and linked to apparently remote theoretical events. The breakdown of the philosophical prohibition of religion, for this is what it comes down to, coincides with the dissolution of the great systems that accompanied the development of science, technology and modern social organization, but thereby also with the breakdown of all fundamentalism – that is, of what, so it seems, popular consciousness is looking for in its return to religion. Naturally, and this too is a widely shared view, it may be that the new vitality of religion depends precisely on the fact that philosophy and critical thought in general, having abandoned the very idea of foundation, are not (or no longer) able to give existence that meaning which it therefore seeks in religion. But such a reading (which has many supporters, even where one would not expect to find them) presupposes a solution to the very problem of the return with which we began. It thinks, that is, the historicity of our present condition simply as an erring that has carried us far away from an ever-present and accessible foundation, producing at the same time, and for the same reason, an 'inhuman' science and technology.

From this point of view, the return to be achieved is simply the abandonment of this historicity and the recuperation of an authentic condition that can only be understood as a resting in the essential. The problem that presents itself is thus whether religion is inseparable from metaphysics in the Heideggerian sense of the term; whether, that is, one can think of God only as the immobile foundation of history from which everything arises and to which everything must return – with the consequent difficulty of making sense of all this coming and going. It may be noted that difficulties of this kind were among those that led Heidegger to call for a re-thinking of the meaning of Being outside of the objectivistic schemes of metaphysics. During the crucial years in which *Sein und Zeit* was being prepared, Heidegger was, as we know, deeply interested in a reflection on religion, precisely in relation to the problems of historicity, temporality and, in the final analysis, of freedom and predestination.

The task of philosophy when faced with this not merely apparent contradiction between the need for foundation expressed in the return of religion in popular consciousness and its own rediscovery of (the plausibility of) religion following the dissolution of metaphysical meta-narratives is, it seems, to detect and throw light upon the popular roots of the two forms of 'return'; yet without surrendering its own theoretical motivation and indeed while establishing this motivation as the basis for a critical radicalization of popular consciousness itself. (There is no need for me to say that what we find expressed here is a general conception of the relation between philosophy and the popular consciousness of the age that cannot be more fully argued for, but which refers less to an Hegelian-style historicity than to Heidegger's reflection on the relation between metaphysics and the complete unfolding of technoscience as the supporting structure of late modern society. Heidegger, too, indeed above all, thinks of and practices philosophy as his own time grasped in thought, as the reflected expression of issues that, even before they belong obscurely to popular consciousness, are the history of Being, constitutive moments of the epoch.)

The common root of the religious need that runs through our society and of the return of (the plausibility of) religion in philosophy today lies in the reference to modernity as an epoch of technoscience, or in Heidegger's words, as the epoch of the world-picture. If critical reflection wishes to present itself as the authentic interpretation of the religious need of common consciousness, it must show that this need is not adequately satisfied by a straightforward recovery of 'metaphysical' religiousness, that is, by fleeing the confusions of modernization and the Babel of secularized society towards a renewed foundationalism. Is such a 'demonstration' possible? The question is simply a translation of the fundamental question of Heidegger's philosophy, but it can also be read as a variation of the Nietzschean project of the overman, taken as one able to meet the challenge as new possibilities are opened to him of mastering the world. To react to the problematic and chaotic character of the late-modern world with a return to God as the metaphysical foundation means, in Nietzschean terms, to refuse the challenge of the over(hu)man(ity); and, moreover, to condemn oneself to that condition of slavery which Nietzsche regarded as inevitable for all those who, precisely, do not accept the challenge. (If one looks at the transformations that individual and social existence have undergone in the society of mass communication, this alternative between the overman and slavery does not look so rhetorical or so far removed from the truth.) From a Heideggerian point of view, then, it is all too clear that to respond to the Babel of late-modernity by returning to God as foundation is simply to try to escape from metaphysics by setting against its final dissolution the recovery of a 'preceding' configuration; one that appears desirable just because less tightly bound – but only apparently – to the actual condition from which one wishes to escape. Heidegger's insistence on the necessity of waiting for Being to speak to us again, and on the priority of its giving itself with regard to every human initiative (I am, of course, thinking of *Was heisst Denken?* and of the script on humanism) amounts to this: the overcoming of metaphysics cannot consist in opposing a condition of ideal authenticity to the degeneration of modern technoscience. Because Being is given only in its event, and moreover, 'where the danger, there grows also what saves', the overcoming of metaphysics, including the final phase of its dissolution – thus also of the Babel of late-modernity and its apocalyptic fears – can only be sought by corresponding in a not purely 'reactive' fashion (in Nietzschean terms) to the call of Being given in its event, that is, in the world of technoscience and of its total organization, in the *Ge-Stell*. As Heidegger constantly warns, to look at technology knowing that the essence of technology is not itself technological, and in this way to see it as the most extreme point of arrival of metaphysics and of the oblivion of Being in the thinking of foundation, means precisely to prepare to overcome metaphysics by listening non-reactively to the technological destiny of Being itself.

Popular consciousness, in its return to religion, tends to conduct itself reactively. It is articulated as a nostalgic search for an ultimate and unshaken foundation. In terms of *Sein und Zeit*, this tendency would just be the (perhaps structural) propensity for inauthenticity that is ultimately founded in the very finitude of existence. In opposition to this, still in the same text, philosophy places the possibility of authenticity (also structural), uncovered by the existential analytic and accessible in an existential manner by way of a resolute projection upon one's own death. But in terms of the overcoming of metaphysics as a recollection and a listening to the history of Being, such an opposition – which is at bottom Platonic – of philosophy to common consciousness does not seem tenable anymore. Philosophy might do better to think of itself as a critical listening – and thus as recollecting the *Ge-Schick* of Being, its *Schickungen* – to the call that only becomes audible in the condition of inauthenticity itself, which for its part is no longer conceived as structural, but as linked to the event of Being, and in this case to the giving of Being in the final moment of metaphysics. All this may be said far more simply by emphasizing that it is not by accident that religious experience is for us given as return.

It is (only) because metaphysical meta-narratives have been dissolved that philosophy has rediscovered the plausibility of religion and can consequently approach the religious need of common consciousness independently of the framework of Enlightenment critique. The critical task of thinking in relation to common consciousness consists here, and now, in showing that even for this consciousness the rediscovery of religion is *positively* qualified by the fact of presenting itself in the world of late-modern technoscience, and thus that the relation with this world cannot be conceived only in terms of flight and polemical alternatives; or, which would be the same thing, at least from the point of view of the difference between metaphysics and ontology, only in terms of the reduction of its new possibilities to ostensibly natural laws, to essential norms (the Pope's view of technology).

However, the fact that the motif of return, and thus of historicity, is essential to religious experience, and not merely accidental, does not mean only or even primarily that the religion to which we wish to return must be characterized by its belonging to the epoch of the end of metaphysics. Indeed, what philosophy recovers from the experience of the essential nature of the return is a general identification of religion with positivity, in the sense of factuality, event-likeness[2] and so forth. It may be that all this is no more than a translation of what the philosophy of religion has often identified as a createdness contitutive of the essential content of religious experience (moreover, there is no reason to rebuff such a proximity to, or dependence on, traditional philosophico-religious reflection: it is another aspect of the positivity in question here).

Indeed, in general, the philosophical re-thinking of religion seems to be essentially dependent on the connection between the two senses of positivity to which we have referred. First, that for which the very content of religious experience in its recovered form is determined by the fact of its returning in the specific historical conditions of our late-modern existence, and whose relation to this existence is therefore not characterized simply by a leap outside it. And, secondly, that the bare fact of returning denotes positivity as a constitutive feature of religion, in as much as religion depends on an originary factuality that happens to be legible as createdness and dependence (in Schleiermacher's sense, perhaps).

To do justice to the significance of the experience of the return one must therefore hold oneself within the horizon of this twofold sense of positivity: createdness as a concrete and highly determined historicity, but also, on the contrary, historicity as provenance from an origin that, as not metaphysically structural and essential, also has all the features of contingency <*eventualità*> and freedom. To keep oneself in the light cast by this connection is not easy. The history of 'metaphysical' religiousness shows how positivity is resolved into mere createdness, whereupon the concrete historicity of existence is either treated as no more than the finitude beyond which religious experience would have us 'leap', so to speak (into God or transcendence), or at best considered as a place where one is put to the test. I have tried elsewhere to show how this risk, and perhaps it is more than a risk, is present in the thinking of Levinas and, up to a point, characterizes Derrida's position too (at least explicitly in the essay on Levinas in *Writing and Difference*).[3] Naturally – as in fact becomes clear from a consideration of the Judaeo-Christian origins of modern historicism, masterfully brought to light by Löwith – the risk symmetrical to this consists in the identification of positivity with worldly historicity, which would reduce the divine to historical determinism: the history of the world as the tribunal of the world, as Hegel said. The author to which we are appealing with this insistence on positivity is clearly not Hegel but Schelling, albeit without any claim to be faithful to the letter of his later philosophy. To be sure, the conception of religion outlined here at least preserves the attention to mythology found in Schelling's positive philosophy; yet less (and here a difference probably begins to emerge) as a more adequate way of knowing truths that transcend reason, than as a language appropriate to the narration of events that, as positive in the twofold sense we have indicated, can only be handed down in the form of myths. Pareyson's reflection on religious experience and its connection with myth[4] – conducted, moreover, with constant reference to Schelling – is of the highest importance here, although it must be carried through to completion if we are to dispel any residual possibility of reducing the positivity of religious experience to pure createdness (with the consequent tendency to subsume mythical thought under a kind of ahistorical abstractness, and the difficulty even of distinguishing Christian myth from Greek myth[5]). The term *myth*, moreover, stands here as an emblem of all that is positive in both senses of the word. It is the place in which is given a historicity that is at once radical and (precisely for this reason) irreducible to the immanence of worldly historicity. With this, we also rediscover another important aspect of the contemporary (and non-contemporary) philosophico-religious reflection, namely, the insistence on the 'religious' (we have no other term for now) as an irruption of the 'Other' and as discontinuity in the horizontal course of history. Except that, at least so it seems to me, this discontinuity and irruption is too often understood – once again – as a pure and 'apocalyptic' negation of historicity, as an absolute new beginning that renounces every link with the past and establishes a purely vertical relation with transcendence, regarded in turn as the pure metaphysical plenitude of the eternal foundation.

In myth as a general term for positivity are gathered all the typically positive elements of religious experience as it recurs in our present condition; elements that, like myth, are not wholly translatable into the terms of rational argumentation: for example, and most especially, more than the sense of guilt and sin, the need for forgiveness. It should not seem strange that the need for forgiveness is picked out here as a characteristic element of religious experience over and above the sense of guilt and the perception of evil and its inexplicability. In all likelihood, one touches here upon one of the features of the specific historicity in which religious experience re-presents itself to us today: in fact, both the intensity of the sense of guilt and the radicality of the experience of evil seem inseparable from a conception of subjectivity that we do not hesitate to call metaphysical, a kind of inflated vision of freedom that seems to clash with so many aspects of the very same spirituality that is today rediscovering religion. In other words, if it is true that religion today re-presents itself as a profound and also philosophically plausible need, this is due in part, indeed above all, to a general dissolution of the rationalistic certainties that have made the modern subject what it is: namely, just that for which the sense of guilt and the 'inexplicability' of evil are such central and decisive elements. Evil and guilt would be less 'scandalous' were the subject not to regard itself with a dramatic solemnity that stems from an implicitly or explicitly rationalist metaphysical attitude. However, this does not remove the fact that the experience of finitude, above all in the inadequacy of our responses to the 'demand' that comes to us from others (or from the Other in Levinas's sense) takes the form of a need for a 'supplement' that we cannot picture for ourselves otherwise than as transcendent. It would not be hard to see in this need, which is at once the desire to respond to the demand of the other and an appeal to a transcendence capable of making good the inadequacy of our responses, a common basis for both the three theological virtues of traditional Christianity and the postulates of Kantian practical reason (at least those regarding the existence of God and the immortality of the soul).

Within the horizon of myth that comprises positivity as defined here one finds, along with the need for forgiveness, other constitutive features of religious experience: how one confronts the enigma of death (one's own, but above all that of others) and, along with death, pain also, and the experience of prayer, perhaps among the most difficult to translate into philosophically meaningful terms. The need for forgiveness and the lived experience of mortality, of pain and of prayer are characteristically 'positive' in as much as they are ways in which one encounters the radical contingency of existence, ways of experiencing a 'belonging' that is also a provenance and, in some almost ineffable sense that we none the less live out in the very experience of return, fallenness – at least in so far as the return also seems always to be the recovery of a condition from which we have 'lapsed' (in the *regio dissimilitudinis* spoken of by the medieval mystics).

Yet, once again, these positive, characteristically positive, 'elements' of the experience of the return in which the religious is given for us are positive primarily in the sense that it is not via an abstract reflection on them as the outcome of the development of human self-consciousness in general that they are encountered. Instead, they are already given in a determinate language, which, in more or less literal terms, is the language of the Hebraic–Christian tradition, of the Bible. Would it be more correct, then, to speak simply of the return to the letter of the sacred texts, the Old and New Testaments? Why insist, for example, on the need for forgiveness, rather than purely and simply on original sin, the promise of redemption, the story of the Incarnation, Passion, death and resurrection of Jesus? Yet is the return we experience so clearly a return to the truth of Scripture? Could we do justice to the experience of return by treating it as a movement that concerns us alone, and by supposing that we shall rediscover a forgotten object, the Holy Scripture, that has remained intact somewhere waiting for us (our culture, the contemporary world and so on) – for some mysterious reason – to rediscover it? If, as it seems, hermeneutics as the philosophy of interpretation could arise only within the ambit of the Hebraic–Christian tradition,[6] it is also true that this tradition remains deeply influenced by hermeneutics. Here, then, is another aspect of positivity that we cannot skirt around: we experience the return of the religious in a world in which one cannot ignore the *Wirkungsgeschichte*[7] of every text, and of the biblical text above all. One cannot ignore the fact that the sacred texts which mark our religious experience are handed down to us by a tradition, by which I mean also that its mediation does not allow them to survive as unmodifiable objects – and perhaps this irreparably mediated condition is not forestalled by the insistence of all orthodoxies on the letter of the sacred text, but rather confirmed by it. In a way that is just a little dizzying the experience of return is already prefigured in the very sacred text – the Old and the New Testaments – to which we find ourselves returning. And that religious experience is given to us as a return is already a sign and a consequence of the fact that we live this experience in terms of the Hebraic–Christian Holy Scriptures. Beginning with St Augustine and his reflection on the Trinity, Christian theology is in its deepest foundations a hermeneutic theology: the interpretative structure, transmission, mediation and, perhaps, the fallenness do not concern only the enunciation, the communication of God with man; they characterize the intimate life of God itself, which therefore cannot be conceived in terms of an immutable metaphysical plenitude (in relation to which, precisely, the revelation would merely be a 'subsequent' episode and an accident, a *quoad nos*).

Are we simply translating into biblical and theological terms a fairly well-known philosophical thematic, that is, the event-like character of Being? Probably this too. But it would be contradictory, precisely from the perspective of the event-like character of Being, to take this as another marginal given, as though philosophy, having arrived at the problem of overcoming metaphysics, were 'consequently' to discover its own analogical relation to the contents of the Hebraic–Christian tradition. This would amount to an affirmation of the event-like character of Being as a given encountered objectively by two different kinds of thinking or forms of experience, each of which would have reached it by its own means: again, as contingent ways of encountering an independent given, posited from somewhere within Being itself. But the philosophy that discovers its own 'analogical relation' to the theological Trinity does not come from another world. The philosophy that responds to the call for the overcoming of metaphysics comes from the Hebraic–Christian tradition, and the content of its overcoming of metaphysics simply amounts to the maturing awareness of this provenance.

As one can see, it is not a question of articulating philosophical discourse in such a way as to allow for the plausibility of religion *as well*, as at bottom one always finds in philosophy that thinks of itself as 'open' and friendly towards religious experience, beginning with that which sought to illustrate the *preambula fidei*, both as a metaphysically grounded natural theology, and simply as an anthropological theory of finitude, the problematic character of existence that calls for the leap towards transcendence (it may be that even the passage from negative philosophy to positive philosophy in Schelling is little more than this). Religious experience as the experience of positivity in the sense outlined seems rather to lead to a radical placing in question of every traditional figure of the relation between philosophy and religion. The return of the religious experienced in popular consciousness and, in a different sense, in philosophical discourse (where the metaphysical, scientistic or historicist prohibitions of religion break down), presents itself as a discovery of positivity that appears identical in its meaning to the thought of the event-like character of Being taken up in philosophy on the basis of Heidegger. The assertion of this identity, if it is to achieve a radical correspondence with its own content, cannot remain a pure assertion. It is precisely on account of the event-like character of Being that we cannot be dealing here with a single metaphysical structure experienced by two different ways of thinking. For positivity or the event-like character calls our attention back to the provenance. The philosophy that poses the problem of overcoming metaphysics is the same as that which discovers the positivity in religious experience. Yet this discovery signifies precisely the awareness of provenance. Can or must such an awareness come down to a return to its own origin? In other words, is the philosophy that discovers itself to have come from Hebraic–Christian theology called for this reason to set aside its own 'derivative' form in order to recover the original one? This would be so, if the theological element revealed here as origin did not itself wholly renounce the metaphysical superiority of the origin: if, that is, the theology in question were not a Trinitarian theology. That provenance as such is so central to our religious experience, moreover, is a constitutive feature of the return of the religious, and is at once both the outcome of what is no longer a metaphysical philosophy and a 'content' of the religious tradition that has been rediscovered: the Trinitarian God is not one who calls us to return to the foundation in the metaphysical sense of the word, but, in the New Testament expression, calls us rather to read the signs of the times. In short, Nietzsche's 'radical' saying (in section 44 of *Daybreak*, entitled 'Origin and Significance')[8] holds, albeit in different terms, as much for philosophy as for the religion it rediscovers: the more one knows of the origin, the less significant it becomes (an expression that, not too paradoxically, may be heard as a distant echo of Trinitarian Christian theology).

Philosophy, then, does not construe the rediscovered awareness of its provenance from religion as a step backwards, as if it were seeking to recover its own authentic language: for to do so would contradict the sense of that which is recovered. However, will this simply mean remaining locked within that process to which one has found that one belongs, without the awareness of the provenance entailing any more than a reinforcement of this very belonging? As the contradictory character of radical historicism shows, such an attitude would in the end merely accord the process the same authoritarian and compelling status as the *ontos on*, the metaphysical foundation. One meets here the same aporiae that one finds again and again along the path of thinking the overcoming of metaphysics (beginning with the impossibility of completing *Sein und Zeit*): how to speak of the event of Being in a language perpetually marked by the stability of essences; or, more recently (in the thematic of the postmodern), how to pronounce the end of meta-narratives if not by narrating the history of their dissolution?

Perhaps, it is just (and only) when philosophy recognizes its own provenance in trinitarian theology that it begins to overcome these aporiae, or at least to discover a sense in them that is not purely contradictory. That it should be a matter precisely of trinitarian theology, and not some form of 'natural theology' or any generic opening onto transcendence or suchlike, is clearly confirmed (at least according to my hypothesis, which I have set out more fully elsewhere[9]) by the way that philosophies which may be intensely religious in character none the less fall back into metaphysics. Instead of holding to the level of the event-like character of Being, they tend rather to rethink this event-like character in purely 'essentialistic' and structural terms. This is true of positions such as that taken by Emmanuel Levinas. For while he regards philosophy as exposed to religious experience in the irruption of the Other, this irruption ultimately takes the form of a dissolution of the event-like character itself, which thereby loses all specific meaning. It is hard to see in Levinas any attention to the 'signs of the times'; all that time, the existential temporality characteristic of man, points towards is the eternity of God, revealed as a radical alterity that calls for the assumption of a responsibility which can only be regarded as historically qualified by accident (the neighbour is to be sure always a concrete, individual, but that's the point: *always*).

Naturally, the reference to Levinas here is not merely to one example among others of a metaphysical lapse. Of all contemporary philosophers, Levinas is perhaps the most careful to situate the attempt to overcome metaphysics in relation to a recovery of the biblical roots of Western thinking (alongside its Greek roots). The biblical legacy is that of recalling philosophy to what, in Heideggerian and not Levinasian terms, we may call the event-like character of Being, encouraging it to recognize the violence inherent in the metaphysical essentialism of Greek origin. Yet in so far as it remains confined to the Old Testament, this return to the Bible goes no further than the acknowledgement of createdness. If the God that philosophy rediscovers is only God the Father, little headway is made beyond the metaphysical thinking of foundation – indeed, it may be that one takes a step or two backwards.

The radical event-like character of Being encountered by post-metaphysical thinking in its effort to free itself from the compelling power of the simply present cannot be understood in the light of createdness alone, as this remains within the horizon of a 'natural', structural religiousness conceived in essentialist terms. Only in the light of the Christian doctrine of the Incarnation of the son of God does it seem possible for philosophy to think of itself as a reading of the signs of the times without this being reduced to a purely passive record of the times. 'In the light' of the Incarnation is once again an expression that seeks to capture a problematic and unresolved relation that lies at the very heart of the experience of event-likeness: the incarnation of God at issue here is not simply a way of giving mythical expression to what philosophy will in the end reveal via rational enquiry. Nor is the Incarnation the ultimate truth of the statements of philosophy, demystified and restored to its proper sense. As has already become clear in various ways over the preceding pages, this problematic relation between philosophy and religious revelation is the very sense of the Incarnation. God is incarnated, *and thus* is first revealed in the biblical pronouncement that ultimately 'gives rise' to the post-metaphysical conception of the event-like character of Being. It is only in so far as it rediscovers its own provenance in the New Testament that this post-metaphysical thinking can take the form of a thinking of the event-like character of Being that is not simply reducible to a bare acceptance of the existent or to pure historical and cultural relativism. If you will: it is the fact of the Incarnation that confers on history the sense of a redemptive revelation, as opposed to a confused accumulation of happenings that unsettle the pure structural quality of true Being. That there is a redemptive (or in philosophical terms, emancipatory) sense to history, in spite, or precisely because, of its being a history of pronouncements and responses, of interpretations and not 'discoveries' or the ascendancy of 'true' presences, is only possible in the light of the doctrine of Incarnation.

The present epoch is one in which it became clear that metaphysics could not be continued (this is the history of nihilism narrated by Nietzsche and exemplified for Heidegger by Nietzschean will to power). Responding to the appeal of this epoch, philosophy has sought to overcome metaphysics, but in doing so has found itself called to renounce the reassuring authority of presence – whereupon it has become hermeneutic, listening to and interpreting pronouncements passed down to it (the *Ge-Schick*). That there are no facts, only interpretations, as Nietzsche teaches, is not in its turn a certain and reassuring fact, but 'only' an interpretation. This renunciation of presence confers on post-metaphysical philosophy, and above all on hermeneutics, an inevitably 'fallen' character. The overcoming of metaphysics, in other words, can only take place as nihilism. The meaning of nihilism, however, if it is not in its turn to take the form of a metaphysics of the nothing – as it would if one imagined a process at the end of which Being is not and the nothing is – can only think of itself as an indefinite process of reduction, diminution, weakening. Could such a thinking be thought outside the horizon of the Incarnation? If hermeneutics really wishes to continue along the path opened by Heidegger's call to recollect Being (and thus *Ereignis*), this is perhaps the decisive question to which it must seek a response today.

Translated by David Webb

Notes

1 *Translator's Note*: the Italian term that would normally be translated as 'represent' is '*rappresentare*'. However, here and elsewhere in the chapter Vattimo uses the word '*ripresentarisi*' – literally 'present again'. This has been translated throughout as 're-present'.

2 *Translator's note*: the Italian '*eventualità*', translated here as 'event-likeness', has generally been translated in this chapter as 'event-like character'. However, it can also denote 'contingency' and has been translated as such on two occasions.

3 *Translator's note*: J. Derrida, 'Violence and metaphysics', in *Writing and Difference*, trans. A. Bass (London, Routledge, 1978).

4 See especially the writings of Pareyson collected in *Filosofia della libertà* (Turin, Einaudi, 1994).

5 I have discussed this problem more fully in an essay included in my *Etica dell'interpretazione* (Turin, Rosenberg and Sellier, 1989).

6 I refer the reader here to the hypotheses set out in my essay 'Storia della salvezza, storia dell'interpretazione', *Micromega*, 3 (1992), pp. 105–12.
7 I am of course referring here to the notions of 'effective history' and 'effective historical consciousness' elaborated by Gadamer in *Truth and Method* (New York, Seabury Press, 1975).
8 F. Nietzsche, *Daybreak*, trans. R. Hollingdale (Cambridge and New York, Cambridge University Press, 1985).
9 Cf. my 'Metafisica, violenza, secolarizzazione', in G. Vattimo (ed.), *Filosofia '86* (Rome and Bari, Laterza, 1987), pp. 71–94.

3

Thinking Religion: the Symbol and the Sacred

Eugenio Trías

Reason and Superstition

Recent events at the forefront of media attention, such as the collapse of the authoritarian regimes of the East, the Persian Gulf crisis and the conflict in Yugoslavia, have left no doubt as to the crucial importance of the religious or cultural–religious substrate in sustaining the societies that compete for supremacy in the world today. Calls to join the crusade against a demonized enemy combine with the opportunistic proclamations of (Christian) spiritual reconstruction aimed at filling the void of meaning and value left by the dismantled political regimes.

All this takes place against the horizon of a general crisis in the idea, or the ideal, of reason steadily forged and established by the West since the Enlightenment. It is time, then, to 'take the bull by the horns' and not to be daunted by the magnitude of the crisis. This reason, solemnly proclaimed by our enlightened ancestors, was simply blind to these underlying religious strata, which are emerging today with such exceptional force and energy.

Reason never sought to understand what lay behind or beneath these strata in all their richness. It used them as a *shadow* or a *scapegoat* on which to establish and constitute itself as sovereign reason. Indeed, it is in the struggle against religion that reason has sought to secure its own legitimacy. Religion has been judged and controlled by the use of a term of opprobrium devised for the purpose by our Roman ancestors: the word *superstition*.

The term *superstitio* was coined by this people of lawyers, jurists and bureaucrats as the (condemned and rejected) dark other face of the Roman *religio*, which was the only form of religion that they considered legitimate. While *religio* channelled the precise and scrupulous rituals of the public sphere or the family, the term *superstitio* denoted the orientalizing and exotic forms of religion that, especially in the Late Empire, had by this time begun to undermine the purely conventional character of the official *religio* and give new life and meaning to the popular demand for immediate salvation.

Superstitio probably signified survival, a kind of fossil leftover of the ancestral world from before Rome's supremacy. According to Max Weber, this word was a translation of the Greek *ékstasis*. In contrast to the ecstatic (superstitious) religions that were archaic relics of the cult of the Goddess (Cybele, Isis, Ishtar, Aphrodite Celeste), with their bloody ceremonies, such as the famously terrifying orgiastic rites of the temple of Hierapolis, to the shameless rampages of the *galli*, who were given to self-mutilation in tragic identification with Attis, son of the Goddess, and to the esoteric cults of the (gnostic or Christian) followers of Mithras, the 'rational religion' of the genuine and naturally ritualistic and juridical Romans emerged both as the official cult of the state and as the private and familial practice of *pietas* to the forefathers. This religion owed its widespread vitality and meaning all to Stoic and late Platonic philosophy.

When European self-consciousness was in its splendour, satisfied and content at humanity's coming of age (Kant), this old Roman distinction reappeared. The Enlightenment, above all in France, was looking for just such a 'religion of reason', vaguely deist in character with sentimentalist overtones, a religion at one with 'human nature' and with nature in general, yet radically distinct from all the 'superstitious' trickery employed by the priestly castes and unscrupulous despots to manipulate the uneducated masses. This strict demarcation provided the basis for the clarity of mind with which the so-called *philosophes*, the genuine forerunners of modern journalism, committed themselves to spreading the ideas of the Enlightenment.

The so-called 'philosophies of suspicion' of the age of Romanticism and positivism were more refined in this respect. They took the inquisitorial practices inherited from Voltaire and rendered them more subtle and sophisticated. Their critique of religion is indirect and sleuth-like: instead of condemning it for being 'superstitious', they strive to interrogate it and to prepare the case for a trial in the course of which it will reveal to the scientist and the expert the truth and meaning that it in fact possesses, albeit unwittingly. The key to this truth and meaning is, of course, in the hands of the investigator: he knows it even before the trial begins. And while the keys to their hermeneutic practices may be different, Hegel, Marx, Freud and Durkheim all adopt the same methodology in their respective approaches to religion.

It is no wonder, then, that religion has been understood as ideology and false consciousness, the narcotic displacement activity of a soulless world, a form of vicarious happiness, of *bonheur*, within a socioeconomic framework that generates dissatisfaction and unhappiness and whose meaning and truth are sought and found in the class struggle and property relations. This, in short, is how Marx and Engels (and their followers) conceive of religion.

Religion could equally be conceived as a revelation of the *absolute essence* in *representational* form or figure, halfway between art and philosophy: a revelation that has, however, yet to attain the form most adequate to the Truth, its conceptual form. This is how Hegel and his orthodox disciples conceive of it. One could also see in religion an abstract and alienated projection of the human essence, or of man as a *being in general*, even the very paradigm itself of each and every human alienation in an abstract and separated world. In a certain sense, the Christian doctrine of the Trinity had already revealed this truth of the humanist gospel, but in a still alienated form. Christianity, as a religion of the human being as such, could be said to have anticipated, albeit erroneously, the *anthropological* discovery of true science and philosophy: this is Feuerbach's view.

Religion could also be seen as the expression and the symptom of a declining *will to power*, the manifestation of a sick will that wants to infect every affirmative will with a feeling that poisons its interiority: a feeling that is in truth *resentment*, a yearning for revenge and a struggle to the death against everything that is filled with life and of superior value. This attitude gives rise to the power of the priests, the capacity to overturn valuations and values alike or to conceive of what is simply bad, harmful and undesirable (*schlecht*) as malign and evil (*böse*).

Religion will therefore be, in its most visible forms, this counter-value created by the priestly caste. In its most sublime forms (Gautama Buddha, Jesus of Nazareth), it could be the quintessential expression of a will to power that plunges into decline and then, in a final lament before annulling itself completely, proclaims the Gospel (or the 'bad tidings', the *dysangel*)[1] of the Nothing. This is Nietzsche's view.

Finally, one could treat religion as an *illusion* vainly set in opposition to necessity and destiny (as expressed in the 'reality principle'). In times of secularization it is the inner man that prevails and this illusion shelters in the most intimate and private dimension of the individual, giving rise to all the burgeoning and varied material of our common neuroses.

The *religious illusion*, then, acts as an unconscious force. It wounds and immobilizes the body via complex mythical systems, just like hysteria. It regulates the most intimate and shameful aspects of the private sphere by way of complex ritual ceremonies, as we find in obsessive neurosis. It generates theological and theogonical constructions that attack the subject from all sides and split it into the circular double figure of the persecutor and the persecuted, as does paranoia. And as in melancholia, it raises to the status of idol the dead and lost aspect of the split subject, on which the living side of the subject gazes sorrowfully, dressed in mourning.

The Hegelian *absolute spirit*, that is, the *trinity* of art, religion and philosophy, is suitably unmasked in this Freudian diagnosis. The artistic side of religion is manifested in hysteria; its philosophical and theological mode in paranoia; its cultural and specifically religious aspect in obsessive neurosis and melancholia.

The explanatory force of all these variations on the *philosophy of suspicion* is undeniable. In them, the phenomenon of religion and religious experience stand in the place of judgement and the verdict of a determinate concept of reason (idealist, materialist, genealogical or psychoanalytical). All these approximations to religion plainly rest on a wholly problematic approach: in each case religion is explained *in terms extrinsic to religion itself.* The common point of departure is the rationalist–Enlightenment premise that religion is, as such, illusion, ideology, an inadequate concept, sickness, false consciousness.

Its truth and meaning are not to be found within the horizon of experience and the (pragmatic or language) game in which it manifests itself. One imagines truth and meaning as to be sought behind, always behind, in an unconscious and underlying substratum which it is the task of the philosopher, the scientist or the analyst to discover (and also to unmask).

Religion is brought before the tribunal of science, of reason (or of the genealogy of the *will to power*), to be examined, interrogated, tested and placed under enquiry, as if it were reason's guinea pig. All the richness and variety of religious experience and of the 'language games' that follow from it are now led back, beyond their unconscious truth, to that one-way street which is presented in authoritarian fashion in these discourses as the sole form of reason.

The moment has perhaps arrived to state resolutely and as plainly as possible that *logos* is not the same as *reason. Logos* is specific to the *human* subject; it defines and empowers the human as such. It manifests itself in the rich variety of what the later Wittgenstein defined as 'language games'. Each of these games has in principle its own inner logic, its own meaning and truth. Moreover, they are 'language' games in the radical (anthropological and ontologial) sense of the word, which makes us think that language itself may be the characteristic element of human nature.

Religion of the spirit

Perhaps it is a matter of preparing for the emergence of a new religion: the true *religion of the spirit* already prophesied in the twelfth century by the Calabrian abbot Joachim of the Flowers and invoked afresh by Novalis and Schelling in the century of Romanticism and Idealism. Perhaps the only way to counteract the wars of religion breaking out everywhere is to lay the basis for a new foundation. But such an event does not come about by force of will alone. For it to occur, a number of different factors must come together. It is a matter, perhaps, of simply preparing the ground in order that the *event* at some point may come about.

For the shards of religion that survive, in their diversity, clearly seem to be incapable of giving unity and solidity to an ever more regional and fragmented world. On the contrary, they heighten feelings of mutual suspicion, mistrust and hatred. The world that is emerging with the end of the Cold War and the Eastern/Western blocs is plainly polycentric. *Ideological* differences have made way for *cultural substrata* and these, in turn, are always rooted in the enduring ground of *religious* traditions. Properly understood, culture always consists in the development of a specific cult within a given society. And the cult, as Hegel aptly puts it, is the inalienable centre of the complex syndrome that we are in the habit of defining as *religion*.

It has been shown, above all in the bitter Yugoslavian conflict, that the real 'point of difference' in a culture, that which can give rise to the Hegelian 'struggle to the death', is not language at all (as a certain romantic nationalism maintains) but religion. One can speak the same language and yet be thoroughly convinced that one belongs to a different and even opposed national reality. If this is so, there must exist an important difference, and only religion can produce it. The diversity in the characters of the *written* word (Cyrillic, Latin) has shown itself to be more important than the (common) *spoken* language. The differences in *writing* have shown themselves to be more significant than the communities of speech: for once, at least, the 'grammatologists' are right. Or is it perhaps the case that the *sacred* appears above all in writing, transforming it into *sacred writing*? To read Cyrillic or Latin: this is the 'point of difference'! (Incidently, if the Basques were Huguenots and the Catalans Shiites, they would have been independent for centuries by now: likewise, if both groups, while all speaking the imperial *koiné*, had learnt to read Cyrillic or Gothic characters instead of the canonic Latin.)

What is certain is that this polycentric world is in want of open vistas. No existing cultural form enjoys any privilege. The interesting question for the future will not be 'in what cultural and religious context did the form of (capitalist) society develop that now seems to prevail unopposed?' (the traditional response, put forward by Max Weber, though somewhat controversial today, is that it arose in the milieu of Calvinist Protestantism). Rather, it will be a question that is far more portentous for the future: 'Which religious and cultural context will prove most capable of adapting to the new forms of victorious technological capitalism?' (A provisional response may be: Shintoism and Japanese *Zen* culture, or perhaps, in general, the synthesis of Confucianism and Taoism found in the Celestial Empire.)

We have already said that, for the time being, it is a matter of smoothing the way for thinking to adapt to this cultural polycentrism, prior to some new yet unforseeable reformulation. To this end, various distinct strategies are necessary. In my most recent book, *Le edad del espiritu*,[2] I tried to formulate a true *archaeology* of the principal intellectual movements that have generated both the great universal religions and the main philosophical systems. Without claiming to be exhaustive, I none the less wanted to examine in depth some of the most important enclaves of our world: the thought and religion of India, the worlds of Iran, Israel and Greece, the birth of Christianity, Islam, the medieval world, the Renaissance, the Reformation, the *Age of Reason*, the Enlightenment and Romanticism. This kind of archaeological excavation is undoubtedly necessary, but of course must also be integrated with other perspectives more directly relevant to the world we live in. Perhaps more than ever, it is urgent that we regain a *universal, world* perspective. More than ever before, it is vital that engagement in one's own particular reality be counterbalanced by a wider *global* vision.

At a time when the faded idea of Europe is in decline, in thrall to blind economic and bureaucratic forces, and when there is a resurgence of the nation-state, and of the whole band of nations aspiring to become states, only two possibilities remain: that of withdrawing completely from the whole wretched process of decomposition and regression to a still worse past, or that of opening one's eyes and mind wide to universal vistas. In all likelihood, one will have to look beyond the strictly European unity, which has of late shown itself to be less potentially cohesive than was thought. As Rafael Argullol and I said in our paper entitled *El cansancio de Occidente*, it may be that there is no such thing as Europe without an *adjective*: Eastern Europe, Latin Europe, Northern Europe, Anglo-Saxon Europe, Central Europe, and even, if you like, Orthodox–Byzantine Europe (Bulgaria,

Russia, Greece, Serbia), Catholic Europe and Protestant Europe. It is impossible to embark on a really substantial and ambitious project based on a foundation as unstable and hazardous as the economy. Europe is paying today for its most closely guarded treachery: that of seeking to construct itself without putting the debate over *culture* first. Less than a year ago, I (with Rafael Argullol) thought of Europe as an organism that had become tired and weary. Today, I believe that its condition has simply become terminal. I say this with real bitterness, since my being, my life and my destiny are, of course, European.

A Europe in evident decline, shouldering the cross (of its own making) of a civil war that rips open its heart; a Spain newly united in its distress, that is, in the mad determination to bring to light its secular demons, its unresolved conflicts of *identity*. Perhaps if we opened our eyes and minds to the complexity of the world and all the important differences in culture and civilization, we may find Ariadne's thread. The fact is that the world as a whole is simply a labyrinth in which each point of transition and rest represents a specific *cultural enclave*, formed and informed by a certain religious (*cultic*) foundation with its own glorious past: Christian–Orthodox, Reformist, Islamic, Shiite, Hindu, Jewish or Buddhist. And so I come back to the initial intuition of this essay: serious thought must be given to the *possibility* that the ground be prepared for the birth of a new religion – the *religion of the spirit*. As one as wise and great as Rafael Sánchez Ferlosio well knows: 'Nothing will change as long as the gods do not change.'

The symbol and the sacred

Clearly, religion appears within our horizon and challenges us to think its truth. It is not enough to play safe, *à la* Voltaire, and accuse religion of superstitiousness. Nor is it enough to speak of 'the opium of the people', of 'Platonism for the people' or even of the 'future of an illusion'. We shall make little progress if we restrict ourselves to repeating *usque ad nauseam* this old Enlightenment refrain, born of the philosophy of suspicion.

The task is to approach the religious phenomenon by way of reflection, to make religion something that may *be thought*. To this end, some phenomenon must be highlighted to make the task easier. In what follows, I will try using a 'key word' as a guiding thread to help me to perform this reflection. This word will be *symbol*. How are we to understand this term? And why have I privileged this word, as that most suited to guiding a possible reflection on the religious phenomenon?

What is it that can be defined as *symbol*, and in what does it consist? For me, this term signifies above all the sensible and manifest revelation *of the sacred*. Religion is, in my view, a re-linking *<re-ligacion> relative* to the sacred (given, naturally, the radical ambivalence inherent in this word: *sacer/sanctus*, the sacred and the holy).

It is a matter of thinking about the symbol and of defining the categories that can be drawn from this reflection. To such an end, we shall look at the original etymological meaning of the term and speak not of symbol (noun), but of 'symbolizing' (verbal form), in reference to the act of 'throwing-together' (*sym-ballein*) the two parts of a broken coin or medal that betoken and secure an alliance.

One of the two fragments can be thought of as available (the fragment one possesses) and the other, by contrast, lies 'elsewhere'. The *sym-ballic*[3] event constitutes a highly complex process or progression in which the two fragments may combine and fit together. The fragment in one's possession may be thought of as the 'symbolizing' component of the symbol. The other fragment, not in one's possession, represents the other half, in the absence of which even the first half lacks any established meaning. It is to this second fragment that the first refers to gain significance and meaning (which is what the symbolizing component symbolizes, or in other words, that in it which is symbolized).

The symbolic event

The symbol is thus a (*sym-ballic*) unity that presupposes a break. There is in principle a disjunction between the symbolizing form as a manifest and manifestative aspect of the symbol (given to vision, to perception or hearing) and the symbolized form in the symbol, which constitutes the horizon of meaning. We have certain forms, figures, lines and words. But the key to the correct perspective on what they signify is missing. And this originary break, this fracture, is what lies behind the whole drama of the symbol. The scene of exile was set up and arranged by a given alliance prior to the culmination of the drama in which the two separate parts act as *dramatis personae*: the part that symbolizes and the part that withdraws. The drama leads towards the final scene of reunion and reconciliation, in which both parts are 'pitched' into their desired coming together.[4]

The symbolic *categories* lend a specific form to this piece of theatre, and to the process or course that constitutes its argument. They shed light on and reveal the conditions that permit or make possible the final event, the resolution of the drama.[5] Such categories present themselves in stages: the first prepares the second, which constitutes the condition of the third, and so on. It is a matter of different *revelations*, by virtue of which the conditions of the symbolic event are brought fully to light. They form a kind of *scale* that one can imagine, in musical terms, as the scale of musical intervals (still on the supposition that the first revelation determines the second, and this the third, and so on).

In the course of all this, a symbolizing form or figure emerges that is conditioned in its turn by a determinate foundation: the matrix of the entire symbolic process. This matrix or matter provides physical support for the symbol. To present itself as a symbolic *form* or *figure* it must, of course, be formed or transformed.

This symbolic matter is the primary condition or category and opens the path and movement that culminate in the symbolic event. This cannot be produced without presupposing the material dimension, which works a little like the lowest and most fundamental interval of the scale (to pursue the musical analogy). This material dimension constitutes the *basso ostinato* that supports the entire tonal edifice. In this sense, the matter or matrix shows through in every symbol.

It is with regard to this symbolic mattter that the second condition stands. For there to be a symbolic event, the underlying (maternal) matrix has to be ordered and delimited until it begins to look like a *cosmos*; a world has to be 'created' or 'formed' (the *undifferentiated matter* has to be assigned limits and demarcated so as to determine it). These material demarcations may be presented as a spatial section (*temenos, templum*) or as a temporal sign (now, *tempora, tempus*: an indication of festivity).[6] The temple and the festival are thus the effects (in space and time respectively) of this transformation of matter into cosmos or world.

Everything is now in place and the scene is set that serves as a condition of possibility of the *symbolic event*. The event itself is always an encounter, or rather a (*sym-ballic*) relation between a *presence* of some kind that reveals itself and its recognition by a particular *witness* (defining its form and figure). The presence (of the sacred) and the (human) witness are correlates in an authentic *relation of testimony <relacion presencial>* that is clearly the hallmark of this encounter. It is thanks to this *relation of testimony* that what is manifested acquires its form and figure: as a theophany, a figure that can be represented, or as an *aura* of glory, or a brilliant light.

This relation of testimony is the condition for the possibility of a genuine communication between the presence and the witness (in the spoken or the written word). The symbolic manifestation culminates in an oral or written communication of this kind, which brings the *symbolizing* activity of the symbol to a close and leads to a revelation in the form of (sacred) words or (sacred) writing. The ongoing series *<seria escalonada>* of symbolizing categories is then locked and sealed.

This last (oral and written) category is the (material) condition of the primary category relative to the *symbolized*. The (oral and written) revelation accomplished via its communication now requires an exegesis, that is to say, a referral or assignment of the manifest symbolizing aspect (the word or the text in its literal value) to the (hermeneutic) keys that may reveal its meaning. Such a referral is only possible if there has already been a prior manifestation or (poetic, prophetic, inspired) revelation. As soon as this manifestation is over, there has to be a clarification of the (exegetical or allegorical) method leading to the keys (which serve as ideal forms of sense).

But from the very beginning these (Platonic, Gnostic, neo-Platonic) forms or ideas strike a final Obstacle that checks the impulse to exegesis and allegory. The assignment or referral takes us from this explanation of *ideas* or *forms* to the final moment, in which every enquiry into meaning seems to be annulled. This is why the symbol (unlike the allegory or the conceptual schematism) always retains a *mystical* quality; its lot is precisely to show how the symbol remains structurally bound to a secret, occult and holy substrate (to the sacred as such, that is in its specific ambivalence).[7] The ideal conditions are, therefore, those which condition such an ascent to the mystical.

However, this mystical encounter, in order to be accomplished in a symbolic event, must return to a situation in which the *union* of the two parts in question (the symbolizing and the symbolized) may be produced. In this sense the mysticism highlights the necessity of pulling back from that negative and sublime ascent towards what is essentially transcendent in order to stop at the *frontier space* in which the symbol can put itself to the test, can try to realize itself as a possible, *sym-ballic*, encounter between the symbolizing part and that which is symbolized in it.

It is in this *frontier* space, then, that the accomplishment of the symbol takes place: the two parts of the symbol, the symbolizing and the symbolized, are here re-conjoined and co-incident. Only here, then, does the symbol actually present itself as an event, and in fact become concrete *as symbol*, in the sense that it realizes its own immanent teleology. It makes its own all the conditions that have underlain its preparation, predisposition and presentation as a *symbolic event*.

Symbolic categories

Let us try now to think the symbol in all its dimensions. The term 'symbol', in the present context, means a verbal event by which two fragments (of a medal or a coin, broken in half) are 'thrown together'. It is a matter, then, of offering a precise definition of the conditions for the possibility of this symbolic event by which the two halves may come to coincide. One (the fragment we possess) serves as the *symbolizing* component of the symbol. The other (withdrawn from the sphere of appearing) is something to which the available half refers in order to acquire its full meaning: something in which the *meaning* of the available part can be determined, that provides the keys and hermeneutic tools by which it may be given meaning, thereby allowing the available part to fulfil the finality by which it is defined, the process of symbolization.

To be a symbol, however, is not to be a thing or an object, or at least not in the first instance. Rather than speaking of this or that symbol, one should speak here of this or that symbolic event. It is in the event that the two fragments of the coin or the medal, originally separated, will be found and shown to fit together or not to fit together. If they fit, the symbolic event is accomplished.

The dimensions of the symbol are those *conditions* which make it possible for the event to take place, for the two parts to coincide, as that which was previously split is stitched together. Such conditions operate as genuine *symbolic categories* (where *category* has a strictly Kantian sense).

Ultimately, one must determine the specific categories on the basis of which the act or event in which the two parts of the symbol are reunited can take place. These categories can only be defined by repeating the route of the movement that ends in the coincidence of the two parts: they are simply the different steps or levels on the way towards the decisive proof or experiment in which the symbolizing and the symbolized are 'thrown together'. They are the actual stages, or phases, of this symbolic process: the individual milestones of an argument whose conclusion or resolution lies in the final symbolic proof, which amounts to the symbolic *act* itself.

This ongoing character makes it possible for these categories to be formalized in musical terms, as different *keys* ranged over the symbolic space, the region that must be crossed if the symbolic act or event is to take place. In the first instance, one must examine the conditions for the possibility of the symbolizing part, then those pertaining to that which is symbolized in it and finally the conditions for the possibility of their reunification or coincidence. Only by way of an analysis of all these conditions will it be possible to move gradually through the series of different *symbolic categories*.

The categories are not derived from an analysis of the forms of combination in judgements, as in Kant; nor do they follow from an examination, conscious or unconscious, of the generic forms of language, as in Aristotle. Rather, what permits the formulation of a *table of categories* is the analysis of the process in which the symbolic event is realized (the interlocking of the two parts, the symbolizing and the symbolized).

There are four necessary conditions for the constitution of the symbolizing part:

1 that this part possess a *material* substrate;
2 that this substrate is none the less ordered and organized in an expository domain which must be called *cosmos*, *world*;
3 that this cosmos may then be established as the setting that makes possible an encounter between a determinate (sacred) presence that rises out of the darkness and a determinate (human) witness that can testify to its existence;
4 that this encounter or relation of testimony may be verified by way of communication (oral or written).

These four conditions determine the symbolizing part that is accessible and manifest. Yet we are referred or sent on by this to the symbolized part, which is not available. Consequently, (a) the symbol, in its presence, must refer to those hermeneutic keys that permit the establishment of the (ideal) figures thanks to which it can acquire a precise meaning; (b) the exegetical keys must necessarily find an upper limit, which undermines any further enquiry into meaning that showed how the referral could only be fulfilled in *mystical form*.

Once the conditions of the symbolizing (matter, cosmos, presence, *logos*) and the symbolized (keys of meaning, mystical substrate) have been established, all the essential requirements for the realization of the symbolic event are in place. All that is required is to define the conditions of the consequent reconjunction of the two parts of the symbol. But just at this point the ultimate and decisive category comes to light, namely, that which establishes the necessity of this reconstitution of what was previously distant and separate.

And so, finally, here is the whole table of the symbolic categories:

SYMBOLIZING CATEGORIES

1 Matter
2 World
3 Relation of testimony (between a present given and its witness)
4 Communication (oral or written)

CATEGORIES RELATIVE TO THE SYMBOLIZED IN THE SYMBOL

5 (Exegetical) keys of meaning
6 Sacred and holy (or mystical) substrate

UNIFICATORY CATEGORIES

7 Reconjunction of the two parts of the symbol

Translated by David Webb

Notes

1 *Translator's note*: the expression is from F. Nietzsche, 'The Anti-christ', in *Twilight of the Idols and the Anti-Christ*, trans. R. J. Hollingdale (Harmondsworth, Penguin, 1979), p. 151.
2 *Translator's note*: E. Trías, *La edad del espiritu* (Barcelona, Destino, 1995).
3 *Translator's note*: this neologism translates the Spanish *sim-balic* that Trías uses to denote the active dimension of the symbol.
4 The symbol was originally a token: a coin or medallion broken in two and offered as a pledge of friendship or alliance. One of the two parts was retained by the giver. Whoever is in receipt of the other part possesses a half that may be produced at some future time as proof of the alliance only if it is matched to the part that is held by the giver. To this end, the two parts are thrown together to confirm whether they match or not. Hence the expression *sym-bolon*, which means precisely 'that which is thrown together'.
5 The Kantian concept of 'category' preserves here its sense of 'condition of possibility' (in the present context, it concerns the condition of possibility of the production of the symbolic event). Such categories may be considered necessary conditions, in the sense that as an ensemble they are indispensable if the event spoken of here is to take place. Moreover, these categories are successive and gradual *revelations* of the event itself.

6 *Temenos* (temple, in Greek) means 'demarcation, section' (from the root *tem-*, which means to cut). The demarcation and section or delimitation of a sacred space; for example, the creation of a 'clearing' in the centre of a wood by felling the trees, or else by taking advantage of an opening. At this point, the confines of the space acquired by cutting down the surrounding trees must be redefined, since the limits of this sacred space are *tabù* or in any case may only be crossed in a ritual form. The temple is thus the *place* of the sacred, distinct from the 'natural' (wild and wooded nature). It introduces a 'lightening' of the density of the wood, by which a space for the sacred is cleared, or rather the sacred itself carves out its own place. In short, the temple is *the sacred as place*. As for the festival, it constitutes the time of the sacred or *the sacred as time*. 'Time', *tempus*, derives from the same root as temple; cf. E. Cassirer, *The Philosophy of Symbolic Forms*, vol. 2 (New Haven, Conn., Yale University Press, 1955).

7 This ambivalence is recorded in the Greek and Latin languages (and in Castilian): *hagion* (*sanctus*, holy) and *hieron* (*sacer*, sacred). It is a matter of two dimensions articulated by a single *phenomenon* (the holy-and-sacred). The holy refers to what is most profound and sublime; what cannot be touched, even indirectly, by testimony (nor 'looked upon'). The sacred, by contrast, can be touched: it can be used (for example in the cultic or sacrificial object), and in this way may even be destroyed or consumed. The sacred can come to signify 'execrable, repulsive, sinister' (hence we have *sacer* in Latin). In this connection, see F. Freud, *Totem and Taboo*: *The Standard Edition of the Complete Psychological Works of Sigmund Freud*, ed. J. Strachey (London, Hogarth Press and the Institute of Psychoanalysis). Regarding the twofold way in which the sacred manifests itself, as a mystery that provokes horror (*phobos*) and/or fascination, see Rudolf Otto, *The Idea of the Holy*, trans. J. Harvey, (London, Oxford University Press, 1958). He theorizes the 'sacred-and-the-holy' as a reference to an experience of radical alterity, the experience of the 'Totally Other' (*ganz Anderes*). It concerns a radical Alterity found closed within the mystery, that is hidden, enclosed and obscure (*mystes*, the arcane as such). Such mystery lays the basis for the twofold experience of the *mysterium fascinans* (the bewitching and enchanting aspect of the sacred) and of the *mysterium tremendum* (the terrible and threatening aspect of the sacred): two dimensions that are in fact closely interlinked.

4

Religious Experience as Event and Interpretation

Aldo Gargani

The danger facing reflection on religion today, and it faces no greater danger, is that of tying the subject matter of religion into a preoccupation, rooted as much in the metaphysical tradition as in positivism, with establishing the reality and presence of the objects of religious discourse. Does philosophy itself not specifically risk making the meaning and value of religious discourse dependent on the inspection of things that can be determined as present and somehow verifiable, with the instruments of reason, or of experience? Shall we make the meaning of religious discourse, like that of any other discourse, depend on the method by which we control the matter addressed, as it is addressed? Shall we thereby leave the destiny of religious discourse hanging from the destiny of a methodological rule that gives legitimacy and credibility to those objects which conform to its own canonical procedures? Yet, conversely, if we free ourselves from the notion of rationality as a state constrained by rules, shall we be left chasing phantasms where, as it were, everything is more or less permitted? In reacting to the traditional metaphysical aspiration to determine the presence of beings as the preliminary condition of their meaning, in rebelling subsequently against the tough neo-positivistic discipline by which one could speak of God and of all the other objects of relevance to religious discourse only where there were available *sense data* or *Erlebnisse* (as Russell and

Carnap would say respectively), we might consign ourselves to anaphoric discourse, where the reference or denotation of what is said is established exclusively by discourse (as when, in the *New Essays*, Leibniz observed in the Hanoverian winter that while there were no cherries in nature, cherries none the less remained as referents of discourse in virtue of discourse itself)? But anaphoric discourse merely points towards the difficulty that we are addressing, since it is merely symptomatic of the nostalgia for a referentialistic schema according to which names and propositions have meaning if and only if they correspond to objects and facts respectively. Anaphoric discourse amounts to a vicarious and compromised form of the referentialistic semantic paradigm of presence.

With the re-introduction of religious discourse, which depends as much on specific historical circumstances as on subtle speculative and psychological factors, the first question and the first source of unease that immediately confronts the philosophical mind – and remember that immediacy does not exclude the emotional and instinctual spheres – is the following: can we speak of God without addressing all the existing arguments for and against the proof of his existence? And, furthermore, how can one speak of religion without somehow committing oneself to some thesis concerning the existence of God? If God is an unreal and phantasmal object that has been eliminated by the empirical, Enlightenment and neo-positivistic tradition, shall we still be capable of the unimaginable effort required to forge a discourse on religion, or shall we be condemned to prattle on like one who insists on or persists in speaking of religion, even as he or she feels the pangs of speculative conscience for making what seems to be a leap in the dark, no longer able to find the path of a semantic and epistemological reference to God?

It seems that religion has not enjoyed the same emancipation of the discursive field as other cultural disciplines: take ordinary language, for example, where we have learnt to use words outside of the object-designation schema, to use words like 'help!' or 'I beg you' without having things or substances at hand to support our expressions; or mathematics, from which we have learnt that we do not need debts in order to understand negative algebraic numbers, and from which we have learnt the use of transfinite numbers without claiming to exhibit the infinite as an actual totality of objects; or the natural sciences, where one speaks of existent objects only that they are ultimately needed to satisfy the propositional functions of theories that are understood holistically – if it is true, as W. O. Quine maintains, that in and of itself the concept 'electron' is no less mythical than the concept 'the wrath of Jupiter' in explaining lightning, whereas it is in fact less mythical when internal to J. C. Maxwell's electromagnetic theory.[1] To be sure, we can say that our employment of words is prompted by causes, but the cause neither contains nor predetermines the meaning of the word it prompts. By this I mean that the causal forces that lead us to speak of DNA or the quantization of energy are of the same type as the causal forces that lead us to speak of 'postmodern experience', the 'crisis of democracy' or 'the crisis of the novel'. If one is not to philosophize with a hammer, it must be conceded that there are causes for saying what we do, causes which are not responsible for the meaning of the words they prompt. In these terms, the world does not become a text, which is a metaphysical assertion perfectly inter-changeable with its specular, or at least metaphysical, counterpart 'only atoms exist'. But anyone who is actually concerned with the text knows too that there is no text without an outside of the text.

The recently renewed philosophical reflection on religion would be restricted in its scope were it to be expressed in a discursive movement that tailors its own message to the distinction, taken as crucial and inevitable (on account of the ontotheological cultural tradition that weighs upon philosophy), between what exists and is present and real, and what on the contrary lives by the phantasmal breath of myth, by the murmur of unfounded belief and by the account that confers no more than an anaphoric existence on the objects of which it speaks. A discourse aiming at the theoretical refoundation in logico-metaphysical and epistemological terms of the beings that have historically occupied theology would make no sense and lead nowhere. Yet attempts to shake off this presupposition and shackle meet with stubborn resistance. So must religious discourse lose the wider sweep of its meaning and surrender its concreteness in order not to have to give up its ontological commitment to its objects? In other words, must we speak of God as an idealized anthropomorphic entity that transcends the empirical spatiotemporal world and subsists in another ontological region? Must we live faith as an attitude that projects itself beyond finite and limited reason, in reality to accomplish with a leap into immediacy what reason is not able to do, and that is to establish the presence of such things as God, angelic spheres, kingdoms of beatification, expiation and infernal punishment? Must we imagine Hell, punishment and guilt against the setting of a real fire that burns the punished souls and Heaven as a completely distinct state infused with love? Is there nothing in common between Hell and Heaven? These are just some of the questions that could be posed in the course of this enquiry.

Our vision will remain inevitably superficial as long as we do not overcome the metaphysics of presence of theological objects and as long as we do not return to that supreme moment which coincides with our actual experience of the significance of religion and which recognizes in religious discourse a hermeneutic perspective from which to look at life. We shall see the traditional dichotomies between terrestrial and heavenly life, between Hell and Heaven, humanity and divinity, collapse as inert, at which point we may ourselves enter into that highest and most fecund play between their affinities and differences. Now, these differences do not mark insuperable rifts or abysses between the regions of discourse, but, on the contrary, their inner involvement in the economy of a discourse that sees itself as such and proceeds as a discourse without end. This might look like an attempt to overcome or to abandon the tradition, but what is at issue here is rather a recovery of the signs of the religious tradition that have not been thought through to the end. Abandoning the metaphysical commitments regarding the ontological status of the referents of theological discourse may therefore signify a recovery of the signs and the annunciations immanent within the history of a religious tradition. Once the metaphysical charge is defused, the objects of the religious tradition become *figures for an interpretative perspective on life*. It is in this capacity that they may be seen to interpret the movements of existence in which we are immersed, and not in so far as they attract the processes of life and history, sucking them back into a further ontological domain of transcendent beings, which is presented today as the most suitable vantage point from which to re-think religious experience philosophically.

Contrary to the general trend, and to all those today for whom religion is an occasion to hand themselves over to a blind immediate feeling – like a leap into transcendence that they call faith, but which formally speaking can be anything that is not discursively and rationally mediated – the recovery and realization of religious experience occurs by way of a movement in exactly the opposite direction. To be precise, it consists *in the movement of reflection and experience that brings religion nearer again to immanence, picking out its symbols in the figures of our life*. Not, that is, in the inverse movement through which the human world is overturned by the antecedence of transcendent entities and events. Religious transcendence could not even be named were it not a difference that emerged from the actual figures of our experience. Transcendence as the division of the ontological boundaries between classes of entities is therefore effaced; and yet it is not effaced as a critical point of interpretive activity at the heart of the flux of the phenomena of life and history. In the end, religion will not be the discourse that discovers and makes manifest an Other Object, an Other Entity, but rather a term of comparison according to which the situations, figures and processes of our life come to be re-interpreted. Not something immense <*immane*>[2] to see, extraordinary in being distinguished from all objects in the ordinary experience of life, but rather a non-object, a paradigm that renders the objects and the situations of our life extraordinary, making them ascend to the level of an extraordinary symbolic force.

Moreover, the movement towards immanence outlined here concerns the true movement within religious transcendence. Examples work just as well, as a result of which, and this may seem paradoxical, religious transcendence achieves its meaning in the fold of a reflection that reconstructs the immanence of its terms. *Transcendence immanences itself*. The crucial feature of what I would call the metaphysical and objectivistic perspective on transcendence, handed down to us all the way from Platonic ontology to the empirical realism of positivism (the attitude that inspects and secures the actual presence of entities), establishes sharp dichotomies within religious experience. It is a matter of expropriation by a crucial and fecund core of thoughts that are betrayed and corrupted in what psychoanalysis calls *phallic language* (for example, the patient who is unable to bring eros to the level of the symbolic and consequently persists in speaking of the length, in inches, of the penises of men she has known).

To partition the destiny of a soul, of a psyche or of a mind into the realms of Hell and Heaven is equally *phallic language*. In Heaven, the souls advance peacefully and with favour on a journey towards the love of God. In Hell, they are gripped by the punishing flames and contorted in infinite pain. These are two distinct and separate ontological realms, and their separation, which seems to represent the high point of transcendence, betrays the meaning of religious transcendence. By contrast, the meaning of religious experience is restored by the movement of thought that reassigns a condition of immanence to the terms and the relations at stake. Let us say, then, in this second version, that the fire of Hell is not the torment inflicted by God on men who have not known how to acknowledge him, but that it expresses men's resistance to the love of God. This implies that God's love in Heaven is the same fire as that which torments those souls damned for resisting love. There is no ontological place or site of Heaven, just as there is none of Hell. Heaven and Hell describe two contrasting destinies in relation to the same flame. The fire of Heaven is the same reason as the fire of Hell. Now the blessed and the damned are no longer divided by metaphysical regions, spatial distinctions, ethico-juridical discriminations (all of which are, in the end, expressions in phallic language), but by a difference in attitude towards the same essential fact of the love of God. Beyond all destinies, it is this love that constitutes the immanent framework of this affair.

How, then, is the commandment 'Do not take the name of God in vain' to be interpreted? As a prohibition against naming a super-entity and supreme transcendent authority that is simply outside the horizon of our existence? Or as a *crucial signification* and a *crucial history* that emerges from a tradition of annunciations and messages to touch the present condition of our life and that can be neither verbalized in any way nor treated as homologous to the ordinary expressions of normal discourse? And so, as that of which one cannot say how or when it is, but which is kept safe in a silence respectful of its profundity and difference? But in this second acceptation, the commandment in question is, on the one hand, made authentic in that it is not normalized in expressions ordinarily pronounced, spoken or written in any circumstances whatsoever, and thus not in the ordinary currency of verbal exchanges. Yet, on the other hand, is involved in the figuration of life. In this sense, 'Do not take the name of God in vain' means safeguard the value of the word from attempts to distort and misunderstand it, to tear it out of its indisputable context and withdraw its links with the silence all around it, with the unreality that is in the end the repository of meaning in contrast to the *presence* of things and persons that no longer have any, that are precisely *present* simply because they are spent and exhausted. In these terms 'Do not take the name of God in vain' safeguards the secret history of the word. The word, for example, of the psychoanalyst that cannot be uttered in vain, namely, outside the session where, so to speak, it found its home: carried outside the session, away from the theatre in which it has been staged, it loses its meaning and is exposed to the insult of misunderstanding and incomprehension. 'Do not take the name of God in vain' is the commandment with which poetic language safeguards itself while keeping at bay all paraphrase, explanation and elucidation that, by explaining it, assimilates it to that language in relation to which poetic expression, in its singularity, sought to establish a point of difference, a leap, a perceptual jolt, a wonder that didactics and pornography (as two kinetic devices typically based on causal–mechanical processes) both normalize via an assimilation to common language.

The commandment 'Do not take the name of God in vain' is inherent to the gesture that protects life from its assassins, from those who would see in life an object to be dominated and bent to their own will and, regarding expression once again, to phallic language and the regime of intolerance, envy and suspicion. Eluding the superego imposed by the parental and social authorities that would like to put a name to everything and make everything explicit and uniform, the commandment in question safeguards the meanings and values by which life protects itself from violence. Thus, the commandment 'Do not take the name of God in vain' is on the one hand the trace of an *annunciation* lodged deep within our culture, whose source lies in the continually re-elaborated tradition. On the other hand, it coincides with the inferiority of life as an unpredictable event that is generative of differences. The annunciation, the gospel, is the essential event of religion. The transcendence of God comes to signify the transcendence of value and the word over the socio-historical circumstances of intolerance, religious fanaticism and the fundamentalisms and persecutions of all-embracing ideologies that would make the phenomena of life conform to a pre-established code of violent normalization.

One can feel nothing but the greatest perplexity at the attitude of many priests who, instead of hearkening to a message, an annunciation, a trace ramified in a tradition and a history, and destined to be taken up in a spiritual and existential elaboration, in effect distance themselves from such things, dangerously distorting their meaning and profile until their own role as priests has been reduced to that of moralists. The term 'moralism' expresses the distortion responsible for the way an annunciation, a gospel, degenerates into a dogmatics of human behaviour. But moralism is consequently also the *loss of theological consciousness* in its highest and richest sense, that is, as reflection, rational mediation of the annunciation and the exercise of doubt. Moralism, or religious experience reduced to a code of behavioural prescriptions, lacks the love that sets theological enquiry alight. In the highest and most decisive signification established in seventeenth-century liberal theology, under the influence of Socinianism by Chillingworth and John Locke,[3] tolerance becomes the outward sign of charity, inasmuch as respect for free enquiry conducted into the contents of faith is the distinctive mark of love towards the neighbour. With the affirmation of tolerance not only in social and political terms, but in the theological terms that underline its coincidence with the fundamental attitude of charity, a change occurred in the tradition of Christianity that shifted religious experience from the primacy of the *contents* of the articles of faith to the primacy of the *form* of the enquiry. But what remains surprising, even strikingly paradoxical, is that the *formality* of the attitude of tolerance retrieves the crucial nucleus of the Gospel. 'Do not take the name of God in vain' amounts not to the manifestation of an implacable authority that commands respect for itself, but rather to a defence of values and significations handed down by a history and a tradition. And yet at the same time, the re-elaboration of these values and significations commends them as custodians of the future, to preserve that which is still not yet as opposed to the already-said, the already-done and that which is founded, protected and popular. 'Do not take the name of God in vain' conveys the preservation of what is specifically human and of what is specifically divine as well; more precisely, the phrase establishes an incommensurable difference between the phenomena of life, between that which is visible, accessible, graspable in a direct and concrete fashion and that which withdraws and drags itself off to be mirrored in the silence that stands as the great test bed for every language.

The play and the evolution of these crucial distinctions do not lead to the inscription of human existence within the horizon of pure metaphysical transcendence, nor, on the other hand, to its enclosure within the narrow space of a historicist, sociological or anthropological immanence. Rather, human existence is found to lie in the evolution of the differences between its figures and in their tragic alternation. The signs contained within religious experience are not rigid designators, the certain proof of a given reality, but announce and prefigure the sacrifice of some parts of life in view of others that do not yet exist and whose unreality offers a more decisive signification of existing reality, in view of which the human individual is carried to *another state* to which he feels he belongs, even before reaching it. And all this without coming out of himself, without claiming to have grasped a truth or a reality outside of himself, like something that can be seized by stretching out a hand from non-truth. For it is all a consequence of an interior movement that effects a transition, a leap into the dizzy heights of the not-yet-said and the not-yet-done, into a domain of half-light. If the annunciations and the signs of religious experience were not uncertain, unstable and obscure, they would coincide with the reality indicated. In the first epistle to the Corinthians, Paul notes that if prophecy and faith were certified and complete knowledge, then there would be neither prophecy nor faith. 'For we know in part, and we prophesy in part.'[4] Religious faith, in its essential guise as annunciation, could be likened to a thought in search of thinkers. A thought, a sign that subsists even when unknown. The awaited day of Christ's return is unforeseen. In the Gospel according to Matthew it is written that the day of the advent of God will come unexpectedly like a thief in the night.

> Wherefore if they shall say unto you, Behold, he is in the desert; go not forth: behold, *he is* in the secret chambers; believe *it* not. For as the lightning cometh out of the east, and shineth even unto the west; so shall also the coming of the Son of man be . . . Watch therefore: for ye know not what hour your Lord doth come. But

> know this, that if the goodman of the house had known in what watch the thief would come, he would have watched, and the house would not have been broken up.[5]

Entry into religious experience seems to halt at its inchoate and primary phase. But this is in fact its enduring condition; namely, that of *initiation to the event*, and more precisely of initiation to time itself, to an interpretative perspective and an awaiting marked by unpredictability and pain. In the first letter to the Thessalonians, Paul, referring to the second coming of Jesus Christ, writes:

> But of the times and the seasons, brethren, ye have no need that I write unto you. For yourselves know perfectly that the day of the Lord so cometh as a thief in the night. For when they shall say, Peace and safety; then sudden destruction cometh upon them, as travail upon a woman with child; and they shall not escape.[6]

One should remind oneself tirelessly that the vocabulary of religious experience is not reducible to that of the mechanical laws of scientific causality and epistemological discourse; any more than the Calvinist doctrine of predestination is a historical law enabling one to predict the fate of the elect, and not rather a perspective from which to interpret human history. The destiny of religious experience does not take shape in an annunciation, in a message which is then consolidated, reifying in a transcendental entity. The word does not cease because there before it is the *thing*, the *great*, indeed the *immense thing* of religious mystery. But how could a mystery be contained in the presence of a thing, even were it immense? Here, too, as a result of an inappropriate assimilation of different vocabularies, the referentialistic schema of realist metaphysics and positivistic epistemology is at work: that is, here the word, there the thing; here the word 'Fido', there the dog Fido. The mystery that was to have culminated in the determination of an object of terror such as an immense metaphysical substance, or a case of irresistible authority and command, would be the death of the word. And with the word would be lost the specificity of the human, which, at the very point of conversion, is carried to another state, to that which is other, inasmuch as this other is knowledge, image, word and the annunciation of the new way. Was the mystery of the Christian religion not originally announced as love, as that paradoxical passion which reveals the desperation and the impossibility of salvation in the form of a human life that withdraws from the relation with the other and from the inevitable tension that accompanies it? The religious mystery is in the end announced as a symptom and as an appeal from everything that transcends the identity in which man closes himself and bars himself in; that is, his auto-reflexive identification of self with self, the point at which reality and the history of love and pain vanish, the point of an evasion that over time becomes a prison in which he is destined to suffocate slowly.

It has been said that the love that Jesus Christ preached is essentially a paradox and at the same time is no less essentially an annunciation: a paradox because it is an annunciation and also the reverse, in that it does not stop at the tautology of loving whoever one already loves or whoever is lovable, but, and this is very different, invites one to love one's enemies. Love for enemies, for torturers and persecutors, appears paradoxical and counter-intuitive if it is not understood at the same time as an annunciation, and precisely as the intimation of and the initiation into the course of their drama, their transformation, their pain and repentance, and their redemption. In giving food and drink to his enemy, writes Paul in his letter to the Romans, man distinguishes between vengeance and recompense, which according to biblical wisdom belong to God,[7] and beats evil with good. 'Dearly beloved, avenge not yourselves, but *rather* give place unto wrath: for it is written, Vengeance *is* mine; I will repay, saith the Lord. Therefore if thine enemy hunger, feed him; if he thirst, give him drink: for in so doing thou shalt heap burning coals of fire on his head.'[8] Love for one's enemies is in fact the point of view of an annunciation and also a prophecy, and not at all an attitude of immediacy towards *the presence of what is, to the presence of what each individual is.* It is rather the site of a difference that, in the tension between love and enmity, between war and peace, opens the horizon of an interpretation of our neighbour and of ourselves and our involvement in his destiny – as though we discovered that we too were no longer identical to ourselves, but *neighbours* to ourselves. And so, in discovering a whole domain of differences and distinctions, we can see that the problem represented by others is our problem, that the line that divides each of us from others is the same line that divides us from ourselves: *for whatever story comes to be told in the end, it is of us that it speaks.* And this awareness is essentially generative of a tolerance that is not merely a gift or a donation or a concession to others – which as such would at most be a moralistic project – but rather is constitutive of reason and our own salvation. Not just the avoidance of violence towards others but also the redemption of the violence in ourselves.

In this way, one can see how a reflection arising from a religious motivation might once again fall within the horizon of philosophical analysis, as indeed is happening today. To begin with, take the idea, among others, of not considering evil and pain exclusively as inimical. The religious experience of the Western tradition, and of the Eastern religions too, is characterized by a constitutive element of theodicy, which does not necessarily mean a project of religious politics whose aim is to justify God, to reconcile providence with the sack of Rome, with the plague in Milan and the Lisbon earthquake. Here, the idea of the apologetic is contaminated by the Enlightenment and rationalist model which takes divinity as a scientific legality that must be held up against facts and the natural order. But God is precisely not a scientific hypothesis because he is not a hypothesis at all. The religious apologetic has to be rethought in its essence as the discipline that promotes a different relation to evil. It does not exorcise it or aim to declare its elimination, but instead approaches it, traverses it and sees in it something that is close by, like our neighbour, and that intensifies the principle of responsibility, in that it is when man thinks he has distanced himself from evil, pain and injustice that he runs the highest risk of committing the greatest violence. While one can go along with Richard Rorty regarding the need to revoke the logocentric and metaphysical discourse on human nature as a universal matrix of ethico-juridical rights and values,[9] one can still see that political and ethical theory stands in need, as does everything else, of a reflection that is at once philosophical and also religious.

One must reflect on the fact that ideologies and beliefs that have defended the rights of the oppressed, of mankind and the poor, like Marxism and Christianity, have also brought with them the Crusades, the Inquisition and the gulag. Each of these events justified itself in reference to a supposedly historical law of self-fulfilment by which the torture of the Inquisition should have given rise to a heavenly city and the Soviet concentration camps to the classless society, with no exploited and no exploiters. These are metaphysical ideologies and they work as a catch that opens and shuts within the core of the very evil destined inevitably to turn to the good. What none the less calls for a philosophical reflection, which is quite different from a universal metaphysical definition of human nature, lies in the recognition that ideologies of the humble and the oppressed, such as Christianity and Marxism, have degenerated into instruments of individual and social persecution. The true anti-metaphysical core of politics and the centre of an adequate philosophical reflection are not solely or even sufficiently defined by the alternative of a cooperative society based on shared values and solidarity. In addition, there is the acquisition of an awareness of an *unknown and unfamiliar* tertium *over and above the factions* (if one is not to play the paradoxical and impracticable game of guilt and responsibility) under whose influence the values, cultures and programmes of moral and social emancipation have degenerated into historical forms of social tyranny and cruelty.

If it is hard to speak of political responsibility, it is clearer and certainly more interesting to speak of the intellectual and philosophical responsibility that consists in having followed, as it were, the voice of good without lending an ear to the voice of evil that infiltrates the good, acting in its place and even better than it. Let us say, then, that the authentic and substantial anti-metaphysical core of politics consists in a philosophical reflection and a religious impulse ready to hearken to evil, to deception, to that vague and obscure setting to reality that hangs over individuals, cities, societies and states, enveloping and silently corroding them, like humidity and rust. The fundamental fact in consideration here is that, like metaphysics, politics too has been a discourse at times enclosed in the terms of its own totalizing vocabulary, entertaining practico-theoretical links only with the *positive finality* of its own project, of its own programme, and taking evil and negativity as external factors personified in rival social and political elements. This metaphysical and ideological politics has identified evil in the figure of the adversary, consolidating and crystallizing it in a social–political presence as if it were an entity, a distinct and specific presence. It has overlooked the fact that evil, negativity, is everywhere, that it was and is even within itself. And so, being in itself as well as in the figure of the adversary, the negative is no longer a specific entity, but is rather an unpredictable and indefinable factor by which every ethical and political act is surrounded on all sides.

One should really have lost hope a while ago, in view of how politicians have always looked straight ahead, eyes forward, sweeping away all limits. Better able to run than to walk, they do not look to the side, behind or above, nor even into themselves, into the very mechanism that they set working. They have always looked straight ahead, launching themselves towards what is right, good and equitable, full of moral assurance and social commitment, without realizing that in crashing towards justice, progress and the social good, they brought about all manner of crime and violence: without realizing the inexorable differences that evil and the negative clawed out within their action itself. Interaction with the causality of the outside world, with its unpredictable events, enigmas, pitfalls, hazardous perturbations and turbulence, and with negativity and evil, should, it is worth recalling here, fall within the correct philosophical perspective, according to which ethical, social and political programmes are placed in constant relation to the danger of that metaphysical violence which is always imminent, even as it appears to be acting on behalf of the good and better than the good. To bring that unknown and unfamiliar *tertium* which envelops social processes and political events, and every aspect of human existence, back to our attention and to make it an object of reflection again is what a philosophical and religious reflection that begins with logic, semantics and epistemology and ends with politics and the theory of society is all about. The *tertium* is the seal of divinity, it is silence, the setting of that which is Other, of all difference, paradox and ambiguity, of the capacity of every term or thought to be turned about into its contrary.

It is from the perspective of this *tertium* that words and human relations of all kinds tighten their reciprocal bonds and link up their conditions of meaning. It is possible, and it has in fact been shown to be possible at different times, for people to believe or to pretend, not unlike players of chess who can pretend to be playing in pairs, that the meaningful range of their most important personal relations has been exhausted.[10] Of course, one's reduction to a name without substance represents the most extreme limit of secularization. In reality, however, even where least suspected, people are inevitably infiltrated by a *tertium*, which is no thing, no entity, no individual, no presence, but rather the setting that, like every religious experience, *brings together and at the same time separates*. It gives meaning and breath to their deeds, to their words and to the dreams that they pass between them while inventing a second birth and telling one another about what is going to happen; an appearance of destiny and an initiation to a new movement, an undertaking, and to all that goes by the name of the production of meaning. It can happen that the *tertium* attracts no suspicion from the people it envelops. In this way chess players pretend to themselves that they are alone, but could not play were there not a third protagonist in the game of chess itself with its rules and its possibilities of movement. And so it is that people in the various circumstances of their lives can remain oblivious to the signs of a *tertium* that they have right under their noses without realizing it and without suspecting it, and this is why the awaited day of the Lord will arrive without warning like a thief in the night.

The religious condition is an other state, it withdraws from the linear sequence of time, subsisting rather between times, *zwischen Zeiten*, as the theologians of Tübingen would have said. It does not assure us of a time to which we shall belong. Thus it is anything but a guarantee of presence. As if to say that Jesus Christ will be in the throes of death up to the end. 'And, lo, I am with you always, *even* unto the end of the world.'[11] In our epoch, the religious condition is situated between the rapture of meaning that is every ideology and every fundamentalism, and the loss of meaning that is the ongoing disenchantment of philosophy.[12] Since religious experience today takes place in the supersession of metaphysical entities and hypostases, it presents itself specifically as the unfolding of difference. It is the development of traces of the Other, the *tertium*, in view of the rigid and insular identity (with its own vocabulary) represented by ideology, lay or ecclesiastical, which fuels the flames of fundamentalism, fanaticism and intolerance. 'Trace' and 'difference' are symptomatic of a setting, of a *tertium* that, by its lacunae and its forlorn distances, articulates the production of words, of their meaning and the disequilibriums, responsible for the events and the manifestations of life. Jacques Derrida rightly maintains that the term 'difference' is neither a concept nor a word, but a limit that is in its turn inexpressible and the condition of possibility of concepts and words, the 'common root of all the oppositional concepts that mark our language'.[13] Translating into Wittgensteinian terminology, we could say that 'difference' is the unsayable that makes the sayable possible. Which is to say, the word echoes as if from the distance of a silent setting and this restores its divine provenance, its character as a gift that reveals a mystery, its redemptive and saving power, like the 'resolutive word' and the 'resolutive thought' that produce no proof of reality and certainty in which to rest, yet which soothe, without erasing it, the pain, the nostalgia that they reveal, and which convey the recognition and legitimation of the problem that at times we ourselves are; which is in the end constituted by the right, as it were, to channel what has become and what is into language, into a temporal point of our historical existence, without thereby passing via a feeling of guilt. Will this not be precisely the path along which we heard – we remembered the words, but over time forgot their meaning – that God is love, is charity and that the Word is God? In the end, as Gianni Vattimo maintains, are we, Westerners and others from beyond, not the consequence of these annunciations?

In the course of the seminar at Capri in the winter of 1994, in which Jacques Derrida, Maurizio Ferraris, Hans–Georg Gadamer, Eugenio Trías, Gianni Vattimo, Vincenzo Vitiello and I took part, the question of reason itself addressing the religious thematic was naturally raised; that is, the distinction between philosophical and religious discourse and the comparison of the respective vocabularies in the light of the recognition that a new rhetorical space, a new public space of communication, has opened in this epoch. In the course of the discussion, Maurizio Ferraris remarked that the exhaustion of the work of philosophy as the critical analysis of metaphysics would restore a legitimacy to discourse on religion, which would in turn result in the problematization, at this stage, of the distinction between philosophy and religion. It is also worth noting that there was general agreement with Gianni Vattimo's suggestion that a systematic philosophical analysis of religion should be avoided. Strangely, yet understandably, it was just this observation that saved the autonomy of philosophical discourse. For, by avoiding the practice of categorization and logico-linguistic analysis, it has absolved itself, on the one hand, from the purely speculative choice of themes, positions and theses of the religious traditions or the elaboration of a natural theology on the basis of a closed and totalizing vocabulary of its own, and, on the other hand, from the risk of an apparently neutral technical approach that is in reality subordinated, wittingly or not, to the acceptance or rejection of certain articles of faith and frameworks of belief. Personally, I believe that as philosophy acknowledges the variety of its cultural vocabularies, the constitutive indeterminability of its own discourse and the heterogeneous components – inferential connections, non-inferential associations of metaphor and similitude – by which it is structured, it reveals the limits of its own vocabulary. These limits have the effect of keeping philosophy from the temptation of totalizing discourse, from the assimilatory violence of traditional metaphysics and from the inclination to generate the cosmos on the basis of a handful of self-evident axioms within a regime of autarchic rationality. I believe that this condition contributes to the clarification of the inner work of philosophy as such and to the definition of its distance from religious discourse – a fruitful distance at which it flourishes. These distinctions and moves to discern limits contribute towards the requirement of tolerance that is a constitutive and generative reason behind philosophical discourse as much as any other use of the word. It is precisely these distinctions, these lacunae and delimitations that fecundate the relation between philosophy and religion, the possibility of the first to refer itself to the second without destroying it and without, moreover, falling into it such that all distinction is lost. The disposition towards listening, to what is other, the recovery of wonder as the 'fundamental affective tonality of philosophy' and, more precisely, the *moment of excess in the indistinction* between what an entity is, in so far as it is the entity that it is, and what in such an entity does not have stability, does not have structure, is continually overturned and reveals itself as it withdraws and hides, the repression 'of the instinct to take a position'[14] that keeps philosophy, as another creative power, in a state of indecidability and inexplicability,[15] are likewise clues, traces and partial expressions of the bond that at present ties philosophical discourse to religious experience.

If the traditional referentialistic and representationalist object word schema, *adaequatio rei et intellectus*, the identity of the knower and the known – that is, all metaphysical philosophy of presence – has gone into crisis, it is also true that a substantial part of analytic philosophy of language is perilously close to being a linguistic reformulation of idealism. Moreover, a substantial part of post-analytic philosophy and epistemology, such as Nelson Goodman's 'ways of worldmaking', Kuhn's paradigms, Hillary Putnam's schema of rational decidability and Jehuda Elkana's anthropology of knowledge,[16] have transformed the work of philosophy into a philosophy of culture, into an intellectual exercise that feeds on itself, on its own results, expunging every trace of difference, every confrontation with alterity within or without, in a self-referential methodological normalization of reality, of alterity and of every mystery and enigma. In the end, the deconstruction of neo-positivism gave us versions of the world with no more world. Philosophy lost that quality of friction with reality which gives pause for thought. Philosophy, in fact, thinks in so far as there is something that gives it to think: history, the event, the singularity marking an annunciation and a path. By contrast, post-neopositivist and post-analytic epistemology constructs versions of the world that presuppose the application of conceptual schemes by an interpreting subject to a neutral, unprejudiced and unformed flux of experience, repeating the Kantian dichotomy between schema and content later taken up by, among others, Ernst Mach, Bertrand Russell and Rudolf Carnap. Thus, Nelson Goodman writes that there exist Cartesian and Newtonian worlds, worlds of Canaletto and Van Gogh, none of which is any more objective than another; jointly, on an equal plane, each of them captures an interesting feature of experience.[17]

But the theory of versions of the world, of paradigms and schema of rational decidability, constitute an inadequate system of self-understanding, in the sense that it is in fact hard to draw the motives that generate versions of the world in science, art and politics back to the philosophical and epistemological theory of versions of the world.[18] We believed we had taken a step forwards but instead find ourselves right back at the beginning, where the problem starts over again and the solution is still nowhere to be seen. Theories of paradigms, of versions of the world and of schema of decidability fail to grasp that quality of friction which is the beginning of philosophical enquiry and which is constituted by a *singularity*: an event, an experiential process, a historical occurrence, a message, an annunciation, a gospel. Or else that which gives itself to think and which becomes a part of tradition through the vicissitudes of interpretation. Take physics: Einstein declared that theoretical physics was not exhausted in a hypothetico-deductive system of logico-mathematical inferences from a handful of axioms. At the origin of relativity lay the phenomenon of the singularity of light that shaped the organization of the theory. On a more general methodological level, Einstein held that at the basis of physical science there must exist an empathy, an *Einfühlung*, on the part of the scientist with regard to natural phenomena which precedes the experimental-mathematical elaboration. 'The highest end of physics', wrote Einstein,

> is that of arriving at those universal laws which permit the reconstruction of the universe by way of deduction. There is no logical path to these universal laws. Only intuition, founded on the sympathetic understanding of experience, can lead to them . . . The empirical world determines the theoretical world in practice, in spite of the fact that there exists no logical bridge between phenomena and their theoretical principles.[19]

Einstein believed that, psychologically speaking, axioms rest on experience, 'yet there exists no logical path leading from experience to the axioms, but only an intuitive connection. Moral: if one does not sin against reason, one gets nowhere [*Moral, wenn man gar nicht gegen Vernunft sündigt, kommt man überhaupt zu nichts*].'[20] Hence for Einstein scientific theory is not a reflex, a representation of reality, but an instrument of research ('*ein Instrument der Forschung*').

> The natural philosophers of the time [the eighteenth and nineteenth centuries] were on the whole steeped in the idea that the fundamental concepts and postulates of physics were not, from a logical point of view, free inventions [*freie Erfindungen*] of the human mind, but could be deduced from experience by 'abstraction', that is, by logical means. A clear recognition of the erroneous nature of this notion in reality came only with the general theory of relativity . . . The fictitious character of fundamental principles is clearly demonstrated by the fact that we can point to two essentially different theoretical bases, each of which in its consequences turns out to be

> broadly in accordance with experience. This suggests that every attempt to derive the basic concepts and the laws of mechanics logically from the ultimate data of experience is destined to fail.'[21]

Significantly, neo-positivist and post-analytic epistemology and the philosophy of language consider the mystery, the enigma and wonder as a disturbance and malfunction of ordinary language. Such epistemology and philosophy of language miss the distinction between the subject as legislator and constructor of experience and nature, and the subject as interpreter of events, occurrences, annunciations, appeals, mysteries and enigmas.

From this analysis there emerges a critical and problematic issue that in my judgement runs right through philosophy, epistemology, aesthetics and religion at present, breaking down their respective limits. In fact, there is today a conflict between *heteronomy* (plurality of vocabularies, of languages, a variety of methodological approaches from the philosophy of science to hermeneutics) and *homonomy* (unique method, decision and demarcation between styles of description). Homonomy takes the variety of styles and descriptions employed by heteronomy to be aestheticism; and heteronomy considers the univocal and privileged choice made by homonomy to be aestheticism in its turn. Aestheticism has become a disquieting accusation in present philosophical debate. To give an example, Richard Rorty, a champion of heteronomy, accuses W. O. Quine of aestheticism when the latter accords a position of privilege to the natural sciences, *Naturwissenschaften*, with respect to the human sciences, *Geisteswissenschaften*, that looks to Rorty like the fruit of a 'purely aesthetic' choice.[22] Yet, who is less of an aesthetician than Quine? Even so, Rorty's characterization is at bottom anything but banal. In his turn, Rorty, as a champion of the plurality of interpretations and of vocabularies of culture, can himself be on the receiving end of accusations of aestheticism. In an essay from 1992,[23] and then again in a debate held at the State University of Milan, Gianni Vattimo pointed out, in posing the problem of the rationality of the hermeneutic enterprise, that the critique(s) of ontotheological culture and the philosophy of presence aside, Rorty leaves himself open to the danger of aestheticism, to an arbitrary game of interpretations understood as a *coup de dés*. For his part, Vattimo identifies the element that discriminates among various interpretations in the ebbs and flows of a given historical experience, of a tradition in which is fulfilled a history of the effects of interpretation, what H.–G. Gadamer calls 'effective history'.

The term 'aesthetic' thereby comes less and less to concern the discipline or the form of the beautiful, and ever more to be a style, an intentional strategy of thought. We can trace a homonomic attitude in art and a heteronomic attitude in philosophical or scientific theory (the various equivalent and evenly matched ways of engaging in the game of science, according, for example, to P. Feyerabend). Poetry or literature fashioned as a version of the sole reality on view is homonomic, no less than a referentialistic theory such as that of Saul Kripke, H. Field or a realist theory such as that of B. Williams. Conversely, a philosophical or scientific theory that presupposes a variety of alternative games opens itself to characterization as, or accusation of being, a set of aesthetic choices. The crucial problem is to enquire whether in heteronomy there may be, by way of a covert implication, a homonomic aspect, as in the case of historicism and relativism that do not manage to historicize and relativize themselves (Hegel's absolute spirit, Nietzsche's will to power). In the traditional conception of knowledge as correspondence, and in philosophical and scientific representationalism where subject and world were taken as rigid identities, the aesthetic phenomenon was the heteronomy that as such lacked truth. In contemporary culture these identities have been shattered both in the culture of ideas (the plurality of vocabularies, of methodological approaches and styles of interpretation) and in social life (churches, sects, parties, political movements, associations, divorces and so on). Stated briefly, Goodman's, Kuhn's and Putnam's theory of a plurality of versions of the world generated by a subject that remains identical to itself (the relation subject–world as a one–many relation) constitutes a half step, or even a *revolutionary setback* <English in the original>, a retardatory effect. Once the subject and the world are both susceptible to a plurality of versions, heteronomy is no longer the most distinctive feature of aesthetic experience. Yet the problem remains whether the heteronomic can avoid the homonomic. What does the thinker of heteronomy think? To be more precise, are his reflections on the different stripes of reality that he describes not set against a single background, something like a philosophical aftertaste? (Here lies the temptation and the core truth of realism.) The problem, therefore, is this: to think the variety of versions of the world, does one not none the less need a single vision of the setting, that is, homonomy? By this I mean, is it not required as a prop, a point of support, as a *Halt* or a foothold, if only to give purpose, to weave together the variety and diversity of the world? The mystery of life consists in that towards which the thinker of heteronomy assumes responsibility and which he recognizes as the shadow, but also as a companion that accompanies his thoughts. (The German language uses the term *der Gefährte* to denote who or what accompanies us, at a distance, without having established any pact or agreement between us.) It is here that one finds the point of contact between analytic philosophy and religious experience. A point of scission that institutes a double regime and opens the development of differences, of the pervasiveness of thoughts, words and existential situations, of all that has manifested itself, but which is at the same time surpassed by an ulterior unitary instance: the place of their gathering, the homeland of their co-existence, the dwelling place of their motivation and finally the setting of a unique nostalgia.

It seems that the universalism of metaphysical rationalism harbours a dream of homonomy, of a distinctive unitary setting, in that, in the nostalgia for God of every living person, it sets itself against the homonomy of any established 'conception of the world'. This is the existential condition recounted in the tale of a doctor by Chekhov:

> I'd like to wake up a hundred years from now and cast at least a cursory glance at what's happening in science. I'd like to have lived another ten years or so. And then? The rest is nothing, I go on thinking – for a long time – but can't hit on anything. And rack my brains as I will, broadcast my thoughts where I may, I clearly see that there's something missing in my wishes – something vital, something really basic. My passion for science, my urge to live, my sitting on this strange bed, my urge to know myself, together with all my thoughts and feelings, and the conceptions which I form about everything – these things lack any common link capable of bonding them into a single entity. Neither in my judgements about science, the stage, literature and my pupils, nor in the pictures painted by my imagination could even the most skilful analyst

detect any 'general conception', or the God of a live human being. And if one lacks that, one has nothing. So wretched is my plight that serious illness, fear of death, the impact of circumstance and people, have sufficed to capsize and shatter my entire outlook as I formerly conceived it – everything which once gave my life its joy and significance.'[24]

This is the point of transcendence even of oneself, of what one has been, is and will be, where philosophical reflection and spiritual religious experience begin to look at themselves, to find themselves in their proximity, to exchange bodies, so to speak, without touching in the ultimate horizon of waiting, to become reciprocally involved in one another's future. Novalis wrote that 'philosophy is properly nostalgia, the desire to find oneself everywhere at home',[25] that is to be everywhere and always in the totality, while it tries to pass beyond man and humanism, yet all the while on the basis of our finitude, of our mortality and of the occasional suspicion that we may have stumbled into the universe by chance.

Translated by David Webb

Acknowledgements

I would like to express my gratitude to Dr Maurilio Orbecchi, President of the Jungian School, and to Elmar Salman, Professor of Dogmatic Theology at the College of St Anselm in Rome, with whom I discussed some of the issues addressed in this chapter.

Notes

1 W. O. Quine, *From a Logical Point of View* (Cambridge, Mass., Harvard University Press, 1961).

2 *Translator's note*: Gargani here, and in the remainder of the chapter, exploits the similarity in Italian between '*immane*' ('gigantic, overwhelming') and '*immanente*' ('immanent'). This play, impossible to reproduce in English, should be borne in mind by the reader.

3 W. Chillingworth, *The Works* (Oxford, Oxford University Press, 1838); Carlo Augusto Viano, *John Locke: Dal razionalismo all'illuminismo* (Turin, Einaudi, 1960), pp. 309–7.

4 Corinthians 12:9. All references to the Bible are to the Authorized Version of King James. On this point, cf. S. Quinzio, *Un commento alla Bibbia* (Milan, Adelphi, 1991), p. 483.

5 Matthew 24: 26–7, 42–3; cf. also 1 Thessalonians 5:4.
6 Thessalonians 5:1–3.
7 Deuteronomy 32:35. Cf. Quinzio, *Un commento alla Bibbia*, pp. 415–16.
8 Romans 12:19–20; 2 Peter 3.
9 R. Rorty, *Essays on Truth and Interpretation, Philosophical Papers*, vol. I (Cambridge, Cambridge University Press, 1991), p. 175ff.
10 S. Levi della Torre, *Mosaico: attualità e inattualità degli ebrei* (Turin, Rosenberg and Dellier, 1994), pp. 17–49; also by the same author, 'Ebraismo', in *I viaggi di Erodoto* VIII (1994) 22, pp. 216–20.
11 Matthew 28:20.
12 B. Forte, 'Cattolicesimo' in *I viaggi di Erodoto*, pp. 221–4. I would like to point out that mystical experience, which constitutes what is essentially an 'intoxication of sense', is in no way implicated in the dichotomy between ideology and disenchantment that is discussed here.
13 J. Derrida, *Positions*, trans. A. Bass (Chicago, University of Chicago Press, 1981), p. 9.
14 M. Heidegger, *Basic Questions of Philosophy* (Bloomington, Ind., Indiana University Press, 1996), ch. 5.
15 Ibid.
16 T. S. Kuhn, *The Structure of Scientific Revolutions* (Chicago, Chicago University Press, 1962); N. Goodman, *Ways of Worldmaking* (Indianapolis and Cambridge, Hackett, 1978); H. Putnam, *Reason, Truth and History* (Cambridge, Cambridge University Press, 1981); Y. Elkana, *Anthropologie der Erkenntnis* (Frankfurt-on-Main, Suhrkamp, 1986).
17 Goodman, *Ways of Worldmaking*, p. 3.
18 A. G. Gargani, *Lo stupore e il caso* (Rome and Bari, Laterza, 1986), pp. 25–44; also by the same author, 'L'attrito del pensiero', in G. Vattimo (ed.), *Filosocia '86* (Rome and Bari, Laterza, 1987), pp. 5–22, subsequently included in my *Stili di analisi* (Milan, Feltrinelli, 1993), pp. 43–60.
19 A. Einstein, *Lettres à Maurice Solovine* (Paris, Aubier, 1956), p. 120.
20 Ibid., p. 128.
21 A. Einstein, *On the Method of Theoretical Physics*, The Herbert Spencer Lecture delivered at Oxford 1933 (Oxford, Oxford University Press, 1933), p. 11. Cf. also A. G. Gargani, 'La "buona austriacità" di Ernst Mach', introduction to E. Mach, *Conoscenza e errore: abbozzi per una psicologia della ricerca* (Turin, Einaudi, 1982), pp. vii–xxxiii.
22 R. Rorty, *Philosophy and the Mirror of Nature* (Oxford, Blackwell, 1980), p. 203: 'This tactic makes his preference for physics over

psychology, and thus his concern about "irresponsible reification", purely aesthetic.'

23 In G. Vattimo (ed.), *Filosofia '91* (Rome and Bari, Laterza, 1992), p. 93.

24 A. Chekhov, 'A dreary story', in *The Oxford Chekhov*, vol. V (stories 1889–1891) (London, Oxford University Press, 1970), p. 80.

25 Novalis, *Schriften*, vol. II, Fragment 21 (Iéna, Minor, 1923), p. 179; cf. M. Heidegger, *The Fundamental Concepts of Metaphysics: World, Finitude, Solitude*, trans. W. McNeill and N. Walker (Bloomington, Ind., Indiana University Press, 1995), p. 5.

5

Desert, Ethos, Abandonment: Towards a Topology of the Religious

Vincenzo Vitiello

At the threshold of the third millennium, of the age that we Europeans and Christians call the third millennium, the spectacle that lies before us could hardly look more worrying. If the collapse of the Soviet empire has made plain to us how an ideology founded on the highest values of human solidarity can be capable of the most pitiless oppression of the rights of man, the religious fundamentalisms gathering strength within Europe and beyond seem to provide confirmation less for Lucretius's saying – *tantum religio potuit suadere malorum* – than for Nietzsche's pronouncement on the 'death of God'.

Nietzsche spoke prophetically. 'The desert grows', he wrote, narrating *our* history, which for him was the history to come, 'the history of the next two centuries'. And history is a desert not owing to a lack of values, but owing to their presence. The desert of our history is created by values – this is what Nietzsche *prophetically* told us.

Yet the image of the *desert* is far older than the thought of Nietzsche, and its sense has not always been negative. To understand Nietzsche, and thus our present, it is therefore worth going back to this older image, not least to explain the first appearance of its negative sense: and that is, the primary – the most common and at bottom also most banal – signification of *nihilism*.

Desert and errancy: the Judaic conception of God

Figures

Abraham Let us read these ancient words once more:

> Now the Lord had said unto Abraham: Get thee out of thy country, and from thy kindred, and from thy father's house, unto a land that I will show thee, and I will make of thee a great nation, and I will bless thee, and make thy name great; and thou shalt be a blessing.[1]

In these words is already contained the entire destiny of the Jewish people. There is no need for an *allegorical* interpretation that aims to grasp the 'spirit' beyond the 'letter'. The earth is not a symbol of the body, or related to sensation, and it is not the house of the father of language – as Philo Judaeus of Alexandria believed. Nor is God's command to be understood as the will to the purification of the soul of man, releasing it from the snares of the terrestrial world. The *migration of Abraham* is to be understood in the most *literal* and concrete way: the Judaic God is a jealous God who will share his people with nothing and no one. And so he separates his nation – what will be his nation – not only from the land of the fathers, from sentimental attachments, customs and the ways of the family, but also from the divinities which dwell in that land. Accompanying the command is a promise that will, when he senses his people's faith in him waver, become a pact. Of this pact, this *alliance*, which in the course of time will be renewed on several occasions, his male protégés must carry an indelible sign on their very bodies.

A jealous God, and one who estranges his people. Not only from the land of the fathers, but also from his own gifts. He conceded to Abraham and Sarah, both old, a promised son. But in order that love for the son should not diminish their dedication to him, he commands the ultimate sacrifice.

Kierkegaard, in a page of profound religious meditation, grasped the sense of the extreme solitude in Abraham. He does not speak with Sarah, nor with Eleazar, nor with Isaac. He cannot speak, because, unlike the tragic hero, he cannot give any reason for his act. Agamemnon sacrifices Iphigenia, breaks the ties of blood, in view of a wider interest, *inter-esse*, and a *common ethos*.

Abraham is and remains alone before God: his is an *absolute* relation to the *Absolute* – a relation beyond everything with One who is beyond everything. Abraham loves 'his son with all his soul.'

> When God requires Isaac he must love him if possible even more dearly, and only on this condition can he *sacrifice* him; for in fact it is this love for Isaac which, by its paradoxical opposition to his love for God, makes his act a sacrifice. But the distress and dread in this paradox is that, humanly speaking, he is entirely unable to make himself intelligible. Only at the moment when his act is in absolute contradiction to his feeling is his act a sacrifice, but the reality of his act is the factor by which he belongs to the universal, and in that aspect he is and remains a murderer.[2]

However, Kierkegaard does not have the courage to think the *absolutenesss* of the relation that binds Abraham to God through to its end. He puts in Abraham's heart the faith that the sacrifice will not take place, or if it will take place, that 'the Lord will give me a new Isaac, by virtue . . . of the absurd.'[3] A Christian thinker – in the *historical* Christian tradition that begins with Paul and not with the word of Jesus – Kierkegaard, no different from Philo Judaeus in being Jewish but with a Greek culture, puts an end to the errancy, both a conclusion and a cessation. It is just this that remains foreign to the Jew: for him the Promised Land, the place where milk and honey flows, lies always in the future.

Moses If Abraham's errancy follows a divine command that uproots him from the land of the fathers, for Moses his very birth is erratic. He is born of the waters of the Nile, if we grant that he is admitted to life only after, having been entrusted to the current of the river, he is saved by the Pharaoh's barren daughter. His *natural* birth, which comes first, does not count; it is phantasmal – properly speaking, it *is-not.* At least, it should *not-be.* And yet the phantasm of this natural birth, is always present. But precisely as *phantasm*, as a being that is-not, and which undermines the *reality* of the *socially* recognized birth, the only birth that the Pharaoh's state can acknowledge. At once Egyptian and Jew, and non-Egyptian and non-Jew, Moses' birth is before him, as a goal to be achieved. To do this, he must distance himself from both of the communities to which he belongs without belonging. Moses will find his homeland as a 'stranger in a strange land'.[4] And so it is that when he chooses his *origin* and with this *his* people, he returns to Egypt to take them away. Moses can recognize himself in his people only in errancy.

His only land and home is the desert – the absence of home. The origin is danger and mortal threat. First the Jewish birth, then the current of the river, and finally the land of Egypt. *Finally*? Is there an end for Moses, an end to the danger and the threat? For him every pause is betrayal, every moment of calm a dereliction, every satisfaction sacrilege. When he asks his God to show himself, his God passes before him with his face covered. Moses can see only the divine back. As Gregory of Nyssa comments:

> So Moses, who eagerly seeks to follow God, is now taught how he can behold him: to follow God wherever he might lead is to behold God . . . Therefore, he says to the one who is led, *my face is not to be seen*, that is, 'Do not face your guide.' If he does so his course will certainly be in the opposite direction, for good does not look good in the face, but follows it.[5]

The God of Moses is always beyond, over there. His true root – the good – is not in the *past*, but in the *future*. The past and the present have value *for* the future. The Judaic conception of time diverges profoundly not only from the 'circular' conception of the Greeks, but also from the 'linear' one of historical, Pauline, Christianity. Judaic time is centred not on the *present* of Christ, but on the *future* of God as always other and always beyond, of God as 'otherwise than Being'. If the *past* is a danger and a threat, the *present* is a desert and has no value in and of itself. The land of dwelling is always future. The whole chain of time hangs from the future. The desert is not a period of trial, but a *destiny*. It is the permanent condition of the Jewish people.

But the desert is not only errancy and poverty, it is also a promise. The column of smoke that guides Moses and Israel is already an *encounter*. It is in the desert and only in the desert that one encounters God as Guide. Israel dwells in errancy. And so there must be laws – and hard ones, too, as hard as life in the desert. The God who shows himself in his absence, who veils himself as he appears, calls for fidelity, a fidelity forever renewed.

Isaac is not an episode from the past. Abraham's sacrifice, too, has a value only if renewed – only in the *future* of each and everyone, in the future of the whole of Israel. And so the future God wants the primogeniture of men and animals. It is for him to renew the holocaust from time to time. The encounter with God is always a sacrifice. The sacrifice of the present, which has value only if sacrificed: and so annulled. Only the annihilation of the present gives value and dignity to the present. The desert is *desert* only for the God who degrades it, annuls it, negates it. The encounter with God is the uplifting experience of one's own annihilation for the sake of a total dedication, for a dedication that knows no *end*.

And so when Israel asks for repose, when the harshness of the desert made ever more a desert calls to mind the slightest Egyptian slavery, then God's condemnation falls mercilessly on that people, on *his* people, incapable of receiving him – rebellious against his exacting judgement. But not only the people of Israel *rebel* against their God. Moses, too, knows the weariness of a goal that never ceases to be a goal, of a God that remains closed in his impenetrable cloud, jealous even of his image; that lends support only when his people are at the point of exhaustion, and then immediately commands that the walk in the desert begin once more. It is not impossible to see in the episode of the golden calf some little 'responsibility' on the part of Moses, his involvement in some way, even if indirect. One need only consider the fact that the idea of fusing the gold to form an idol came from Aaron, the 'mouth' of Moses. And yet Moses' punishment, to die without touching the Promised Land, is too harsh to be attributed to the second, unordered, stroke of the staff, on the rock from which God made water burst forth to quench the thirst of Israel.

Interpretations

Hegel The pages on religion written by Hegel as a young man are characterized by a deep hostility towards Judaism. Comparing Abraham with Cadmus, Danaus and other Greek heroes, Hegel writes that where the latter 'went in quest of a soil where they would be free and they sought it that they might love', the former, the founding fathers of the Jewish nation, 'wanted *not* to love, wanted to be free by not loving'.[6] The abandonment of the land of the fathers was just the first act of a liberty that wanted to be absolute, beyond all links with the world. Even the love for the son, for the only son that he had, weighed upon him. He could accept it only when it was certain 'that this love was not so strong as to render him unable to slay his beloved son with his own hand'.[7]

The judgement of Moses is no less heavy: he freed his people from one yoke in order to place on them another, still heavier. The 'does not want to love' of Abraham, who made enemies for his nation of everyone he encountered on their wanderings, is turned by Moses and Aaron against their own people: 'the deeds of Moses and Aaron worked on their own brethren precisely as they did on the Egyptians, i.e. as a force, and we see how the latter defended themselves against subjection by just the same means.'[8]

Clearly, the negative judgement could not but fall equally upon the God of Israel. The comparison between the secrecy of the Eleusinian mysteries and the concealedness of the God of Moses is illuminating.

> And the concealment of God in the Holy of Holies had a significance quite different from the arcanum of the Eleusinian gods. From the pictures, feelings, inspiration, and devotion of Eleusis, from these revelations of god, no one was excluded; but they might not be spoken of, since words would have desecrated them. But of *their* objects and actions, of the laws of *their* service, the Israelites might well chatter (Deuteronomy 30:1), for in these there is nothing holy. The holy was always outside them, unseen and unfelt.[9]

Hegel only sees the negative aspect of the Judaic vision of life, which for him was nihilism and nihilism alone. The *desert* is just the image of the absence of love, of the absence of value and the absence of God. To the annihilation of creation corresponds the Nothing of the Creator. Hegel recalls the disappointment of Pompey, who 'had approached the heart of the temple, the center of adoration, and had hoped to discover in it the root of the national spirit . . . the life-giving soul of this remarkable people . . . [only] to find himself in an empty room'.[10]

On close inspection, all of Hegel's criticisms are centred on the Judaic conception of time. An heir to Pauline Christianity – to historical Christianity – he could not understand a time totally deferred to the future, a time that did not have its centre in the present. His infinite is totality, *positivity, presence*, Revelation, *Offenbarung*. The god that does not show itself, that does not love, that does not reveal itself, the god that is always and only *future*, is for Hegel an impoverished and deficient god. Hegel's future is only in the *certainty* of the present, in the *truth of what has come to be <l'avvento>*. The Messiah has arrived *<è venuto>*. Time is fulfilled. And so all the ills of the world – the *mala mundi* – are defeated and overcome in the overall good. Also overcome and defeated, along with the *mala*, is the *malum*, death. Death is for life: the Friday of the Passion is followed by the Easter of the Resurrection – in the truth of philosophy no less than in the faith of religion.

Benjamin and Jabès Hegel defined the Jewish people as *ausgezeichnet*, remarkable, extraordinary.[11] And yet it seems impossible to understand this recognition of Israel's greatness from within his interpretation of Judaism. Moreover, Hegel's discourse does not fully comprehend the function of the Messiah in the Judaic conception of the religious. He confines himself to observing that 'the ordinary Jew, who was ready enough to sacrifice himself but not his Object, sought it in the hope of the coming Messiah.'[12] But, in fact, the Messiah's role is one of necessary mediation. On account of his remoteness, the absolute extremity of his Being-future, the Judaic God is always on the brink of breaking all relation with the present, and thereby places at risk his own nature as *future*. The Messiah does not bring the future closer, does not *actualize* it. Rather, he sustains its distance – and this is precisely the point: he sustains it. For the prophet – he who speaks to the future in order to weigh the spiritual wretchedness of the *present*: the *infidelity* to God of his people – the link with the divine, in whose name he speaks, should not begin merely with him. It should not be *his*, merely *subjective*, but rather *objective*, and thus willed by God himself. The Messiah is the manifestation of God's fidelity to the alliance in contrast to the *infidelity* of the people of Israel. The Messiah is the presence of the divine *future* in the human *present*. And yet he is the presence of an absence, which is at the same time a condemnation of the present. The Messiah, too, therefore, remains, and must remain, always future.

In him is gathered and expressed all the complexity of Judaic time. Walter Benjamin is among the finest and most acute interpreters of this complexity, and was so from his earliest writings.

Benjamin begins with the distinction between revelatory or expressive language and communicative language: that which, in naming, expresses and is the *essence* of things, and that which, as an image of things, is a useful vehicle of information. This distinction, however, does not belong to actual history, for from the time of original sin, from the time, that is, of the birth of history, man has lost revelatory *paradisiac* language.[13] 'Pure language' is only an *archaic* memory – the memory of a past that has always been past. The fact of the matter is that there have existed and do exist only 'the hundred languages of man', of historical humanity, which are all *betrayals <tradimenti>* – and thus also *traditions, transmissions* – of that pure and original language that has never existed, and which is not even meta-historically and axiologically present in each historical language.[14]

Benjamin's interpretation of time is deliberately opposed to that of Hegel. If tragic time (which really belongs to the *pre-history* of man) is, like messianic time, a fulfilled time (*erfüllte Zeit*), it is none the less fulfilled in a sense exactly contrary to the Hegelian conception. The time of the tragic hero is fulfilled inasmuch as death does not simply signify the end of life, but gives *form to its destiny*. It fulfils the 'principle', that which was there from the beginning. Death confers immortality on the tragic hero. But it is an 'ironic immortality'.[15] Although for Benjamin, too, *the truth of the finite is the infinite* – in Hegel's well-known phrase – in his interpretation of the tragic the infinite lies not in the reconciliation of the divine with the human, the reconstitution of the 'ethical order of the world', but rather in the absolute – not dialectic – negation of the finite. In the silence of the tragic hero is revealed the non-historical character of his destiny. The death of the tragic hero does not open a history, it reveals with the gratuitousness of destiny the 'superiority' of the hero over his gods. Herein lies the *moral* sublimity (in the Kantian sense) of tragedy.[16]

If this is the fulfilment of tragic time, in what does the *unfulfilment* of historical time consist? Here, the divergence from Hegel is, if possible, still more profound. Against the immanence of the concept, Benjamin sets the transcendence of the idea, against the relational character of the symbolic, the finality of the allegoric. In short, against the elevation of history, a radical historical nihilism. The course of history is not a trail of conquest and salvation. On the contrary, it is a boundless accumulation of debris. History is just the space of the ephemeral, of the senseless, and finds its best expression in the shattered language of the *Trauerspiel.* Separated from the Eternal, divided within itself, time can have no other continuity than that of a merely spatial aggregation.[17]

And yet in the wretched createdness of history the nostalgia for God is still present. A human nostalgia, but one provoked by the absence of God. Of the God – present through the Messiah. Each point of time, each second, states Benjamin, 'is the strait gate through which the Messiah might enter'.[18] *Might* enter, and in fact does enter: enters as an awareness of human wretchedness, as a need for the divine as that Nothing which is the measure of our nothingness. Benjamin thereby reveals the *historicizing* function of the figure of the Messiah, without conceding anything to the historicist elevation of history. The Judaic Messiah remains future, and eternal future – hence his divine face. Moreover, it is this eternal future that has the power to call the present to itself while at the same time condemning the present and denying itself to it. The explanation of the power of this *ausgezeichnet*, remarkable, extraordinary people is messianism.

The Judaic experience of the divine as absence finds in Edmund Jabès another interpreter of exceptional quality. The *present* is the negation of God. And not the present only of *man*: the present of the word that claims to speak the silence of God. Before even the present of man, it is the present of God, the *creation*, that is the negation of God.

> God, before the Creation, is All; afterwards, ah, afterwards, is He Nothing?
>
> The All is invisible. Visibility is between the All and the Nothing, everywhere torn up from the All.
>
> To create, God placed Himself outside of Himself, in order to penetrate his Self and destroy Himself.
>
> After creating the world, God was the All without the sky and the earth.
>
> After creating the day and the night, God was the All without the

stars. After creating the animals and the plants, God was the All without the fauna and flora of the world.

After creating man, God was without a face.

No one has seen God, but the steps of His death may be seen by us all.[19]

It is the fullness of God, his perfection or completeness, his being All in One, that reduces the earth to desert. No, not man: no human guilt, no sin of man could be so powerful as to diminish God. Only God can destroy God; and the work of God. No, it is not for man, but as such, for the *divine essence* itself, that creation is the *negation of God.* On the other hand, human sin and guilt are possible only *after* the creation, *after* the desert. Yet in this way the sense of *dwelling in the desert* is turned on its head. From being negative it becomes positive. To migrate, to wander in the desert, to accept exile is the only way that man can correspond to God, to God's creation. The *rejection* of God is itself a correspondence to Him, to his *work.* 'The creator is rejected from His creation. Splendor of the universe. Man destroys himself creating.'[20]

The sin of man would therefore be not to accept exile, nomadism and perpetual migration. But if the earth is a desert, how could man ever not accept errancy? To be sure, the ways of sin are infinite: man is capable of turning even the desert into a dwelling, and the place of exile into a homeland. Thus Jabès highlights the necessity of duplicating his own nomadism, upholding at once the strangeness of the land from which he was exiled and the strangeness of the land that welcomed him[21] – the strangeness even of the language in which he writes. Exile is for him always exile *from* exile: *Voyage dans le voyage. Errance dans l'errance.*[22]

But, however much Jabès insists on being 'a stranger' *<estraneo> – l'étranger de l'étranger, ai-je, une fois, écrit*'[23] – in the end, the cogency of thinking compels him to recognize the *primacy of Hospitality.* To be sure, desert hospitality has no room for familiarity. The welcome is for the stranger as such, for the traveller who is anonymous even when known, unexpected even when awaited.[24] This is to say that the hospitable welcome of the desert harbours the disquietude of the absence of God proper to the place. But in what way does it harbour this? 'Strangeness' is always disquieting: however, it belongs to the person – whether the host or the guest makes no difference – and never to the welcome itself. The *hospitality* itself is secure, even though the disquietude is *within* it. Against his intentions, Jabès turns the desert into a dwelling place of omni-welcome. The presence of man rests always and securely in the absence of God. And hope, in the book testifying to that absence.[25]

> Hope: the following page. Do not close the book.
> I have turned all the pages of the book without finding hope.
> Perhaps hope is the book.[26]

And yet in *Le Parcours* he writes, in an unusually 'strident' fashion:

> God is not God. God is not God. God is not God. He *is*. He is before the sign that signals him. Before designation.
>
> He is the void before the void, thought before thought; thus also the unthought before the unthought – as if there were a nothing before the nothing.
>
> He is the cry before the cry, the trembling before the trembling.
>
> He is the night without night, the day without day. The look before the look, the listening before listening.
>
> He is the air before breathing. The air breathed in and out by the air. Not yet wind, but light air, indifferent, in its primitive laziness.
>
> Oh, vacant infinite.[27]

Is it going too far to hear in these words the echo of another 'cry'? Of a cry that gives birth to and expresses a wholly other experience of the divine?

Ethos: the Greek experience of the divine

If the God of Israel turns his back on his people – is always future, remote, distant; is a guide, at times benevolent, but never a travelling companion – by contrast, the gods of Greece show their faces. Pindar recalls that 'one is the race of men, one is the race of gods' and 'from one mother do we both derive our breath'. Yet 'a power that is wholly sundered parteth us, in that the one is nought, while for the other the brazen heaven endureth as an abode unshaken evermore.'[28] On the other hand, before history began, it was customary for the celestial ones to share their meals with mortals. And even after Prometheus' deception of Zeus put an end to this practice, the gods still deigned to lie with mortal women, and goddesses with men. In Greece, the divine dwelt in the house of man. An anecdote reported by Aristotle tells how some strangers who were on their way to Ephesus went to visit the most celebrated *wise man* of the area and hesitated there, surprised to see such a figure warming himself by a kitchen stove. Heraclitus invited them in: *einai gar kai theous* – 'here too the gods are present.'[29]

Figures

Odysseus Abraham and Moses set out on their journeys to distance themselves from their land of origin, from their past beginnings. Odysseus confronts all the dangers of the journey in order to return to the land of his birth. He knows full well that Calypso triumphs over Penelope in beauty, and yet he longs to go back. Aware that he is turning down the gift of immortality, he agrees to die so that he may see his island again.[30] His truest future is his origin. Nostalgia his most fundamental sentiment. Adventure is a beautiful thing, and risk too. It is pursued like the spice of life, but only if there is return. And, for Odysseus, to go home is less an aim than a destiny. In truth, for him the greatest danger is the illusion of being already at home: such is the spell of love cast by the enchantress Circe. And the hero keeps this at bay not by himself, but through the help of his companions who, worried for their families, remind him of his true homeland.[31] The return, none the less, demands a long trip – longer than the human mind can imagine. A journey through the Land of the Dead. There Odysseus meets his mother. The end is conjoined with the beginning. It is the circle of life that, there in Hades, the blind eyes of Teiresias reads him before time: the return to Ithaca, the victory over the suitors, the journeys to come and the coming returns: and sweet death, also (*thanatos ablechros*). At sea, yes,[32] but everything in a friendly sea, it too a home, brings thoughts of Ithaca. The whole adventure unfolds in the present, in the enchanted circle of an *aionic* now in which the past and the future, passing, *are*.

Apollo The Greek gods dwell in the world of men. Yet in their proximity they remain distant. Heaven envelops and embraces the earth, but in order to dominate it. When myth turns from telling of human affairs to the narration of divine events, the tone is raised – for from the changeable and the accidental one passes to the eternal and necessary. Odysseus descends into Hades to learn his future from Teiresias. What is predicted will come true, but the certainty of future occurrences, already present in the mind of the seer, is only a certainty *de facto*. The words of Teiresias lack the legality of the world's necessary order. The *sight* of Apollo is quite different. The son of Zeus is the custodian of his father's *nomos*. His present is the *legal* order of occurrence. Therefore, strictly speaking, he does not fore-see, he *sees*. Within the horizon of time he sees the ordering of all times.

'Phoebus' Apollo – the 'pure' – because his sight is not contaminated by the accidental character of occurrence. God of beauty: the most beautiful because, *ekphanestaton*, 'the most manifest', he makes manifest all things. He is the light that traces the outlines and the limits of what is. According to the Platonic Aristophanes' tale, it was he who Zeus, having cut the original and magnificent androgyne into two halves, ordered to 'twist every divided person's face and half-neck round towards the gash, the idea being that the sight of their own wounds would make people behave more moderately in the future.'[33] It is with Apollo, then, that consciousness arises. Consciousness of the human limit with respect to the gods. Consciousness therefore of time, of the *divided* and *ordered* time of man. Aristophanes' myth conserves, among other things, a memory of the birth from the tumult of a confused and chaotic primordial nature of the order of time articulated into the past, present and future.

Apollo is the divine figure of the Parmenidean *aionic*. The mythical prefiguration of the epistemic present that the whole of our Western tradition – first *sophia*, then *philosophia* – has striven to 'think'. But he is not *only* this.

Let us remember that the responses of Delphi were ambiguous. This ambiguity was not attributable to the weakness of men's minds, but to the will of the god – the *oblique* one, *Loxias*, as the

Greeks themselves called him. Veiled, up to a point, in the 'truth' of Apollo lay a robust will to falsehood. This was accompanied by violence, since the little rocky island of Delos feared to be the place for Leto to give birth.[34] In fact, the most Greek of Greeks was not of Greek origin. The story of the quarrel with Hera and of the killing of the dragoness to which the goddess had entrusted her monstrous progeny, Typhon,[35] plainly contains a memory of the originary violence directed against the illimitable, formless and orgiastic nature of Mother Earth; a violence out of which was born the cosmic order of Zeus the father, founded on measure and law. The origins of Apollo sink deep, then, in the most ancient *Mediterranean* culture. And even when he came to be taken up onto the Greek Olympus, myth conserved a memory of his most ancient origin. In fact, it tells that the very gods 'trembled'[36] at his first appearance in the dwelling place of Zeus.

Heraclitus, too, speaks of the ambiguous nature of Apollo when he remarks that the oracle at Delphi 'neither speaks nor conceals, but gives a sign'.[37] And perhaps Heraclitus was still thinking of the figure of Apollo when he stated that 'nature loves to hide'.[38] The most beautiful nature, the most manifest.

Interpretations

Plato The word of philosophy is not originary, but secondary. Older than the philosophers are those men of wisdom who – true *legislators* (*nomothetai*) – set names to things; and with names, order.[39] The Greeks, *philosophers*, 'are all children, and there's no such thing as an old Greek'.[40] Aware of this, philosophy speaks above all through the words of *mythos*, which narrates the generation of time. The divine maker of the world, in order to render his creation as similar as possible to the model, took the eternity which endures in unity (*menontos aionos en heni*) and made of it an eternal image (*aionion eikona*) which proceeds according to number – time itself. And with time, he generated the heavens, the days and nights, and the months and years that are parts (*mere*) and forms (*eide*) of time. It is clear that whatever belongs to movement – the 'was', the 'is' and the 'will be' – cannot be attributed to that which, in order to be unmoving and individed, 'is' and only 'is'.[41]

A strange, bemusing story that opens by telling of the birth of the *eternal* – albeit of an iconic and derivative eternity – and closes with the hypothesis of a dissolution of time and the heavens, that is, of the *eternal* image of eternity.[42] It is worth noting here that Plato always expresses the eternity of the time-image by the term *aionios*, from *aion*, a contraction of *aei on*, 'the always being'; whereas the eternity that endures in unity is also denoted by *aidios*. And rightly so, since *a-idios* is precisely the undivided; that which has neither parts (*mere*) nor forms (*eide*), which is not there to see (*idein*). Time is thus the division of the undivided, the image and the form of that which has neither image nor form. It is the vision of the invisible.

The relation of *opposition* that exists between the model and the image indicates that it is precisely by the model that the image is threatened. When it conforms to the model perfectly, the visible image disappears in the invisible, in the indistinct and formless. In the *second* word of philosophy, there reappears the threat presented by myth in the *ambiguous* figure of Apollo – 'beautiful' and 'violent', Greek of Mediterranean origin. Perhaps it is not by chance that at the beginning of the 'story' of the generation of time, Plato refers to the gods as *aidioi*. The invisible belongs to the visible, to the most visible. Just as the terrible belongs to the beautiful, to the most beautiful: '*das Schöne ist nichts/ als des Schrecklichen Anfang*'.[43]

The task of Western philosophy from its earliest beginnings has been to exorcise this demonic threat, to protect itself from the danger of the eternity that endures in the one. Against the formlessness *<l'informe>* and indistinctness of the originary, against the *aoriston* of *dunamis*, Aristotle affirms the primacy of the act, of *energeia*, of the complete, of form: *morphe mallon physis tes hyles*.[44] The demonstration runs thus:

> For how can there be motion if there is no actual cause? Wood will not move itself – carpentry must act upon it; nor will the menses or the earth move themselves – the seeds must act upon the earth and the semen on the menses.[45]

> Therefore Chaos or Night did not endure for an unlimited time, but the same things have always existed [*tauta aei*], either passing through a cycle or in accordance with some other principle – that is, if actuality is prior to potentiality.[46]

The world is eternal – there is no danger of its fading. The god – pure form concealing within itself no formlessness – is the eternal one in which is gathered and reflected the multiple, *eidetic* eternity of the world. Guarantor of the eternity of time and foundation of the absolute character of epistemology. Close to man, by virtue of securing the world inhabited by him, he allows man to be *politikon zoon*.

Hegel's philosophy participates fully in this *ethos* founded on the *proximity* of god. Hegel, a Christian philosopher, a philosopher of historical, *Pauline*, Christianity. Not that Hegel was unaware of the nocturnal, *pre-Greek*, face of the god Apollo. On the contrary, his interpretation of the Greek world begins with a presentation of two counterposed 'ethical substances', the one an expression of the *natural* right of the shadows, the other an expression of the *divine* law of the day.[47] Yet the conflict between the nocturnal and solar faces of god – a conflict that in ever different forms and ways has characterized the entire history of humanity – has just one goal, a single aim: the *revelation of the depths*.[48] The shadow is from the very beginning destined for the light – in the end itself to become light.

Nietzsche and Hölderlin From the very beginning of his genealogical work, Nietzsche was aware that the 'solar religion–epistemology' nexus, which has been at the foundation of Western civilization since Socrates, and thus since the birth of 'philosophy', is the expression of an *ethos*, of a way of living in the world whose demand for certainty stems from mere timidity and extreme insecurity. As a 'philologist', he dedicated himself to our most ancient roots in the desire to see the other face of god, the pre-Greek face of the Greek Apollo. He named this face Dionysus.

That we are dealing with a single God, divided within and struggling with himself, is plain to see. Otherwise, one would understand nothing of their *collaboration*, which is born out of the quarrel and for the quarrel. Moreover, the unity is stated explicitly. Nietzsche calls it *Bruderbund*, 'fraternal union'. Given this *union*, Dionysus speaks the language of Apollo, and Apollo that of Dionysus.[49] For the One – the primordial One – in order to appear, must acquire form, while dividing itself into multiple forms and individuals. Forms, figures, appearances; always appearances, forms and figures of the undivided, the unapparent, the formless. The specific character of the icon lies in this, that it gives figure to that which does not have figure. Were the primordial One already figural, formal <*in forme*>, the icon would be nothing more than a copy, a vain repetition of itself.

But in what way is the Formless <*Informe*> in form, the Undivided <*Indiviso*> in the divided <*diviso*>? Not acccording to the modality of *presence*. If the *formless* being of the One consisted in not having a particular, *dividual* and finite form, it being – as *in-dividual* – all the forms in which it is expressed at different times, then nothing would distinguish the Dionysus of Nietzsche from Hegel's Depth. But Dionysus is not *present*. Dionysus is *always absent*. He is *absence*. This is a delicate point at which we would do well to pause, not least in order to grasp the *priority* – temporal included – of the chorus over the hero in tragedy. This is to say, the priority of the contemplation of action over action itself. But what kind of a paradox is this? One can hardly contemplate something before this something exists. The paradox of tragedy is undoubtedly . . . a paradox: the paradox of the contemplation of absence. For that which is *truly* contemplated in tragedy is *absence*. The absence of god. Dionysus *is not there*. He is never there. All the figures that he takes on at different times, all the heroes that give a face to this god of tragedy – they are never Dionysus.[50] Dionysus withdraws. He is withdrawal itself. And it is this that makes all certainty uncertain, all quiet disquiet. Dionysus is the absence that disquiets. *Das Unheimliche.*

The appearance of the hero – the transition from the *tragic dithyramb* to the dramatic form – already marks the decadence of the tragic, as the *absent* god is somehow consigned to a mask. Tragedy, however, retains its original meaning as long as the chorus manages to sustain its *antithetical* attitude in relation not to the hero, but to the reduction of the divine to the face of the hero. That is, as long as it continues to serve as custodian of the absence of the god Dionysus.

It is instructive to read these pages from Nietzsche's *The Birth of Tragedy* alongside Hölderlin's notes on *Oedipus* and on the Sophoclean *Antigone*. There is in both a similar opposition to a dialectic of the Hegelian kind – an opposition that indicates a common choice of field whose significance is *epochal*, since it presents itself as an alternative to the entirety of Western civilization or tradition.

For Hölderlin, the tragic representation of the union of the divine and the human is realized *im Zorn*, in anger, whereby it becomes comprehensible 'how the boundless becomes one, purifying itself through boundless separation'.[51] It is not union that *purifies* disunion, but exactly the reverse. Hegel – and everything that Hegel stands for here – is overturned! And it is from this perspective that Hölderlin sees the function of the chorus: 'Hence ever-contending dialogue, hence the chorus as contrast to the former . . . Everything is speech against speech, one cancelling the other.'[52]

In terms of abstract logic, we might put it like this: the chorus is the *contradictio contradictionis* that saves the contradiction from the contradictoriness of its existence. That is, the tragic chorus does not calm things, but quite the opposite: it heightens the *disquiet*, the *Unheimlichkeit*.

Yet, however much Hölderlin, in the name of infinite nature, opposes the merely human and finite concept of Hegelian reconciliation, he does not manage to remain faithful to contradiction. His in-finite – the *aorgic* – itself effects a form of reconciliation: through death – in order that new and higher and richer life may arise. Speaking of Empedocles, he writes:

> with his death he reconciles and unites the contending extremes out of which he emerged more beautifully than during his lifetime, in that now the union occurs not in a particular and thus is too close, in that the divine no longer appears in sensuous manner, in that the happy deceit of the union ceases precisely to the extent that it was too close and unique, so that both extremes of which one, the organic, must be deterred by the transitory moment and thus be raised to a purer universality, while the aorgic one, transcending to the former, must become an object of calmer contemplation for the organic, and that the inwardness of the past moment emerges in more universal, controlled, differentiating manner. (Translation modified)[53]

Like Hölderlin, so also Nietzsche: Dionysus, the absent god, is absent because no form, no individuation, no Apollonian figure is equal to him. But from his withdrawal are born all figures and all individual forms. The death of the individual is not the defeat, but the triumph of the principle of individuation. The primordial One, life in its pure state, pure flux, destroys in order to create. And in so doing, it is revealed as a 'primordial pleasure' that recalls 'the shaping force of the world' that Heraclitus likened to 'a child placing stones here and there and building sandcastles and knocking them down again'.[54] To build them otherwise, *without end.* To be sure, elsewhere in *The Birth of Tragedy* Nietzsche declares that music has no need of words, but merely tolerates them.[55] And here, perhaps, one may see the first signs of his critique of the Wagnerian *compromise* between paganism and Christianity, his opposition to Romanticism. But if one breaks the *fraternal link* between Dionysus and Apollo, how are we to distinguish between the orgy of Babylon and Attic tragedy?[56] Clearly, the 'question' exceeds the limits of *The Birth of Tragedy* and bears upon the entire arc of Nietzschean thought. To be sure, he drove himself to elevate movement and becoming over all measure as no one else before him; yet nevertheless in doing so he never ceased to seek a conciliation. Of what kind? That of becoming with itself, of life with itself, of Will with Will. A single quote from *Zarathustra* suffices here: 'And who has taught it [the will] to be reconciled with time, and higher things than reconciliation? The will that is the will to power must will something higher than any reconciliation – but how shall that happen? Who has taught it to will backwards too?'[57]

These were not *rhetorical* questions, for Nietzsche's last years were dedicated to the search for *scientific* demonstrations of the doctrine of the eternal return.[58] The conciliation *beyond* all conciliation, the supreme, ultimate conciliation, the *anulus aeternitatis*, the most modern and most ancient version of the *tauta aei* required an epistemic foundation. Nietzsche saw two paths before him: on one side, that opened by Aristotle, and built by the *epistemic* and *religious* tradition of the West; on the other side, the road of *madness*, of projected madness: the shepherd no longer shepherd, no longer man.[59] And he chose.

Nietzsche closes his intellectual autobiography with these words: 'Have I been understood? – *Dionysus versus the Crucified*.'[60]

'Have I been understood?' – why this doubt? For if in the figure of the Crucified there is a reprise of asceticism, of the primacy of value over fact, of obligation over life, then how, after *Beyond Good and Evil* and above all after *On the Genealogy of Morals*, could one still doubt having been understood? Yet what if, for argument's sake, Nietzsche had addressed his question not to others but to himself? If, for argument's sake, the question translated a doubt regarding his own position? A doubt that he wished to stave off by the very act of formulating it? All this might easily be thought a pointless exercise in psychologism. And yet, and yet . . ., if Dionysus is ultimately levelled off to the figure of Apollo and to Life whose destiny was ever the ceaseless production of *Forms*, if the Will to power has as its supreme aspiration the repetition of itself, and this repetition *wants* to be founded *scientifically*, on solid demonstrations; if, in short, the *ethico-epistemic* model is ultimately that defined in its essential characteristics by Aristotle – then is there really an opposition in the closing lines of *Ecce Homo*? The question forces us to ask: what is *Christianity*? Not least in order to understand that Nietzsche's final *choice* is not *inevitable*. Between *episteme* and *madness – tertium datur*!

Abandonment: the word of Jesus and the Christianity of Paul

Figures

Jesus '*Aperiam in parabolis os meum/ eructabo abscondita a constitutione mundi.*'[61] Jesus *repeats* the words of the prophet – on purpose. But let us ask ourselves, what is the meaning of this 'repetition'? It is a fundamental question, since even the final words – the words cried out in the ninth hour of the Cross[62] – *repeat* the beginning of Psalm 22 from the Book of David.

In Jesus, the repetition underlines the break, the difference. The word of Jesus is not that of the prophet, not that of the Old Testament. It is other. And of an *alterity* that allows for no mediation, but only a strict *aut/aut*. There is much to be learnt here from the story of the disciple who asked Jesus for permission to go and bury his father. Jesus' response was very sharp: 'Follow me; and let the dead bury their dead.'[63] Even the most ancient act of compassion is regarded as vain, if and in so far as it belongs to the world. To the world of the Law, of the *visible*. 'Take heed that ye do not your alms before men.'[64]

Prayer itself is offered in secret, avoiding the eyes of the world.

> thou shalt not be as hypocrites *are*; for they love to pray standing in the synagogues and in the corners of the streets, *that they may be seen of men* ... But thou, when thou prayest, enter into thy closet, and when thou hast shut the door, pray to thy Father which is in secret ...[65]

Accordingly, to render unto Caesar that which is Caesar's and unto God that which is God's is not a banal imperative to keep the two *cities*, the religious and the political, apart from one another. Rather, it has the profound sense of marking the insuperable difference between interior and exterior, consciousness and world: 'the care of this world ... choke[s] the word, and he becometh unfruitful'.[66] Nothing is further from Jesus than the intention to found a church, a community. When they tell him that his mother and his brothers wish to speak to him, he replies: 'Who is my mother? and who are my brethren? And he stretched forth his hand towards his disciples and said, Behold, my mother and my brethren! For whosoever shall do the will of my Father which is in Heaven, the same is my brother, and sister, and mother.'[67] Everyone is a disciple of Jesus: everyone who understands his word. Why this qualification? What is the difficulty in understanding the word of Jesus?

Aperiam in parabolis os meum – the word of Jesus is not a bridge between the interior and the exterior, consciousness and the world. On the contrary, it is the sword that separates them: 'I came not to send peace, but a sword ... *And a man's foes shall be they of his own household*.'[68] Jesus speaks in parables, that is, *obliquely*, because he is aware that what he has to say cannot be said in the language of the world – in the only language there is. The parable is a necessity. And this is the hardest thing to understand; as an episode reported by Matthew attests. To the disciples who ask him why he speaks in parables, Jesus replies that they understand him because the 'mysteries of the Kingdom' are known to them, but not to others who 'seeing, see not; and hearing ... hear not'.[69] Keeping to the letter of this story, one must conclude that Jesus did not come to speak to everyone, but only to a few. Precisely the opposite of what we read a moment ago in regard to his own 'relations'. In truth, Jesus speaks to everyone and for everyone. But he is understood only by those who grasp, beyond the surface meaning of the words, the *mysteria* that is re-*vealed* <*si* ri-*véla*> ever anew in the words: those who understand that the word is always *double*, oblique, false and that the *divine* cannot be translated into language. As John explains: '*lux in tenebris lucet, et tenebrae eam non comprehenderunt*'.[70] This is also the reason why Jesus ordered his disciples to 'tell no man that he was Jesus the Christ'.[71] The disciples themselves did not understand him. When he announced his death to them for the first time – his death to the world, a death *always already taken place* – Peter was upset and said to him 'Be it far from thee, Lord, this shall not be unto thee.' But Jesus replied 'Get thee behind me, Satan: thou art an offence unto me: for thou savourest not the things that be of God, but those that be of men.'[72] Satan names here the world of men and of the things of men. The kingdom of exteriority. Of the Law. '*Skandalon*' in Greek means both 'trap' and 'snare'. For Jesus himself the world is a 'trap' and a 'snare' – and he fears it. This is why he *must* speak of his death. And of his resurrection, which is not a return to life, a rebirth after the death of the body, after physical death. The resurrection is death itself: death to the exteriority of the Law, which is *life* in the interiority of *faith*, or of *consciousness*. This is his teaching: 'But as touching the resurrection of the dead, have ye not read that which was spoken unto you by God, saying, I am the God of Abraham, and the God of Isaac, and the God of Jacob? God is not the God of the dead, but of the living.'[73] This is a teaching that not only the Sadducees but his own disciples do not understand. Because they do not understand the necessarily *oblique* and *false* character of the word. Of the word of truth. Because they do not understand the constant threat that hangs over the word of Jesus, easily transformed – as will soon happen – into Law, community, ecclesiasticism, world. Because they do not understand the difference between the word of Isaiah – 'Himself took our infirmities, and bare *our* sicknesses'[74] – and the *repetition* of these words.

The words of the Old Alliance were a prophecy of salvation, of the redemption of evil to good, but the word of Jesus says that no evil of the world can ever touch the inner man. Sicknesses and infirmities do not disappear, they are not *redeemed*, they remain what they are – in the world, which would not be the world without them, without sicknesses and infirmities. Neither do consciousness and faith keep man from the evil of the world. It is in the evil of the world that the *divine* element of man *lives*. This is why Jesus, in the invitation to universal *philía*, recalls that the Father in Heaven 'maketh his sun to rise on the evil and on the good, and sendeth rain on the just and unjust'.[75]

If we now listen again to the cry of the ninth hour, we understand the abyssal difference with respect to the words of Psalm 22. In the cry of the Son, it is the Father that is revealed. Abandonment is not the punishment of a sin: it is the revelation of the Father. This is the ultimate paradox, the pure contradiction: the Father is just this, the Father, only in and through the abandonment of the Son, of the Son of Man, of all sons, and of the world. This is the *truth* announced by the Messiah – in the only form possible, that of the oblique, false, discourse, of the parable that speaks of 'the things hidden from the origin of the world' – re-*vealing* them <*ri-velandole*>.

Paul 'Why do ye not understand my speech? *even* because ye cannot hear my word. Ye are of *your* father the devil, and the lusts of your father ye will do.'[76] The Devil, or Satan, it is said, is the world of men, the world of exteriority and of the Law. But the seduction of the world, of the word of the world by which the *mystery* of the inferiority of *faith* is articulated via the *exteriority* of the Law, and which tears down the covering veil protecting the true in the profound intimacy of *consciousness* – this seduction soon takes hold of the teaching of Christ as well.

From the Second Letter to the Corinthians:

> we use great plainness of speech: And not as Moses, *which* put a veil over his face, that the children of Israel could not steadfastly look to the end of that which is abolished: But their minds were blinded: for until this day remaineth the same veil untaken away in the reading of the Old Testament; which veil is done away in Christ. But even unto this day, when Moses is read, the veil is upon their heart. Nevertheless when it shall turn to the Lord, the veil shall be taken away [*aufertur velamen*].[77]

Paul turns the teaching of Jesus literally upside down. *Auferre velamen* – this is his aspiration. In order to tear down the veil, to translate the Word into the world, he goes, in Athens, onto the Areopagus, and unveils the *Deus absconditus* to the Gentiles, to those pious pagans who consecrated an altar to the unknown god. According to the story told by his friend Luke,[78] some of the learned Athenians who had heard Paul speak of the 'resurrection of the dead' began to mock him and others simply walked away. It is hard to believe this story: the death and resurrection of the gods had been a part of Greek religious experience from its very inception. No, this was not disturbingly new to the wise men of Athens. Nor was the rest of what Paul told them; to wit, that this god who was unknown to them 'had made the world and everything in it'. This had been not narrated, but *explained* and *demonstrated* to them in their philosophy – above all in that of Aristotle.

Paul joins together what Christ set apart: God and the world, interiority and exteriority, faith and law. Paul *secularized* Christianity. He made of it a historical force. A force creative of histories. And he did this consciously, with utter lucidity. This is where his greatness lies: he, a converted Jew, brought the whole of Jewish culture into the *new* religion, and in so doing he *founded* historical Christianity, the Christianity that we know and in which 'we live, we move and we are'. Christ stated that he had come not to destroy the law but to fulfil it.[79] That his *fulfilment* amounts to a *subversion* is clear to anyone who reads the verses that follow. Jesus fulfils in the sense that he announces the other half of the human universe, the most important half, indeed – from the point of view of religion – the only part of any importance; namely, the divine side of the human, *faith*, the *celestial* half that is other to and beyond, absolutely other to and absolutely beyond, the *terrestrial* part. Paul, on the other hand, sees the law as the completion-realization of faith. *Ho dikaios ek pisteos zesetai*[80] – but from faith arises, already with Abraham, the Law. And prior to faith in Christ, the Law was the Jews' 'master'.[81] The Apostle of Peoples does not deny the superiority of the Jew over Gentiles, even though it is sometimes on account of just this superiority that the Jew is condemned, the sin of the Jew being worse than the sin *against nature* of the Pagan.[82] Historical Christianity, the Christianity instituted by Paul, is thus the religion of the Law founded on faith. The religion of the wholly unveiled word, the religion of *Offenbarung*. The religion of the Jew for whom the Messiah came, the future was realized and the present became the space in which all times are united and made welcome. The desert is no longer deserted: even the face of God can be seen. *Aufertur velamen.*

This is the Christianity that has triumphed. Historical Christianity, the Christianity that has made history, the history of our West. And it is this tradition that reaches its completion with Hegel, at once a Christian and a pagan philosopher, because a philosopher of the present, of presence, of the *parousia* of the absolute. A philosopher of that philosophy which defines itself as 'its own time apprehended in thoughts'.[83]

To be sure, in the Christianity of Paul there is also the *not-yet* of the *second* resurrection, the *future* of the Apocalypse. But this future is already present in the Annunciation. The 'now' <'*ora*'> of Paul's Christ comprehends all times.

Centuries later, an Italian poet, and a faithful interpreter of the spirit of Pauline Christianity, writes:

> *E degli anni ancor non nati/Daniel si ricordò*
> And the years as yet unborn/Daniel remembered.[84]

Interpretations

Augustine The Christianity of Paul is the religious *repetition* of the epistemic present. Which means: Paul intends to redeem the whole of worldly time. However much he distinguishes between the 'animal body' and the 'spiritual body', and however much he declares that the resurrection will not be of the corruptible body but of the incorruptible ('it is sown in corruption; it is raised in incorruption'),[85] he none the less *wants* a resurrection of the body along with the soul. The present of the Annunciation, the 'hour' of Christ has meaning only for the second resurrection. 'But if there be no resurrection of the dead, then is Christ not risen.'[86]

Clearly, Augustine does not deny the second resurrection. How could he, as a bishop and the head of the ecclesiastical community of Hippo? Yet it is clear that he places the emphasis on the first resurrection. This is borne out by the comment he addresses to John's Gospel in *De civitate Dei*. The text runs:

> Mark my words carefully: I am telling you that he who listens to my words and puts his faith in him who sent me possesses eternal life, and does not come up for judgement, but has passed over [*metabebeken*] from death to life. Mark my words carefully, I am telling you that an hour [*hora*] is coming, in fact it is already now [*nun*], when the dead will hear the voice of God and those who hear shall live. (John 5: 24–5; translation modified)

The commentary is as follows:

> [Jesus] is not yet speaking of the second resurrection, that is, the resurrection of the body, which is to come at the end of the world, but about the first, which is here and now. It is in fact, to distinguish the two that he says, 'The hour is coming, in fact it is here already now.' This resurrection, however, is not the resurrection of the body, but of the soul. For souls also have their own death, in the shape of irreligion and sin, the death died by those referred to by the Lord when he says 'Let the dead bury their own dead', that is, 'Let those who are dead in soul bury those who are dead in body.'[87]

Augustine draws a sharp distinction between the two resurrections, and it is to the first that he accords the fundamental role: 'And so anyone who does not wish to be condemned in the second resurrection must rise up in the first.'[88] *Venit hora, et nunc est.* Augustine underlines this present – which is now. The present of the resurrection, of the reawakening of the soul to itself, to its *interiority*. This 'resurrection' *from* impiety and iniquity has no bearing on the world. The world is and remains in iniquity, in the abandonment of sin.

The 'now' of the first resurrection is the *present* of the Cross; the *future* of the second resurrection is the Pauline *time* that rests on the certainty of faith not in the Cross, but in *after* the Cross.[89] But the 'now' that is *now* is not a *momentum*, it does not indicate a crossing or passage. Rather, it indicates the standing, the standing of the *in-stans*, of that which *stands* in time without participating in it. '*Erchetai hora kai nun estin*': the Greek *hora* expresses the season of youth, of spring, of blossom, and thus of reflowering; at the same time, it names the age of the harvest, of fullness and of fruit. This is to say that the *now* which is now awaits nothing else because it is already fulfilled. For the soul, the now of reawakening is the now of maturity. The *now* is not a time that passes, not because the soul cannot fall back into the time of sin and iniquity, into the time of the world, but because in its *instant* of grace it is not affected by movement. The *now* neither passes, nor lasts – *it is, it simply is*. If it ebbs, it is because it comes to be swept away by time and the world (or by something else, as we shall see further on).

In this way, the second resurrection is added to the first, but does not fulfil or perfect it. It is an uncalled-for extra, as John's Gospel makes quite clear: '*Qui verbum meum audit* . . . transit *a morte in vitam*.' The crossing from death to life occurs in the *instans*, in the present of the *now*. And it is important to highlight the significance assumed by the *first* resurrection in a work dominated by the *apocalyptic future* of the second resurrection.

That the Christianity of Augustine goes beyond that of Paul is made even clearer by *De Trinitate*. This work was conceived under the inspiration of Paul's *auferre velamen*. It aims, that is, to demonstrate the identity between the divine essence and revelation. *Trinity* means just this: '*a Patre et Filio missus est idem Filius*. If the eternity of the Angels, as an indication that there has never been a time in which these purely spiritual beings were not present, does not eliminate but on the contrary presupposes the difference between creator and creature, between the eternity of God and that of the Angels,[90] then the *generation* of the Son from the Father implies rather the identity of their *eternal being*, their *common eternity*.[91] Through and through to the very depths, God the Father is, as One and Triune, the Son. But in what, then, does the difference between them consist? In this, and in this alone: that the Father as such, while containing in himself all the perfections present in the Logos of the Son, none the less has them *differently* from the Son, namely, without distinction. If, in the Son, in the Revelation, justice and truth, goodness and pity, are distinct, in the Father they are as one. The force of Plotinus' thought bears upon Augustine against his own will and intentions. Yet if the Father is the Father as wholly gathered into himself, in the form of the *simplicissima complicatio*, then the Logos explicating the most *Simple, to haploustaton*, is the truth, the tradition and the transmission of it only in so far as it is equally its betrayal <*tradimento*> and falsehood. It is in the nature of the Trinitarian essence that the truth be given only *in parabolis*, and that is, as a falsehood. The Son's cry of abandonment is thus the most authentic revelation of the Father. The Spirit is nothing more than the union of this divine essence of the Father with the Son, of the revelation, or *mission*, and of the truth with abandonment and falsehood.

Revelation, or *mission*, is abandonment – truth is falsehood: this is the *unprecedented* meaning of the divine *kenosis*, of the scandal of the Cross – which in the end bears even upon Augustine, in spite of his fidelity to the Apostle.

Kant It is in Kantian philosophy that the experience of the word of Jesus – and not therefore of the Christianity of Paul – finds its highest and most coherent *interpretation*.

Kant begins from the radical separation between infinite and finite, noumenon and phenomenon. That which appears, shows itself, that which has figure and determination, is what it is – *phenomenon* – in so far as it is in relation to other figures and determinacies, other phenomena. The phenomenon is in itself multiple, because it multiplies the relations that *bind* it to other phenomena.[92] Relation thus means: bond, condition, necessity. The phenomenal, the world of *objects*, is therefore the world of necessity. Nothing that happens in time and in space can be free because it is always conditioned by something else. All that is free is the in-finite, or that which has no *figure* or form – that which cannot be *schematized*. That which has no time: in short, the noumenon. It has no past other than its own conditions, nor any future. And, in fact, Kant makes it quite clear that in the noumenal world – that is, in the world of *freedom* – *nichts geschieht*, nothing happens.[93] And, we might add, nothing can happen. However perilously close Kant moves to Spinoza in the solution to the *Third Antinomy* – particularly where he speaks of the 'causality of reason'[94] and of the 'empirical character' as the *schema* of the 'intelligible character',[95] i.e. of the empirical world as the *figure* of the noumenal world – his position is none the less *radicitus* different from that of Spinoza. The infinite in Spinoza has a *positive* signification, denoting the Substance explicated in the attributes and in the finite modes, the *natura naturans* that is actualized in the *natura naturata*. The in-finite in Kant is by contrast a *negative* concept. It denotes the *not* of the finite, the negation immanent within the finite. This, too, is made quite clear by Kant, and moreover at a fundamental point in the first *Critique*, where he deals with the amphibologies of the concepts of reflection, and thereby the *transcendental topic*. Of the inner noumenon, Kant says that we can say nothing, not even that it is inner or outer; not even that it is still there when our own concepts and intuitions are not.[96] The noumenon is a negative concept that delimits the power of sensibility,[97] the claim, that is, to give figure and *visibility* to what truly is, to the *alethos on*. Kantian philosophy is the rigorous foundation of apophatic theology. Of the unsayability of the true: '*aperiam in parabolis os meum*'. Nothing is further from Kant than the Pauline '*aufertur velamen*'. But to say this is not enough. The division of the two worlds – 'I came not to send peace, but a sword' – does not mean that their separation is possible. The negativity of the in-finite indicates that there is no life for the finite beyond the conditionedness and necessity of the world. John's '*ut consummati in unum sint*'[98] is merely the death-drive, the *Todestrieb*. For God reveals himself only in abandonment, in the wretchedness of the world, in the unhappiness of constraint. And this is the most profound, though also most elusive (to Kant himself, indeed above all to Kant), meaning of the second *Critique*.

It appears that the categorical imperative in its most explicit formulation may open for freedom a space of action: '*Handelte* . . .', 'Act . . .'.[99] But precisely the opposite is true. The imperative grounded in reason turns to nothing other than reason itself, to the will supported by reason. And who, in the grip of the passions, is ever able to listen to the voice of reason? To listen to the command – which commands simply that one free oneself from the proclivities of sensibility – one must already be free from them. As if to say: to respect the command one must have already respected it! And yet, not only is there no freedom of choice – for only the man who is already good can act in a morally good way – but there is not even an action to accomplish. Kantian morality – as a pure morality of intentions that can in no way be fulfilled, perfected or even cultivated by acting in time and in the world – is concerned not with *doing*, but with the *knowledge* that accompanies all doing. This is where the *divine* in and of man lies: in the *negative Selbstzufriedenheit*, in the negative satisfaction with oneself felt when, living in the world, subject to the constrictions and necessities of time, one is aware of not being *of* the world, of not belonging to it, of being a stranger to it, and in this sense, and only in this sense, free.[100]

The moral strangeness of man, his constitutive utopia, explains why the '*aperiam in parabolis os meum*' cannot be translated, even into symbols. Yet the symbol still evinces an originary co-belonging of truth and word, eternity and time, God and world – a co-belonging that, even when interrupted, can always be recomposed, if only in the form of metaphor and allegory, of saying what is other, of giving a sign to what is other, of the referral back. By contrast, speaking *obliquely*, in parables, bears witness to an originary separation – and is for this reason falsehood, giving *figure* and *image* to what *phusei* withdraws from all figure and image, giving limits to the Unlimited, *horizei to aoriston*, dividing the Indivisible, *polla epoiese ten mian.*[101] A *necessary* falsehood, moreover, since it is only the veil of falsehood that protects the finite from the constant danger and threat of the killing truth, of the blinding divine light (no one can see God except *per speculum et in aenigmate*), of God who in his *absolute positivity* negates all negation, and thus, if *omnis determinatio est negatio*, all determination: who *necat*, in and for his *perfection*, the finite as such. Thought in his *truth*, God is the death of the finite.

Yet Jesus' speaking obliquely, in parables, is false in the highest and most noble sense. Covering the face of Truth, it safeguards the awareness that the word of man, the *finite* word, is such only through its *negative* relation with the *Infinite*, with *Silence*, with the *Simplest* and *most Perfect*. Only the eternal, as a *possible* negation of time, stands in the way of the reduction of difference to the epistemic identity of the 'always the same things' (*tauta aei*). For this reason the highest word is the falsehood that says the truth in betraying it, aware of being unable to say it otherwise. Nor is this awareness *other* than falsehood: on the contrary, it comes to be thought as the falsehood of falsehood. Falsehood folded back upon itself, *re-flected*, a fine expression of the twofold strangeness of the word of the Son of Man – strange to the Father and strange to the world, to eternity and to time: a fine expression of the *ou-topic in-stant* of the Cross.

Translated by David Webb

Notes

1 Genesis 12:1–2. All references to the Bible are to the Authorized Version of King James.
2 S. Kierkegaard, *Fear and Trembling*, trans. W. Lowrie (Princeton, NJ, Princeton University Press, 1974), p. 84.
3 Ibid., p. 124.
4 Exodus 2:22.
5 Gregory of Nyssa, *The Life of Moses*, trans. A. J. Malherbe and E. Ferguson (New York and Toronto, Paulist Press, 1978), pp. 119–20.
6 G. W. F. Hegel, 'The spirit of Christianity', in *Early Theological Writings*, trans. T. M. Knox (Philadelphia, University of Pennsylvania Press, 1988), p. 185.
7 Ibid., p. 187.
8 Ibid., p. 189.
9 Ibid., p. 193.
10 Ibid., p. 192
11 Ibid., p. 192.
12 Ibid., p. 203.
13 W. Benjamin, 'On language as such and on the language of man', in *One Way Street*, trans. E. Jephcott and K. Shorter (London, Verso, 1985), pp. 107–23.
14 W. Benjamin, 'The task of the translator', in *Illuminations*, trans. H. Zohn (New York, Schocken Books, 1969), pp. 69–82n.
15 W. Benjamin, *The Origin of German Tragic Drama*, trans. J. Osborne (London, Verso, 1985).
16 Benjamin, 'Fate and character', in *One Way Street*, pp. 124–31.
17 Benjamin, *Origin of German Tragic Drama*, chs 1, 4.
18 W. Benjamin, 'Theses on the philosophy of history', in *Illuminations*, p. 264.
19 E. Jabès, *The Book of Questions: Yael, Elya, Aely*, trans. R. Waldrop (Middletown, Conn., Wesleyan University Press, 1983), pp. 224–5.
20 Jabès, *The Book of Questions: II and III*, p. 194.
21 E. Jabès, *Un Étranger avec, sous les bras, un livre de petit format* (Paris, Gallimard, 1989), p. 107.
22 Ibid., p. 18.
23 E. Jabès, *Le Parcours* (Paris, Gallimard, 1987), p. 16.
24 E. Jabès, *Le Libre de l'hospitalité* (Paris, Gallimard, 1991), pp. 84–5.
25 Jabès, *Le Parcours*, p. 30.
26 Jabès, *The Book of Questions*, p. 178.
27 Jabès, *Le Parcours*, p. 35, translated by the present translator.

28 Pindar, *Nemea* 6, 1–4, in *Nemean Odes, Isthmian Odes, Fragments*, trans. W. H. Race (Cambridge, Mass., Harvard University Press, 1977).
29 Cited by M. Heidegger, 'Letter on humanism', in *Basic Writings*, ed. D. F. Krell (London, Routledge, 1993).
30 Homer, *The Odyssey*, trans. R. Lattimore (New York, Harper Collins, 1991), V, vv 203–24.
31 Ibid., *X*, vv 472–4.
32 Ibid., *XI*, vv 134–6.
33 Plato, *Symposium*, 190e.
34 Homer, *Hymn to Apollo*, vv 66–9.
35 Homer, *The Odyssey*, vv 331–69.
36 Homer, *Hymn to Apollo*, vv 1–4.
37 Heraclitus, B93
38 Heraclitus, B123
39 Plato, *Cratylus*, 390a–391d.
40 Plato, *Timaeus*, 22b.
41 Ibid., 37d–38a.
42 Ibid., 38b–c.
43 R. M. Rilke, *Duino Elegies*, trans. S. Cohen (Manchester, Carcanet, 1989), I vv 4–5.
44 Aristotle, *Physics*, II, 193b, 6–7.
45 Aristotle, *Metaphysics, X–XIV, Oeconomica, Magna Moralia,* trans. H. Tredennick and G. C. Armstrong (Loeb Classical Library) (Cambridge, Mass., Harvard University Press, 1990), Book XII, 1071b, 28–32.
46 Aristotle, *Metaphysics*, XII, 1072a, 7–9.
47 G. W. F. Hegel, *Phenomenology of Spirit*, trans. A. V. Miller (Oxford, Oxford University Press, 1977), p. 317f.
48 Ibid., p. 493.
49 F. Nietzsche, *The Birth of Tragedy* (Harmondsworth, Penguin, 1993), §22.
50 Ibid., §9.
51 F. Hölderlin, *Friedrich Hölderlin: Essays and Letters on Theory*, trans. T. Pfau (Albany, NY, State University of New York, 1988), p. 107 (translation modified).
52 Ibid., p. 107.
53 Ibid., p. 54.
54 Nietzsche, *Birth of Tragedy*, p. 115.
55 Ibid., p. 35.
56 Ibid., p. 17.
57 F. Nietzsche, *Thus Spake Zarathustra*, trans. R. Hollingdale (Harmondsworth, Penguin, 1955), p. 163.

58 F. Nietzsche, *The Will to Power*, trans. W. Kaufmann and R. J. Hollingdale, ed. W. Kaufmann (New York, Vintage Books, 1968), esp. §§1062–7.
59 Nietzsche, *Zarathustra*, p. 180.
60 F. Nietzsche, *Ecco Homo*, trans. W. Kaufmann (New York, Vintage Books, 1985), p. 335.
61 Psalms 78:2; Matthew 13:35.
62 Matthew 27:46.
63 Matthew 8:22.
64 Matthew 6:1.
65 Matthew 6:5–6 (emphasis added).
66 Matthew 13:22.
67 Matthew 12:48–50.
68 Matthew 34–6 (emphasis added).
69 Matthew 13:10–13.
70 John 1:5.
71 Matthew 16:20.
72 Matthew 16:23.
73 Matthew 22:31–2.
74 Matthew 8:17.
75 Matthew 5:4–5.
76 John 8:43–4.
77 2 Corinthians 3:12–16.
78 Acts 17:19–32.
79 Matthew 5:17–20.
80 Romans 1:17.
81 Galatians 3:24.
82 Romans 1:2–3.
83 G. W. F. Hegel, *Philosophy of Right*, trans. T. M. Knox (Oxford, Clarendon Press, 1949), p. 11.
84 A. Manzoni, *Inni sacri: la resurrezione*, ed. R. Bacchelli (Milan and Naples, Ricciardi, 1953), vv 55–6. (Translated by David Webb.)
85 1 Corinthians 15:42.
86 1 Corinthians 15:13.
87 St Augustine, *The City of God*, trans. H. Bettenson (London, Penguin, 1984), XX, 6, 1.
88 Ibid., XX, 6, 2.
89 *Translator's note*: in the following lines, the term 'now' is a translation of the Italian '*ora*', derived from the Greek '*hora*', which in addition also signifies 'hour'. The impossibility of rendering this ambiguity in English robs the passage of some of its elegance. However, I felt this was preferable to switching between terms.
90 Augustine, *The City of God*, XII, 16.

91 Ibid., I, 6, 9–7, 14.
92 I. Kant, *The Critique of Pure Reason*, trans. N. Kemp-Smith (London, Macmillan, 1983), esq. A 285, B 341.
93 Ibid., A 541, B 569.
94 Ibid., A 551, B 579.
95 Ibid., A 553–4, B 581–2.
96 Ibid., A 288–9, B 344–5.
97 Ibid., A 255, B 310–11.
98 John 17:23.
99 I. Kant, *Critique of Practical Reason*, trans. L. White Beck (Indianapolis, Bobs-Merrill, 1983), p. 154, §7.
100 Ibid., pp. 117–18.
101 Plotinus, *The Six Enneads*, trans. S. McKenna and B. S. Page (London and Chicago, Encyclopaedia Britannica, 1952), VI, 7, 15.

6

The Meaning of Being as a Determinate Ontic Trace

Maurizio Ferraris

Qui giacciono i miei cani, / gli inutili miei cani, / stupidi ed impudichi, / nuovi sempre et antichi, / fedeli et infedeli / all'Ozio lor signore, / non a me uom da nulla. / Rosicchiano sottera / nel buio senza fine / rodon gli ossi i lor ossi, / non cessano di rodere i lor ossi / vuotati di medulla / et io potrei farne / la fistola dì Pan / come di sette canne / i'potrei senza cera e senza lino / farne il flauto di Pan / se Pan è il tutto e / se la morte è il tutto. / Ogni uomo nella culla / succia e sbava il suo dito / ogni uomo sepellito / è il cane del suo nulla.

Gabriele D'Annunzio, October 1935[1]

(1) 'The Humanity of the Son of God' is the title of a poem by Folengo that is typically humanistic in its orientation. And humanization is still at the heart of the Christian religion, which combines so intimately with the political and the anthropological, as in Rousseau's 'The Creed of a Savoyard Priest' or Kant's *Religion within the Limits of Reason Alone*. To deliberate over the future of an illusion and to declare oneself inevitably Christian are the same thing from this perspective: whether we are Buddhists, Taoists, historicists, vegetarians, environmentalists or sentimentalists, first and foremost we are Christians. This fact, established from the very beginning, and polemically so, as the utilitarian essence of Christianity (Suetonius: *Christus* is *Chrestus*, useful), sheds light on the attempt to save religion from the objections of reason. In accordance with Enlightenment critique, Rousseau acknowledged that there are in the Gospels teachings repugnant to reason and, in the *Lettre à M. Beaumont*, he finds mediation useless (was it necessary for God to use Moses to speak to Jean-Jacques?); Christ is not a mediator, but a great example of humanity, greater even than Socrates. The imitation of Christ is thus possible, but everything here hangs on the avoidance of deism in order to save a theism of some kind (the counterpoint to this is the Hume of *Dialogues Concerning Natural Religion*, which Kant, for one, regarded so highly).

The God that is too human is, in fact, not even useful. To be sure, the reduction of God to the moral God is functional to religion itself; but it is an insidious functionality, in that it ultimately destroys religion, besieging it and finally overcoming it with alternative forms of morality and still more effective ideologies. Perhaps Bonhoeffer had this in mind when he proposed to abandon the moral God. Yet one could still object that this itself is the mark of modernity, the greatest *hubris*: the proposal to abandon the moral God as a projection of the I is still, and in a quintessential way, to pose the problem of what to do with God; it postulates that one can do without God, that one must find a place for him. Here more than ever, God has need of man, who for just this reason no longer has, in principle, any need for God. If God spoke from a burning bush, if he transformed one who looked at him into a statue of salt, then the problem of what to do with him and where to place him would certainly not arise. But, on the contrary, Christianity emerges before a dead God, whose resurrection is progressively diluted by *kenosis*. The true believers, then, are not the Christians; not those who behave morally and who would do so even if there were no God, but those who have seen miracles, or who believe in them, or who are in fear of God. And yet, with the abandonment of pre-established harmony, which already sets God at the margins of the universe, nothing remains but theodicy, which is itself the end of God placed into the hands of mankind.

It is here that we touch on the problematic core of secularization. It is suspended between the reduction of God to a moral God, which detracts from the necessity of religion, and the call to a religion that exceeds plain reason; for secularization constitutes the hostile foundation of religion but also its driving force, thereby forfeiting the possibility of a rational critique of religion. '*I am God, I have made this image*' (Wagner, Christianity, The Redeemer, Parsifal): Nietzsche was absolutely right to want to divinize himself. After centuries of Moral God (human God), he had every right. In a process that, perhaps with a certain ethnocentric pride, is identifed with Christianity, religion as we have known it in history (burnings at the stake, abjurations, wars of religion and to be sure also happy and ecstatic deaths in a history whose historicity finds its own conditions of possibility in religion) is disappearing. That is, the Christian religion as a faith whose defences include that of being the most rational, the most true, of a truth that has an essential relation with the truth of history and of science, is in the process of dissolving. Nothing will be able to make it rise again, except the occurrence of crises such as can carry us back to a time prior to world history – or, rather, such as can suspend that historical provenance on which the Christian religion is founded. It could indeed come about that, to satisfy demands that are ultimately psychological or philosophical, secularization may want to hang on to a moral theology and a political theology. On the basis of the logic of secularization we should however conclude that a fully realized secularization may well be able to assimilate without incongruity the mythical or extramoral remainder of religion – of a religion destined to be wholly consummated in reason and thereby also to find a place at its side for every form of resurrection and archaism that are at present destitute of rationality and of morality, and justified precisely by this absence. From the perspective of a definitive break between secularization and theodicy, the day of the Antichrist or the kingdom of Heaven on Earth would be that in which the Gospels – not the Apocrypha and not the Gnostics, but the Synoptics and John – were published in a series on Eastern spirituality: and perhaps it is not far away. In such a case, religion would be, *at once*, absorbed by plain reason and, in the same gesture (or by a rational decision), referred back to pure myth in a celebration of memory. The return of God as an event wholly and in every respect reducible to custom would be here a secondary phenomenon of secularization.

That Christianity seems to take the edge off the harshness of religion, and that this is not extrinsic to its essence, is clearly behind the exhortations to tragedy and the abyss by which it is periodically traversed; these are the demands of reason, in search, perhaps, of an alterity. If, however, we can turn towards the God of Abraham, it is only because we have consulted the God of the philosophers, just in view of the simple fact that the counterposition between the God of Abraham and that of the philosophers is in principle intraphilosophical, even when it is taken up by sacred or even merely religious writers charging philosophers with spiritual disgrace or stupidity.

However, the problems are not only religious: for the call to Christianity, as to the more rational faith, or the generic faith of the rational animal, is not so *philosophically* straightforward either. It is with some difficulty that, with a view to tolerance, the equidistance between religions proposed by Lessing in *Nathan the Wise* has been maintained – and one might also note that this equivalence, made in the name of reasonableness and of humankind, is still faithful to the essence of Christianity. Its unstated presupposition is, in fact, that of Voltaire: it is precisely because we are secure in the true faith that we must tolerate unbelievers. A more needy and unsettled faith would probably be remote from tolerance. Perhaps one should invert the perspective set out in the article 'Tolerance' in the *Dictionnaire philosophique*, according to which it seems paradoxical that Christianity should be the least tolerant of the religions, since it should, in view of its truth, be the most tolerant. Clearly, in this claim to rational truth, the greatest intolerance is at work.

This ambivalence is carried to an extreme in Kant. There is only one religion, for all humanity and for all times.[2] It is in *pure* Christianity that the idea of the moral religion took on reality. For there the Church gave form on earth to the invisible kingdom of God;[3] the greatest merit of Christianity was its agreement with the purest rational moral faith,[4] and the ecclesiastical faith would grow progressively nearer to pure religious faith: the struggling Church would turn itself into the Church triumphant.[5] One can see, however, that the distinction is not between moral religion and various other forms of religion, but between religion and paganism. Religion is the faith that situates what is essential to the cult of the divine in morality; paganism is the absence of this condition[6] and, as religion with no moral scruple, amounts merely to superstition.[7] The essence of Christianity coincides *from the very beginning* with the essence of reason, and this in turn with the essence of subjectivity – and the beginning finds itself in the end. Broadly speaking, this argument (which is also that of Mme Bovary's physician: I am for the religion of Voltaire, the religion of progress etc.) was developed by the ideologies of the pure heart that were the heirs to mysticism. It suffers, however, from that characteristic weakness documented so well by Nietzsche: what do we do with a human God, when we turn to God precisely because we are disgusted by mankind? What do we do with a spider God, one that is hospitalized (God of the lazar houses) or onto-theologized (God of the philosophers).

Hence the original version of the humanity of Christ in Nietzsche, who sees in the Redeemer not the example of an eminent man but rather (like Dostoevsky) an idiot, a man who has hallucinations, a childlike character etc. In this, however, Nietzsche shows himself to be at least in part an heir to the Enlightenment (the disorders of the Redeemer, in the *Antichrist*, are the same as those of Socrates, in *The Birth of Tragedy*); for in completing the Enlightenment (*Rêve d'Alembert*, Sade) with what he believes to be a new Enlightenment, but which is in reality the direct outcome of it, Nietzsche declares his preference for a terrible God. We do not know what to do with a brother, we want a cruel father (Maistre and Baudelaire agree on the essence of this argument). What do we do not just with a God that is human and our brother, but with a religion in which there is no mystery? What sense is there to a Christianity à la Toland? *Le prêtre est immense parce qu'il fait croire à une foule de choses étonnantes. Que l'Eglise veuille tout faire et tout être, c'est un loi de l'esprit humain. Les peuples adorent l'autorité. Les prêtres vent les serviteurs et les sectaires de l'imagination.*[8]

The sectaries of the imagination. Baudelaire is really the anti-Feuerbach (that is, he shares his presuppositions, but overturns what follows from them); for Feuerbach, in fact, imagination is the illusory basis of religion and representations of the divine have their source in feelings of dependency, ignorance, anxiety and fear. The aim of the critique of religion is thus the genuine liberation, religious and not political, of humanity. For true human desires are not actual, but precisely imaginary (and here Feuerbach comes back to concur with Baudelaire, for whom true progress lay not in technical evolution, but in the reduction of the burden of original sin). Philosophical occultism and the search for transcendence within humanity continue to respond to this general human need not to have everything clear, to go beyond the simply human. It was already central to Kant's polemic against the enthusiasts, without Kant excluding any appeal to mystery on that account; quite the contrary. One only has to think of §49 of the *Critique of Judgement*, where the imagination proceeds at once from laws based on analogy and from the elaboration of principles that have their foundation in spheres superior to reason, and that draw on analogy only to transcend it, demonstrating its insufficiency. In this same sense, Maistre remains exemplary as a critic of the philosophy of Bacon: to deride modern experimentalism from the perspective of a reactionary apologia is not a 'cultural' attitude but a truly speculative one. What is it for a life to be fully present? This anthropological enquiry also implies a particular inflection of modern religion that tends to present itself as a religion of the other. Yet it is highly incoherent to proclaim the end of transcendence and vertical relations, and then call for the thematization of the transcendence of the other; this other, as the mature fruit of modern subjectivity, is the heir to Christianity, and its premises lie in the subjectivity and intersubjectivity of Augustine and Descartes.

(2) However, religion within the limits of plain reason turns out to be another name for Christianity; conversely, 'What may I hope?' is a fundamental question *for the philosopher*.[9] This sentence can be read in two senses.

The first is that of secularization. The transition from church-going faith to pure religious faith is a movement towards the kingdom of God:[10] the further one advances in secularization, the closer one gets to the kingdom. Here, the religion of the heart arrives at atheism: religion must come first, and the determinate concept of God follow. Which religion? 'Religion is conscientiousness (*mihi hoc religioni*). The holiness of the acceptance [*Zusage*] and the truthfulness of what man must confess to himself. Confess to yourself. To have religion, the concept of God is not required (still less the postulate "There is a God").'[11] The same principles are to be found in Heidegger: the gods have need of Being, and Being has need of man.

This theorem is a system.

1 First there were temples and then churches; it is what happens naturally, observes Kant, before adding that morally speaking it should happen the other way around (as in the alternative between the historical and theoretical forms of exposition since Descartes).
2 The Bible is explained as having morality as its aim; and morality is not to be interpreted via the Bible, but on the contrary, the Bible via morality. In this way, biblical teachings may be understood as universal practical rules of a religion of pure reason,[12] since the God who speaks through our (morally practical) reason is an infallible interpreter.[13]
3 The invisible church, as idea of all upright people, serves as an archetype for all the visible churches.[14] The true visible church is that which expresses the kingdom of God on Earth. In terms of quantity, it is universal; in terms of quality, it is purity, i.e. that is its way of being; in terms of relation, it is liberty (submission to an invisible and moral father); its modality is its invariability, in the submission to originary laws and not to arbitrary symbols.

This table of categories, underpinned by the axiomatic purification of the sensible, is easily compared with that of the aesthetic judgements in the *Critique of Judgement*: the beautiful is disinterested (quality), universal (quantity), free (relation: finality with out end); and it is characterized by universal communicability, rooted in the presupposition of a common meaning (modality). It is therefore not surprising that the Christian religion needs to be aesthetically attractive, since it needs to be a beautiful symbol. The Church is, like beauty, a symbol of the moral good, a sign that points to its own overcoming. The perfect church would be that which succeeded in introducing the religion of good conduct as an authentic aim, such that dogma might one day be left aside.[15] Nor is it surprising that, as both cases – religion and beauty – concern the departure from the sensible towards the intelligible, the third *Critique* and the essay on *Religion* are the two places where Kant speaks of *parerga*, of that which materially surrounds the essence (frames and telamones as the parerga of works,[16] the effects of Grace, miracles, mysteries, media of Grace like *parerga* of religion[17] what is essential to revealed religion becomes accidental here, like a frame to a picture). Grace is thus a *parergon* that undergoes secularization. For, like hope in the progress of the good, revived by the belief in the presence in us of an originary disposition towards the good, and *through the example of humanity pleasing to God in the person of the Son* (we shall see the problematic nature of this exemplarity shortly), Grace can draw strength from this holy example.[18] Yet, the instruments of Grace as such are superstitious illusions and a fetishistic cult: prayers, divine offices and sacraments have value only as instruments of the senses for strengthening the spirit.[19]

Pure religious faith is a plain rational faith, whereas every revelation is an historical faith[20] and, as such, is void of moral value.[21] Corresponding to this secularization, in a unique gesture, is a mythicization by which the moral subject takes on the role of God. The concept of God is entailed neither by physics nor by metaphysics, but by morality. The moral relation in us[22] – God exists, but precisely, only in us.[23] One can see here the Cartesian argument to which we shall return later: it is psychological evidence that proves the existence of God; God depends on man, because one can only speak of morality in man. We, humanity, must acknowledge free will in order to render the possibility of God comprehensible. Pure practical reason forces us to forge a concept of God for ourselves, whereas theophany makes an idol of the Platonic idea.[24] The 'more subtle', symbolic, anthropomorphism,[25] in virtue of which we speak of God analogically, rests on just this foundation of God in the *cogito*. It is a case of a regulative idea that has value in relation to a systematic and finalistic sphere; an idea that therefore has no absolutely objective value. In this way, the knowledge of God is symbolic and not schematic (and anyone who believed otherwise would lapse into anthropomorphism).[26]

Once the objectivity of God is removed, humanity stands at the centre: humanity, and every rational being, exists as an end in itself, and not just as a means, for rational beings are objective ends.[27] Theology treats nature as a kingdom of ends; morality treats a possible kingdom of ends as a kingdom of nature.[28] Similarly, in the *Critique of Judgement*, only the form of man can embody the ideal of beauty, since only man is an end in himself. On the other hand, the speculative interest of reason leads us to regard every ordering of the world as if it arose from the design of a supreme reason, and to order the things of the world according to teleological laws. There is thereby a *focus imaginarius* in which man and God converge: the end in itself is the end of creation. This is the general form of teleology and there is no point condemning it as humanistically impious, for this is precisely what the religion of Abraham means – at least as it is understood by Hegel (the ascendancy of Christianity over paganism as a degradation of the hunted animal, sacrifices and metamorphoses since 'man must be able to eat what does him good': the bond between God and Abraham as the capacity to name animals, imposing his own dominion over them), Husserl (in the nexus between spirit, science and European humanity) and Heidegger (man as the end of being, being as the end of man).

(3) For Kant, then, the key point in this theandric affair is whether or not Christ is exemplary. Unlike a programme of government, which without exemplification would be pure *fictio*, morality does not need examples, for the law comes first and exists, and one is not to imitate the saints, but to judge whether their actions are in conformity with the moral law.[29] It follows that to require such an example, or else miracles, would be an expression only of incredulity.[30] The relation is thus inverted (precisely in accordance with Christian exemplarism): faith in the existence of the moral law is not acquired from examples, and to pretend that it were would be simple incredulity. On the other hand, precisely because the moral law exists, it needs to manifest itself, and this is the task for every moral man, even in the knowledge that the manifestation of the idea is inadequate.[31] Yet it is precisely because we are not to imitate the saints, but to set an example of sanctity, at a certain point a Messiah had necessarily to come down to earth; not to create faith, but to demonstrate its existence.

The inappropriateness of the divine genesis of Christ is what most obviously follows from this basic perspective.[32] The Redeemer must be human. It could be said that Christ descended and suffered for the good of creatures, casting his majesty aside, and that this is why we can love him and regard this rule of perfect morality *as a rule* that holds for us as well; 'but this divine man could never be given to us *as an example* to imitate, nor, therefore, as a proof that *we* too could complete and achieve a good so pure and sublime'.[33] What is Christ for, then? 'All human knowledge begins with intuitions, proceeds from thence to concepts, and ends with ideas.'[34] The history of religion and of revelation, the transition from faith to reason, is a process whose principle of operation lies in the laws of psychology, as was the norm in the eighteenth century (see Condillac and Vico, to mention only the most important examples), and is still a long way from being overcome. So it is that the history of the world, the advent of the Messiah, the end of time, is the exact repetition of the vicissitudes of the soul. Lessing, discoursing on the education of humankind, will take as his first principle that revelation is for humankind what education is for the human individual; the heart of revelation too may, in effect, be taken back to a question of phylogenesis and ontogenesis. This was substantially accepted by Kant, for whom the need for a Messiah is for a representational limit of the soul: it is on account of the limited character of human reason, writes Kant,[35] that we can never attribute a moral value to others without representing them to us ('*dio oudepote noei aneu phantasmatos he psyche*', Aristotle *De anima* 431a, 16–17). It is in this kind of representation that Scripture too indulges, and necessarily so. But it concerns a schematism of analogy, not to be confused with the schematism of objective determination, which would lead to a lapse into anthropomorphism.[36] On the other hand, one might observe that also in Kant, in the argument of the sublime, there is a residue of the ontological proof. Or, rather, the example works negatively, in the manner set out in the *Critique of Judgement*: the inadequacy of the sensible arouses in us the feeling of the supersensible. Is this the contrary of the beautiful or is it not in fact an extension of the symbolic law by which the beautiful is regulated (as indeed in the relation between the starry heaven and the moral law)? Derrida is absolutely right to see a relation between the law of this inadequacy and the God of Anselm (*aliquid quo nihil majus cogitari potest*):[37] the experience of the infinite as the representational limit of the finite and the description of the sublime in Kant are the same. In both cases, the image plays a role of primary importance: in putting itself forward, it also points to that which transcends it, simply because every image can be the representation of one thing and the sign of another. This may seem to be no more than an empirical fact. And yet the empirical is constitutive, if God has need of man (moral religion), and man has need of the image (concepts without intuitions are empty).

In this way, God stands as an ideal of pure reason too. These days, writes Kant, the summit of perfection is called the ideal. In Plato it was the idea. But God, as the ideal of perfection, is the principle of knowledge and, in so far as he actually exists, he is also the principle of the realization of every perfection in the universe.[38] The idea gives the rule, the ideal serves as an original for the perfect determination of the copy.[39] The idea is a concept of reason, the ideal the representation of a single being adequate to the idea.[40] The ideal of reason is the original (*prototypon*) of all things, from which they derive their own possibility as imperfect copies (*ektypa*).[41] This singular transcendental ideal of reason is the sovereign real being, the object of transcendental theology.[42] This Platonism also holds for beauty, where the archetype (*Urbild, archetypon*) of taste is the ideal of the beautiful, the indeterminate idea that reason has of a maximum; it cannot be presented in terms of concepts, but only via a simple ideal of the imagination.[43] It is easy enough to see the powerful inverse relation between the ideal of reason (God) and the aesthetic ideal of the imagination. Now, as we have alluded, this ideal is man. The ideal is not in fact a free-ranging beauty, but an adherent beauty, fixed to an object via a concept of objective finality: only one who carries the end of his own existence in himself is susceptible to such an ideal.[44]

The following problem now arises. An idol is a divinity represented to us in a way that is not just moral but also anthropomorphic.[45] If, however, humankind is unique in its capacity to be moral, then even symbolic anthropomorphism, the subtlest kind of all, will be in every respect assimilable to the crudest anthropomorphism. If, in addition, one assumes that revealed religion is merely a sensible manifestation, necessary on account of humankind's inability to think without images (whereas moral religion would be its perfection, still just as human) and that this scansion represents both historical and psychological progress (the soul as the site of an ongoing liberation of images from their servitude to the sensible), then the transition from revelation to moral religion simply extends or illustrates in a historical and factual sense the act, phenomenologically attributable to imagination, of conserving the image without the sensible presence of the object, only then to appropriate it as an abstract trace (a concept like *eidos aneu morphes*).

(4) It is a matter, then, of revoking any sensible determination of the idea. Hence the nomenclature proposed by Kant:[46] the *repraesentio* (representation in general), can be *perceptio* (represented with consciousness), divided into *sensatio* (subjective perception) and *cognitio* (objective perception). The *cognitio* is *intuitus* (singular and referred immediately to the object) or *conceptus* (referred to the object via a feature which several things may have in common). The *conceptus* can be empirical or pure: the pure, which originates in the intellect alone ('not in the pure image of sensibility'), is said to be *notio*, and *idea* when it transcends the possibility of experience. Anti-empirical in intent (directed against Locke in particular, and from this point of view a comparison with the table of definitions contained in the second book of Leibniz's *New Essays* might be profitable), Kant's outline of the nomenclature reaches its final objective when he declares that, in view of these distinctions, it should ultimately appear absurd for the colour red, for example, to be described as an idea. Yet one has only to recall the twofold nature of the Platonic idea, which designates at once the greatest degree of aesthetic presence and the greatest logical distance, to see that the fundamental difficulty remains. Owing to the soul's inability to think without images, this entire differentiation takes place *in the image* (and in the modifications derived from it). The concept is not an image; nor is it a determinate modification, even in Kant and despite many affirmations to the contrary. Just consider the approving reference to Locke (and thus also to Leibniz: '*Ces mots métaphoriques de soutien ou de substratum*') in §59 of the *Critique of Judgement*. *Grund* and *Substanz* are symbolic hypotyposes: the concept of concept is a metaphor, and the concept would (in accordance with the movement of the imagination) simply be the *Aufhebung* of the sensible.

The logical idea cannot be exhibited. However, the sensible is mathematically or dynamically extended, pushed towards the inexpressible, and this is why the proscription of images is the most sublime precept of the Jewish religion.[47] Just as the example holds only as a negative example, so the image holds only to be overcome. The logical idea lives off the death of the aesthetic idea, yet its own resources lie there. This is not only why the logical idea leads to an inverse but real proportionality with the aesthetic idea, but more generally why the idea as such is difficult to distinguish from the ideal and from the idol. Yet once it is recognized that all these modifications and differentiations occur in the image, it seems problematic actually to hold to the (critical and theological) distinction between idea, ideal and idol. The ideal is not just the idea *in concreto*, but *in individuo*: what is for us an ideal was for Plato an idea of the divine intellect, 'an individual object of its [the intellect's] pure intuition'.[48] The Platonic idea is now defined as a noetic intuition, and the problem in general is to know whether philosophy can dispense with intellectual intuition. If, then, Kant had at first likened his own notion of idea to Plato's (to oppose the concept of idea as a *faint image*), now he underlines an intuitive side to Platonism, and proposes that the Platonic idea be considered an ideal. Yet, unlike the Platonic ideal, the Kantian ideal is not productive, but practical:[49] with this, however, Kant draws the teleological sense of the idea closer to the notion of exemplary cause. Moral concepts are referred to the sensible (pleasure and pain); but 'when we attend merely to their form' (again the form as abstraction), they 'may well serve as examples (*Beispiele*) of pure concepts of reason'.[50] What Kant is describing is precisely the abstraction from the sensible by which the rule is drawn: virtue and wisdom are ideas, the wise stoic is their ideal. This wisdom exists only in thought, but, of course, by way of our abstraction from, or ordinary comparison with, wise stoics from the past. Again, we are dealing with an interlacing of exemplary and final causes, where the model (past and empirical) has a teleological and transcendental significance: 'As the idea gives the *rule*, so the ideal in such a case serves as the *archetype* (*Urbild*) for the complete determination off the copy (*Nachbild*).'[51] Yet once this idea breaks off from the sensible, the distinction between the ideal and the sensible itself becomes problematic. It is no wonder, then, that there may be an ideal of reason and that this ideal is God. In his description of the transcendental ideal (*prototypon transcendentale*) Kant takes over the Cartesian determination: it regards a *natural idea*[52] and describes the movement back from the conditioned to the condition on which this ideal rests.[53] Even in definition, the transcendental is said to comprise the insufficiencies of the empirical ('the inner insufficiency of the contingent'[54]). Kant demurs only from the conclusion regarding the existence of God, or rather regarding existence in general (hence the difference between the sovereignty of mathematics and philosophy's dependency on the sensible, dissimilated in Kant and assimilated in Descartes). Nothing prohibits the admission of a being endowed with supreme self-sufficiency, but one cannot turn the hypothesis into a certainty.[55] On the other hand, in becoming a teleological hypothesis of the unity of reason, God ceases to be impenetrable[56] and the mystery passes instead to the schematism, a consequence of the reduction of theology to psychology.

(5) Cohen underlines that for Kant our sensible concepts ultimately rest not on images of objects, but on schemata.[57] The concept of dog is a schema, and does not pertain to any concrete dog. The schematism is not a problem of logic, but above all of psychology, and one that has its origins in the conflict between Berkeley and Hume over general ideas. Thus, in Kant, the individual is represented by the image, the universal by the rule. Since the categories are schematized, it is necessary that concepts be more than single representations like concrete images. On the other hand, however, they must be able to link up with the forms of sensible givenness.[58] They must be monograms. And, for Cohen, it is just here that the obscure and mysterious meaning of the schematism lies. But this mystery, perhaps the mystery *par excellence*, is a resource of the image; the fact that the sensible can make itself intelligible by simple iteration or inscription, as is usual in the case of idealization. In other words, the passage from the image to the schema is still a resource of the image. The polemical impulse driving the necessity of the schematism, as Philonenko stresses,[59] is to be found in the refutation, presented by Berkeley in the introduction to the *Principles of Human Knowledge*, of abstract general ideas, which in turn takes up the difficulty underlined by Locke in the *Essay on Human Understanding* of thinking the general idea of a triangle (that is, not an isosceles, scalene or equilateral triangle, of a certain dimension etc.). Moreover, for Berkeley, the general and abstract idea is a logical monstrosity: if I represent a dog to myself, it is either big or small, not at once big and small. In the end it is a psychological difficulty, which Berkeley presents experimentally in the invitation that he extends to his readers: try to represent a general triangle.[60]

It is to this that Kant must respond, and he does so by contrasting the method to the image: five points are image of the number five, whereas the number five, or one hundred, is a method, precisely the schema of the concept.[61] The problem, however, is to establish whether this method is wholly distinct from the image or rather follows from it, just as the trace left by the sensation is the idealization of its permanence; whether, that is, Kant, in his engagement with what is loosely called empiricism, has not derived from it the resources and ultimately the very condition of possibility of the schematism.

We can see, meanwhile, that the reasons underlying the rejection of the exemplarity of Christ, and of idolatry in general, are also at work in Kant in the distinction between image and schema, and that the difficulty in principle of distinguishing idol, ideal and idea prolongs the aporia. From this point of view, it is significant that, for Levinas, idolatry is characterized as contempt for the *Torah*, which is the antithesis of idolatry, its absolute contradiction. For the essence of Judaism is conceived as an uninterrupted exegesis of the book, of immutable letters traversed by the breath of the living God. God, here, is not incarnate but, writes Levinas, inscribed. His life is lived in letters.[62] By this, Levinas means that the sign is the opposite of the golden calf. If, however, we consider the meaning of the image from the beginning of the philosophical tradition (the twofold meaning of the *eidos* in Plato, the meaning of the image as a sign of itself and of what is other in Aristotle, up to the double nature of the symbol as a thing and referral, and indeed the 'wonderful' double nature of the word meaning in Hegel), it becomes difficult to distinguish, by right and in principle, between image and concept. In fact, they both issue from the trace – such that the opposition between the *Torah* and the golden calf seems instead to be a complementarity arising from a common genesis; the idea, simply, of the trace as a principle at once originary and derivative.

It is precisely this ultimate indistinguishability between image and trace, and between trace and sign, that represents the fundamental reason (before any historical argument concerning secularization) why it is difficult to distinguish not only philosophy from theology, but philosophy from religion. It is interesting to see that the motivation for this seems to lie less in the philosophy of history than in the static features of a psychology of perception.

Every empirical inscription implies idealization. If, then, Heidegger's claim to distinguish ontology from ontotheology, from religion and from Christianity itself (to the point of refraining from any consideration of the huge theological and generally religious reception of Heideggerian thought), is problematic, it is just as difficult for Levinas to trace a distinction between his own vision of religion as metaphysics and the ontological atheism that he imputes to Heidegger. According to Levinas, philosophy as ontotheology in the sense intended by Heidegger thinks the possibility of God's meaning; and in so doing it determines him immediately as an entity *par excellence*. This is why the history of Western metaphysics is a history of the destruction of transcendence. In opposition to this, Levinas puts forward his own way – which is that, also found in the tradition of Christian apologia, of the *credo quia absurdum*: God does not have a meaning and is thus irreducible to a determinate Being and to philosophy. Levinas also counters that meaning overflows Being, and that to return it to ontology is already to carry out a fatal reduction. This issues in the usual critique of philosophy as the cult of presence and immanence, which is why religious thinking that wishes to appeal to experience, even in opposition to philosophy, will ultimately have its foundation in the same ground as philosophy. If we accept what has been said so far about the trace, not least in the above regarding its psychological dimension, we see how just this is what can be overturned: nothing is present, everything is trace, presence constituting itself in the form of ideality. It is all the more remarkable, therefore, that Levinas perceives a challenge to philosophy in the question of the idea of the infinite in Descartes, which introduces precisely the hypothesis that nothing is present because nothing is simply finite. In Descartes, the idea of God might explode the unity of the 'I think', which is radicalized in Malebranche: there is no idea of God, or God is his own idea: '*L'idée de Dieu, c'est Dieu en moi, mais déjà Dieu rompant la conscience qui vise des idées, différent de tout contenu.*'[63] Moreover, referring to Descartes' second metaphysical meditation, Levinas writes that the *in* of in-finite signifies, at the same time, *non* and *within*. Rather than adopting a reductive attitude, Levinas does not speak of a genesis of the infinite on the basis of the finite, but instead underlines the fact that the negation of the finite is already implied in the infinite, inscribed in the finite as a trace, or – in Levinas' terms – as an inscription that is neither empirical nor transcendental, older than both: a significance older than signification, an arche-originary signification. In the end, via an analysis that moves in a similar manner to Heidegger's characterization of the transcendental imagination in the *Kantbuch*, Levinas maintains that the precession of the trace with respect to the empirical and the transcendental must lead us to see in the trace something transcendent. For our part, and in fundamental agreement with reductionism, we would be inclined rather to see the transcendentality of the trace as a consequence of its empirical and anthropological character. From this perspective it seems permissible to understand the meaning of Being not as an originary non-meaning, nor ultimately as a past that has never been present, but precisely as a determinate ontic trace that generates meaning by simple iteration.

Metaphysics in its modern sense is little older than the *Disputationes metaphysicae* of Suarez and, roughly speaking, comprises the whole domain of theoretical philosophy. Its borders are ill defined. For the university scholastics, it is Aristotle's first philosophy; for Cartesians, it is the three sectors of the supersensible – psychology, cosmology and theology. It is revealing from this perspective that Heidegger, for whom ontic knowledge is dependent on ontological knowledge, asserts in *Being and Time* that fundamental ontology 'must be sought in the *existential analytic of Dasein*',[64] adding immediately that the priority of *Dasein* is first and foremost an ontical priority. Is this a contradiction, or more likely a circularity that follows from the fact that the ontic priority of *Dasein* is understood at the same time as an ontological priority; for *Dasein* is that being in whose decision Being is an issue. What is, then, a transcendental anthropology? It is the nexus between psychology and metaphysics in which the meaning of transcendental philosophy is enclosed. Metaphysics is the unconditioned in man, the obscure space made possible by his self-transcendent constitution. On the basis of similar considerations, Samuel Alexander, in his Gifford Lectures of 1916–18 which were subsequently published under the title of *Space, Time and Deity*, elaborated a notion of deity as coincident with the schematism: the deity is not God, but God in us, as the connection of space and time. 'Deity is not spirit.'[65] It is the possibility of matter and of spirit. Accordingly, *deity is also an empirical quality*.[66] We are infinitely finite, or, in Alexander's terms: we are finitely infinite, whereas the deity is infinitely infinite. We are finite because our minds are only limited parts of the space and time in which they are extended. We are infinite because, as in the *Monadologie*, our minds are mirrors of the entire universe.

(6) The only analytical attribute of the soul is *ego sum, ego existo*.[67] According to an argument found in Vico and that was also common to the period, marking the break with Aristotle, nothing is easier for me to know than my spirit; thus, inner sense is immediately familiar, and this is why Kant can say that the reality of time is superior to that of space. At this point, I close my eyes, abstract myself wholly from the senses and try to give order to what I know. Some things are like the images of things, and only these can properly be named ideas; with these, I represent to myself (*cogito-représente*) a man, a chimera, the heavens, an angel or God himself.[68] This sensationalist definition paves the way for Locke, and also for Gassendi's polemic against Descartes, in which he denounces an ambiguity in Descartes' argumentation. His point is well made, for Descartes' argument rests on an ontological and semantic equivocality in the idea – between sensible representation (from which he derives evidence) and intelligible principle (from which he derives necessity). Descartes goes on to say that other ideas are representations conjoined with an affection, with will or a judgement. Ideas are always true in themselves, as the defence of the senses that runs from Greek philosophy down to Kantian anthropology rightly has it. It is important to see that in Hume all feelings are true as well, owing to an extension of representation to judgement. Nothing remains but judgements in which I must seek carefully to avoid mistakes. The most common error is to think that things which are in me are also outside of me, and for this reason it is important to broach the genetic examination of the origin of ideas: some are born in me (*nées avec moi, innatae*),[69] others seem to be foreign and to come from outside, others again are made by me.

Yet one can see how hard it is to separate these three types of idea, and how all three fall under the regime of representation. Moreover, the style of analysis followed by Descartes is psychological. Husserl will censure him for this, but without thereby succeeding better than he in achieving independence from psychology (or from anthropology: Husserl is wrong to reject Heidegger's anthropologism as misdirected). The source of these ideas, to continue, is empirical (psychology); and that on which my certainty is based (distinct from psychology) is the natural light, which I cannot extinguish, for it is from this light that the inference from doubt to certainty proceeds. The natural light, then, is like the schematism, or, more precisely, like the synthetic unity of apperception. The light is natural: empirical with a transcendental or constitutive function. Such a light cannot be placed in doubt: and yet we have to see that there is a difference between the object and its idea, and the difference in question resembles that between analogical and digital, between physical resemblance and logical identity (indeed, Descartes takes as an example the difference between sensible knowledge and the astronomical knowledge of the sun). The idea of an omnipotent God who is the creator of all things definitely has a greater objective reality than that of the finite substances which I represent to myself. Now, on the strength of the natural light – or, rather, as just noted, of an empirical given that is transcendental precisely on account of its empirical character, since the senses never lie – it is plain that there must be at least as much objective reality in the total efficient cause as in its effect. The nothing, in fact, could not produce anything. Thus, according to an Augustinian argument that one rediscovers, for example, in Leibniz and Baumgarten, if we presuppose that there is something in the idea that is not derived from the cause, we must assume that it comes from the nothing. Now, that which I think subjectively may easily be false, but this does not mean that it has no cause. From here one has to go back to a first idea, which is like its master or its original (*patron ou original, instar archetypi*),[70] or rather to God. All ideas of other people, of things, animals and angels can come about in combination with the idea of God, but not the idea of God itself. God has here the same substance and function as the productive imagination in Kant, in the way that it mysteriously sets itself apart from the reproductive imagination.

Apparently, everything proceeds from God. In fact, however, the empirical stands as constitutive of the transcendental: God exists because otherwise I, who am finite, could not have the idea of an infinite substance. The mechanism is that of the constitution of presence via the possibility of disappearance, as analysed by

Derrida in *La Voix et la phénomène*, and with the same results (presence is interwoven with absence; here, the transcendental is interwoven with the empirical, or vice versa). Now, one attains to God in a way that is empirical twice over: he is an idea (psychology) of a finite being. Descartes was careful to emphasize that one does not reach the infinite by a simple negation of the infinite, as there is plainly more reality in infinite substance than in finite substance. One might object that there is at least as much reality in the cause as in the effect.[71] However, the point is not the filiation or naturalistic derivation of religion or suchlike, but the recognition that it is in precisely this play of empirical and transcendental that religious feeling consists. How could I know that I lack something, that I doubt and desire, if there were not the infinite? Clearly, I could lack some other finite thing; the argument does not in any way show that what I lack is infinite, nor even that it exists (cf. the example of phantom limbs taken up by Descartes himself).[72] The trace, the lack which institutes the infinite in the finite, emerges here as the structure of religious feeling.

The circle tightens: if I were the author of my own being, I would not doubt anything. With my doubt I thereby become proof of the infinite. Conversely, it pertains to the nature of the infinite that I who am finite cannot understand it. Between finite and infinite the relation is, precisely, that of a trace and of an impression. I am the image and likeness of God; I bear the mark of the one who made me ('*la marque de l'ouvrier empreinte sur son ouvrage – nota artificis operi suo impressa*').[73] It is from this mark that the innate character of the idea of God in me arises (it is the trace of God in me that provokes the feeling of the infinite in the finite). In Augustinian and Platonic terms, the will (we might say *cupiditas, Streben, per l'assoluto*) is the image of God in me. The empirical–transcendental relation (and reproductive–productive imagination) is exemplified by the triangle: I can imagine a triangle whose nature is what it is, and is eternal, even though it is born in me. And there is no point in objecting that I may have received it from the external world of sensibility because I can imagine forms that I have never seen in nature and that would none the less be endowed with rational and eternal properties. From this Descartes concludes that an analogous argument could be used to demonstrate the existence of God.

Clearly, the problem lies in the fact that the triangle is in me as something that I may have seen, whereas the image as such is something empirical that I cannot avoid, and the empirical itself is transformed by this very unavoidability into a transcendental. In fact, I cannot think of God without existence, just as I cannot think of a mountain without a valley – and this expresses an aesthetic impossibility, not a logical one. In other words, I could very easily think of God without existence, and consider his existence as an aesthetic consequence and a sensory deficiency akin to that which renders a chiliagon and a myriagon indistinguishable to me. At this point, one comes back to the triangle. If I think of a triangle, I cannot conceive of it without certain properties; this is still an aesthetic argument transformed into a logical one – the empirical transformed into transcendental, as is inevitable. The unavoidable function of the image leads one to conclude that, in fact, *abstracting* from the empirical, I can imagine – without imagining – a chiliagon that would be somewhat more aesthetically complex than a pentagon, and indistinguishable from a myriagon. The whole of the Sixth Meditation is, accordingly, dedicated to the imagination, on which the entire demonstration rests (the sensible passivity, which, via retention, produces idealization).

(7) In *Faith and Knowledge*, Hegel reaches a conclusion that could in effect have come from Kant: the transcendental imagination is the intuitive intellect, and the intuitive intellect is the archetypical intellect. But it is archetypical only in that it is category immersed in extension, which becomes category when it separates itself from extension (they are the characteristics of the Christian God as withdrawal from the sensible). And the same is found in the *Enzyklopädie §55* and with reference to the schematism in the *Lessons on the History of Philosophy*, where Hegel believes this union of sensibility and intellect in the schema, via the transcendental imagination, to be one of the most beautiful moments of Kantian philosophy; albeit one misunderstood by Kant himself who did not fully thematize the priority of the imagination with respect to intuition and the intellect. Not having recognized this priority, the synthesis that Kant performed was extrinsic, as when one binds a table leg with a cord. This is quite right, given that the *syn* of synthesis, being at once empirical and

transcendental, cannot be characterized in the originary manner envisaged by Hegel. Conversely, all that is valorized in Hegel under the heading of life and the living spirit could more usefully, and without equivocality, be understood in terms of the cooperation between empirical and transcendental (of which life is a determinate modification: the fact that the living being has its beginning and end in itself).

Returning to *Faith and Knowledge*, it is also clear why Hegel is concerned to underline the originary value of the imagination. Protestantism establishes the true faith, leading it back to consciousness. Yet it also absolutizes the form of the finite, in Jacobi and Fichte just as in Kant, such that no philosophy of this kind can achieve knowledge of God, only knowledge of man. 'Truth, however, cannot be deceived by this sort of *hallowing* of a finitude' (my emphasis).[74] The absolute is not made up of the finite and the infinite; in it the finite and the infinite 'are one', and finitude disappears since whatever negativity there is in it is negated.[75] As one can see, Hegel *repeats* the Cartesian argument, or, more precisely, the logical structure by which it works; it issues, however, not in the proof of the existence of God, but rather in an absolute immanent to man in the form of the transcendental imagination. This makes Kant's examination at once illuminating and misleading.

The Kantian programme, as an analysis of the finite intellect, is for Hegel wholly comprised in the project of Locke; in short, it remains inscribed within a psychological domain that it exceeds only in the question of how synthetic *a priori* judgements are possible. But it is precisely here that the imagination, as the possibility of judgements, intervenes. The imagination, in fact, is the synthetic unity of intuition and intellect, or rather of activity and passivity, of empirical and transcendental.[76] Hegel has every right, then, to underline the excessive character of the transcendental imagination. Through it a psychological examination of the finite intellect can, at the same time, define the possibility of synthetic *a priori* judgements, which are realized precisely 'through the absolute originary identity of the heterogeneous':[77] or, in view of the originary identity of the empirical and transcendental, reproductive and productive, non-dialectizable and dialectizable.

The problem is, however, that it is inappropriate to use the term 'originary' here. The imagination is originary (it effects the synthesis of intuition and intellect) only in so far as it is secondary: judgement is transcendental only in so far as it is also a *judicium sensuum*. Hegel maintains that one has understood nothing of the transcendental deduction if one does not see in the imagination not the medium introduced between subject and object, but rather that which as primary produces the subject and object. Equivocating over the originary (by ignoring that there is no longer any necessity for the originary to refer to the notion of origin as *prius*) allows Hegel to highlight as the limit of Kantian imagination what is, in fact, its primary resource (Heidegger will do the same with regard to originary temporality, which in his view cannot intermix with vulgar spatialized temporality). 'Productive imagination has been allowed to get by easily in the Kantian philosophy, first because its pure Idea is set forth in a rather mixed up way, like other potencies, *almost in the ordinary form of a psychological faculty, though an a priori one*.'[78] That this suffers from the difficulty of explaining the exchange between soul and body in Kant is certainly quite clear to Hegel.[79] But, once again, Hegel – taking the same approach that led him to criticize the extrinsic character of the synthesis, the fact that Kant does not thematize its originary character and so forth – reinforces the critique of the psychologism that compromises the *a priori* nature of the imagination and makes of the Kantian system a formal idealism no different from that of Locke. As such, to posit the intellect as subjective is to negate it as absolute and thereby also to deny it access to the absolute. From this follows, quite consistently, the valorization of the imagination in the third *Critique*, in reference principally not to the judgement of taste, but to teleological judgement (which transposes the problem of imagination from the merely psychological or aesthetic sphere to the theological), where the identity of the transcendental imagination and the intuitive intellect is reaffirmed. And this, of course, leads to the theological conclusion:

> If we remove from the practical faith of the Kantian philosophy some of the popular and unphilosophical garments in which it is decked, we shall find nothing else expressed in it but the Idea that Reason does have absolute reality, that in this Idea the antithesis of freedom and necessity is completely suspended, that infinite thought

> is at the same time absolute reality – or in short we shall find the absolute identity of thought and being. (We are here thinking only of Kant's doctrine of faith in God . . .).[80]

With this, the problem of religion in our own time seems to have been set out with sufficient clarity. The absolute is seen to have an empirical and psychological genesis, but (in a tacit furtherance of a Cartesian argument) it is assumed that the infinite must have more reality than the finite.

(8) The common and unfamiliar root that 'perhaps' generates sensibility and intellect:[81] this, according to Heidegger, is the unknown that Kant wants to penetrate. We should like to ask whether the Heideggerian horizon, just because it postulates a correspondence between Being and subjectivity and between transcendence and the self-transcendence of the subject, does not move towards a conception of the transcendental imagination that is originary precisely in so far as it is derived (in accordance with what Derrida has called a logic of the supplement). We have spoken of 'subjectivity' in the tacit assumption of its equivalence with *Dasein*, since the Heideggerian critique of subjectivity is for the most part a deliberate move borne out of a historiographical hypothesis. The self-overcoming of *Dasein* is, in fact, just what one sees at work in the *Meditationes*. Yet self-transcendence is characteristic of the imagination (the trace retained, passively, which thereby becomes spontaneous, active and idealized). And, in turn, the imagination is characteristic of *Dasein*. Thus, in the course of the winter semester of 1922–3, Heidegger proposed to translate *Peri Psychés* not as *Von der Seele*, but as *Über das Sein in der Welt*.[82] The soul is the seat of the imagination. The retention of the trace secures temporality, and subjectivity would be merely the outcome of a sensible retention which in its turn becomes protension and idealization (exactly what Heidegger will thematize some years later as the self-overcoming of *Dasein*, but with the qualification that *Dasein* already is self-transcendence, or follows from an idealizing retention). The same motif, seen here in relief against imagination, recurs in the relation between *Dasein* and Being. In *Sein und Zeit* Being is defined as transcendent – as the *transcendens schlechthin* – yet as that which is thought in *Dasein* (whose condition lies in *Dasein*). This is clearer still in the

valorization of the Nothing in 'Was ist Metaphysik?', which could easily be transcribed into a Cartesian horizon: 'Being itself is essentially finite and reveals itself only in the transcendence of Dasein which is held out in the nothing.'[83] 'Going beyond beings occurs in the essence of Dasein. But this going beyond is metaphysics itself. This implies that metaphysics belongs to the "nature of man" . . . Metaphysics is the basic occurrence of Dasein. It is Dasein itself.'[84] In its turn, *Vom Wesen des Grunds* may be characterized as a thematization of the self-transcendence of the empirical as possibility of the transcendental: the Nothing is the not of the being; the not of the being (the Nothing) reveals Being; Being is the difference from the being, made possible by the being. 'The ontological difference is the "not" between being and Being.'[85] Here, implicitly, we find the definition of imagination as a faculty conserving the trace of sensible things in their absence.

The foundation is lacking because the foundation is the difference between being and Being. It is the Nothing of this difference produced by the self-transcendence of *Dasein* which, surpassing itself, carries itself towards the transcendental. What we find here is an exact repetition of a Cartesian movement, with an analogous outcome: that which, as empirical, turns out to be constitutive of the transcendental presents itself as constituted by the transcendental which has been emancipated through idealization. If we were positivists, we could claim to have discovered the origin of religious feeling, but this all too obvious thought is not the point here. From the impulse towards the originary is derived everything that Heidegger says when speaking of mystery, of the abyss, of withdrawal – and, indeed, the whole reflection on *Ereignis*. What might confidently be described as a further step, although in the form of a thematization of the speculative aspects of the imagination, would lead essentially to two points. First, there is absolutely no guarantee that the mediation between finite and infinite will be resolved into a decision for the infinite or the finite; the dialectic between the dialectizable and the non-dialectizable is still dialectical – indeed, it is the most intimate possibility of dialectic – but is not therefore resolved into the predominance of one pole over the other. This is what happens in the imagination, which takes the form precisely of both retention and idealization, of finite passivity and the possibility of infinite iteration. Secondly, there is no need to call this activity 'originary' (in Hegel's or

Heidegger's sense), for the simple reason that originary and derivative are themselves constituted as a pair following from the passivity–activity of the imagination; the originary, here, would just be something archaeological recovered from a teleological perspective, in the manner of Freudian *Nachträglichkeit* or of Levinas' 'past that has never been present'. To speak of the self-transcendence of the *cogito* or of *Dasein* means therefore to describe the physiological activity of the trace. A trace inscribes itself, and the act of inscription is empirical and passive. None the less, as inscribed and thus idealized, the trace becomes at the same time transcendental. This unique move is what defines the transcendentality of the imagination.

The constitution of the present is made possible by the disappearance of the empirical. This is why Derrida can write that the infinite difference is finite (a phrase not to be understood as a general eulogy of the finite, but as the co-implication of the finite and the infinite). Presence is never present to itself, because it is constituted linguistically and, in a deeper sense, grammatologically as a trace. Spirit thus has its origin in iteration, or in the letter (in iteration as the possibility of both the letter and the spirit alike); which is precisely another way to say that the empirical (a certain guise of the empirical) is transcendental, is the possibility of the transcendental. The sign makes a sign: semantically, it indicates itself and something other, according to what is in fact already the resource of the image. Ontologically, it is suspended between presence and absence. Like the imagination, it is at once passive registration and active idealization. In this sense, preceding ontology and phenomenology, prior to the empirical and prior to the transcendental, the sign precedes the truth; it has existence, therefore, but no essence.

This is why Heidegger proposes to translate '*anima*' as 'Being-in-the-world'. The deferral made possible by the trace is not a modification of the *cogito*, but constitutive of it.[86] Thus in Kant, moreover: I produce time in the moment in which I experience it, or rather, I produce inner sense in the moment in which I place it together with outer sense – Aristotle was right to define time as the number of movement according to the before and after. One may still ask whether the origin of God *as much as of man* does not lie in precisely this mystery (the condition of the empirical and the transcendental) immanent to the trace. From it is derived all 'theological' ('metaphysical') notions that nourish the world of the spirit: image or representation, sensible or intelligible, nature or culture, nature or technology. And, conversely, we should note that the very attempt to go back, to reach the possibility of the trace, leads to the unifying structure characteristic of mysticism. Yet for just this reason, once again, there is no point in going back to originary time (to adopt the form that Heidegger gives to the general need for the origin) because there is no vulgar time, or, rather, even originary time would already be derivative. That everything can be sacred or profane, full of meaning or perfectly senseless, seems here to be the simple consequence of what will look like the most mundane evidence and the most problematic of mysteries: the passage from the sensible to the intelligible by way of the inscription of the trace.

Translated by David Webb

Acknowledgement

This essay was made possible by the support of the Alexander von Humboldt-Stiftung Institute.

Notes

1 Here lie my dogs / my useless dogs, / stupid and wanton / forever new and old faithful and unfaithful / to Sloth their master, / not to a nobody like me. They chew away underground / in the endless dark / they gnaw the bones, their bones, / they never stop gnawing their bones / emptied now of marrow / and with them I could make / Pan's fistula / as with seven canes / I could with neither wax nor linen / make Pan's flute / if Pan is all and / if death is all. / Every man in the cradle / sucks and slobbers over his finger / every man entombed / is the dog to his nothing. (Originally published in the 'Introduzione' by L. Anceschi to *Opere di Gabrielle D'Annunzio*, Milan, Mondadori, 1982. Translated here by David Webb.)

2 I. Kant, 'Toward perpetual peace' in the Cambridge edition of Kant's works, *Practical Philosophy*, trans. and ed. M. Gregor (Cambridge, Cambridge University Press, 1996), p. 336.

3 I. Kant, *Religion within the Bounds of Mere Reason*, in the Cambridge edition of Kant's Works, *Religion and Rational Theology*, trans. and ed. A. Wood and G. di Giovanni (Cambridge, Cambridge University Press, 1996), pp. 178–9. All page references for this essay will be to this edition.

4 Kant, 'The conflict of faculties', *Religion and Rational Theology*, p. 242. All page references for this essay will be to this edition.
5 Ibid., p. 275.
6 Ibid., p. 272.
7 I. Kant, *Gesammelte Schriften* (Königlich-Preussische Akademie der Wissenschaften, Berlin-Leipzig, 1900; and subsequently Deutsche Akademie der Wissenschaften, Berlin, 1967), vol. IX, 494–5.
8 C. Baudelaire, *Oeuvres Complètes*, ed. Y.-G. LeDantec and C. Pichois, vol. II (Paris, Gallimard, 1975–6), p. 1248.
9 I. Kant, *Critique of Pure Reason*, trans. N. Kemp Smith (London, Macmillan, 1983): references to this text will be given to the original A and B edition page numbers; A 805, B 832–3. Cambridge edition of Kant's Works, *Lectures on Logic*, trans. and ed. M. Young (Cambridge, Cambridge University Press, 1992), p. 538.
10 Kant, 'The critique of practical reason', *Practical Philosophy*, pp. 232–3.
11 I. Kant, Cambridge edition, *Opus Postumum*, ed. E. Förster, trans. E. Förster and M. Rosen (Cambridge, Cambridge University Press, 1993), p. 248.
12 Kant, *Religion within the Bounds of Mere Reason*, pp. 159–61.
13 Kant, 'The Conflict of faculties', *Religion and Rational Theology*.
14 Kant, *Religion within the Bounds of Mere Reason*, pp. 135–7.
15 Ibid., pp. 193–4.
16 I. Kant, *Critique of Judgement*, trans. J. C. Meredith (Oxford University Press, Oxford, 1986) p. 68.
17 Kant, 'Critique of practical reason' in *Practical Philosophy*, pp. 182–3.
18 Kant, *Gesammelte Schriften*, vol. VIII, p. 43.
19 Kant, *Religion within the Bounds of Mere Reason*, pp. 210–11.
20 Ibid., pp. 136–41.
21 Ibid., pp. 141–2.
22 Kant, *Gesammelte Schriften*, vol. XXI, p. 149.
23 Ibid., vol. XXI, p. 114f; vol. XXII, pp. 105, 122, 126f.
24 Kant, *On a newly Arisen Superior Tone in Philosophy*, ed. and trans. P. Fenves (Baltimore and London, Johns Hopkins University Press, 1993), pp. 51–72, esq. n5, pp. 64–5.
25 I. Kant, *Prolegomena to any Future Metaphysics*, trans. P. Carus, Rev. J. W. Ellington (Indianapolis and Cambridge, Hackett, 1977), p. 97.
26 Kant, *Critique of Judgement*, p. 223.
27 I. Kant, 'Groundwork of the metaphysics of morals' in *Practical Philosophy*, pp. 77–81. All further references will be to this edition.
28 Ibid., pp. 87–8.

29 P. Menzer (ed.), *Eine Vorlesung Kants über Ethik* (Berlin, Pan, 1924), p. 137.
30 Kant, *Religion within the Bounds of Mere Reason*, pp. 105–6.
31 Ibid.
32 Ibid., pp. 106–7.
33 Ibid., p. 107.
34 Kant, *Critique of Pure Reason*, A 702, B 730.
35 Kant, *Religion within the Bounds of Mere Reason*, pp. 107–8.
36 Ibid., pp. 107–8.
37 J. Derrida, *The Truth in Painting*, trans. G. Bennington and I. McLeod (Chicago, Chicago University Press, 1988), p. 137.
38 I. Kant, 'Inaugural dissertation: on the form and principles of the sensible and the intelligible world', in the Cambridge edition, *Theoretical Philosophy 1755–1770*, trans. and ed. D. Walford and R. Meerbote (Cambridge, Cambridge University Press, 1992), p. 388.
39 Kant, *Critique of Pure Reason*, A 567–8, B 595–6.
40 Kant, *Critique of Judgement*, p. 76.
41 Kant, *Critique of Pure Reason*, A 578, B 606.
42 Ibid., A 614, B 642.
43 Kant, *Critique of Judgement*, p. 76.
44 Ibid., pp. 76–80.
45 Kant, *Critique of Judgement*, §89 (28) 'The use of moral argument'; and also Kant, *Religion within the Bounds of Mere Reason*, pp. 201–2.
46 Kant, *Critique of Pure Reason*, A 320, B 377.
47 Kant, *Critique of Judgement*, p. 118.
48 Kant, *Critique of Pure Reason*, A 568, B 596.
49 Ibid., A 569, B 597.
50 Ibid.
51 Ibid.
52 Ibid., A 581, B 609.
53 Ibid., A 584, B 612.
54 Ibid., A 589, B 617.
55 Ibid., A 612, B 640.
56 Ibid., A 614, B 642.
57 E. Cohen, *Kants Theorie der Erfahrung* (1871) (Berlin, Cassirer, 1918), p. 490.
58 Ibid., p. 495.
59 A. Philonenko, 'Lecture du schématisme transcendental', in J. Kopper and W. Marx (eds), *200 Jahre Kritik der reinen Vernunft* (Hildesheim, Gerstenberg, 1981), pp. 291–312.
60 G. Berkeley, *Principles of Human Knowledge* (Glasgow, Collins/Fontana, 1979), Introduction, §13.

61 Kant, *Critique of Pure Reason*, A 145.
62 E. Levinas, *In the Time of Nations*, trans. M. B. Smith (London, Athlone Press, 1994), pp. 57–9.
63 E. Levinas, 'God and philosophy', in *Basic Philosophical Writings*, ed. A. T. Peperzak, S. Critchley and R. Bernasconi (Bloomington, Ind., Indiana University Press, 1996), p. 136.
64 M. Heidegger, *Being and Time* (1927) (Oxford, Blackwell, 1994), p. 34.
65 S. Alexander, *Space, Time and Deity*, The Gifford Lectures at Glasgow, 1916–18 (New York, Dover, 1966), vol. II, p. 349.
66 Alexander, *Space, Time and Deity*, p. 358.
67 R. Descartes, Meditation II, *A Discourse on Method: Meditations and Principles*, trans. J. Veitch (London and New York, Everyman Library, 1978), p. 89. All further page references will be to this edition.
68 Ibid., vol. III, p. 102.
69 Ibid.
70 Ibid.
71 Ibid., p. 106.
72 Ibid., vol. VI, p. 139.
73 Ibid., vol. III, p. 109.
74 G. W. F. Hegel, *Faith and Knowledge*, trans. W. Cerf and H. S. Harris (Albany, State University of New York Press, 1977), p. 65. All further page references will be to this edition.
75 Ibid., p. 66.
76 Ibid., pp. 70–1.
77 Ibid., p. 72.
78 Ibid., p. 73.
79 Ibid., pp. 75–6.
80 Ibid., p. 94.
81 Kant, *Critique of Pure Reason*, A 15, B 29.
82 This seminar remains unpublished at present.
83 M. Heidegger, 'What is metaphysics?' (1929), in *Basic Writings*, ed. D. F. Krell (London, Routledge, 1993), p. 108.
84 Ibid., p. 109.
85 M. Heidegger, *The Essence of Reasons*, trans. T. Malick (Evanston, Northwestern University Press, 1969), p. 3.
86 *Translator's note*: the Italian term '*differimento*' has been translated here as 'deferral'. However, it is the noun form of the verb '*differire*', which may convey the sense of differing or of deferring, depending on whether it occurs as intransitive or transitive. Both senses are at play here.

7

Dialogues in Capri

Hans-Georg Gadamer

As the only German participant in this small discussion group, I found myself in a somewhat difficult situation. None of the other participants spoke in German, and with my old ears I was only able to follow the broad outline of the contributions which were so rapidly delivered in French, Italian and Spanish. Even now, I have only put pen to paper after having read the written transcript of the contributions by Derrida and Vattimo.

Derrida has described our friendly discussion so accurately and so well that I have nothing further to add. None the less, the dialogue between Gianni Vattimo and Jacques Derrida has assumed such a central position in my own reflections that I was glad to be able to read their contributions more closely.

Clearly, the selection of participants was also one-sided since, with the exception of myself, everyone came from the Latin world. I was the only Protestant. More problematic, as Derrida rightly pointed out, was the absence of any representative of Islam. Equally problematic was the fact that no woman was present, especially since women – and mothers in particular – certainly have a privileged contribution to make to the theme 'religion in our world'.

None the less, the atmosphere was one of concord and collective endeavour. Despite the diversity of languages, none of us felt tied to any sort of dogma. The common word 'religion' remains, now as before, a privilege of Latin culture, the origins of which probably lie in the rural civilization of early Rome. In general, I do not hold etymologies to be of such great importance. Neither Heidegger nor Derrida has yet succeeded in convincing me that an etymology can tell us something important if what is uncovered does not somehow continue to speak to us in the living language of today. This is the case even if the etymology is correct, whatever 'correct' may mean in this context.

I believe that I have now come to understand the principal themes which led to our meeting here in Capri. They were clearly articulated by the first two speakers, Derrida and Vattimo. For reasons which I have already indicated, my own contribution was concerned only with a very general perspective. Undoubtedly, the title under which our various contributions are gathered needs to be grasped in a broader sense. It should, in fact, be termed 'Religion and the Religions'. For this expresses the situation in which the problem of religion has become a central concern in the modern world. Ours can hardly be termed an age of religious wars, but the catastrophe of the Second World War certainly had something of the madness of a bloody religious conflict about it. This point was also expressed by Vattimo in recognizing the important role played by dogmatic atheism in the background to the conflict of the Second World War. This background has since changed to a significant extent and atheism no longer possesses the same force now that the racist madness of National Socialism and the compulsory state religion of the Soviet Union have met their end.

None the less, we need to recognize how difficult it is to reform totalitarian economic and social structures in countries such as Soviet Russia if Western economic and political models are successfully to be introduced in place of the old model of a powerfully centralized government and a command economy. The same difficulty is undoubtedly confronted by intellectuals in many other 'advanced' countries. The 'rationally organized' character of the old social system continues to survive even after the break-up of the Soviet state in so far as the idea of a planned economy is still considered to offer a rational solution to problems of social and political organization. The dream of a 'true' socialism is far from having been fully renounced. Before such dreams, the prosaic reality of everyday life finds itself in a difficult position. The ideal of democracy, with its acceptance of dependency, risk and unstable economic conditions, and its modest system of adaptation, is not easily accepted in modern mass society. The realism underlying this system of permanent compromise may well be unable to satisfy the dreams and illusions of a society accustomed to pliant obedience. Such realism may be more difficult to learn than obstinately persisting in the promise of salvation held out even by an oppressive dictatorship which still dreams of world revolution.

Even after the breakdown of the Marxist doctrine of ideological self-deception promulgated from the standpoint of a dogmatic atheism, the various religions still find difficulty in reaching out to people. The battle lines have, of course, changed and things are different today in so far as dogmatic atheism no longer forms one of the fronts. In the place of Marxism, with its global denial of all forms of religion, we encounter a new type of atheism which is based on indifference. It is this indifference which increasingly seems to characterize the attitude of the younger generation in the industrialized world. Certainly, as a proportion of humankind as a whole, they still do not yet represent the majority. Moreover, the nature of this indifference varies greatly across the different Christian confessions. None the less, we can no longer conceal from ourselves the fact that the industrialization of society itself sometimes takes on the form of a religion of the world economy which also prefigures future developments. Nor are we so surprised by this. From Max Weber we have learnt how capitalism and industrialization were to a large extent inspired by Protestantism. The doctrine of predestination, in particular, served to legitimate the striving for commercial success which characterizes modern industrial societies. The undeniable progress in science and technology has allowed the consequences of this development to grow into an independent power over which we are no longer fully in control. The inner law governing developments in industry and technology determines our destiny to an ever-increasing degree and we Europeans are confronted with the problem of hardly knowing any longer how to respond to this. The same holds true for the United States of America.

Over time this system has, in fact, led to an increasingly high standard of living in the industrialized countries, although it originally led directly to acute impoverishment and the development of an industrial proletariat. This was what Marx and Engels so vigorously denounced, especially in Great Britain which paradigmatically represented both the new machine technology and the destitution of those it rendered unemployed. With the industrialization of the economy, entirely new social tensions arose which presented the social policy of the modern state with new challenges. In general, it led to an increasing regulation of social relations, something which became even more inevitable with the introduction of the welfare state. Thus, for example, the regulation of the struggle between employers and employees led to the introduction of negotiating procedures which, to a large extent, are still operative today. Prevention of the abuse of the unemployed and the provision of benefits to those who lose their jobs have become fundamental challenges which society and the economy have to meet. An army of civil servants has grown up and with it a rampant bureaucracy and a concomitant transformation of our entire way of life. The senseless destruction wrought by the terrible wars of this century has repeatedly stimulated the technological revolution through the process of 'reconstruction' of what was destroyed. Despite all the ravages and devastation of war, prosperity in the industrialized countries has continued to grow, encouraging the emergence of the new concept of 'quality of life'. On a global scale, however, the gulf between rich and poor countries continues to widen all the time. In particular, in our own industrialized countries the traditional basis of the family and its unifying influence on society has been weakened. This is the case throughout the various social strata, from the aristocracy and the bourgeoisie through to all the other classes which constitute modern society. The notion of 'service', too, has to a large extent lost the dimension of honour which was once associated with it, and which also exerted an influence on the Christian Church and its continued vitality.

However, there are also other religions and other great civilizations whose origins are quite unconnected to the world of Puritanism, even if they too are touched, and increasingly touched, by the 'religion of the world economy'. We do not know whether the people who make up this larger part of humanity will be able successfully to defend their own religiously grounded social and cultural world under the thin and seemingly transparent industrial skin within which, to a greater or lesser extent, we all now live. Although what we term the Enlightenment was a process which took place in the modern period of Christian Europe, we really need to think further back into the past. We are gradually beginning to realize that it is only relatively recently that great ancient cultures such as those of China or of India have begun to enter into dialogue with the later European Enlightenment. Once we ask why it is that the Christian Enlightenment proved victorious in Europe rather than other areas or civilizations of the globe, we have already taken an important step towards understanding the historical destiny of the West. Even in the very beginnings of the West we encounter an original Enlightenment which clearly documents the self-conscious reflection upon human speech and language. In this context it is not without significance that the background to the modern Enlightenment is described as a 'Renaissance', a name which refers back to that origin with the re-birth of Greek and Roman antiquity. None the less, we must learn to think on a broad scale if, under the title 'Religion and the Religions', we seek to reflect on the destiny of humankind and to consider what the future may bring. We must properly ask ourselves whether other religious and cultural worlds can provide any response to the universality of the scientific Enlightenment and its consequences which is different from the 'religion' of the global economy. Will the world, perhaps, be able to discover an answer which, as yet, can only be guessed at?

I do not venture to express an opinion on this question. However, I am convinced that the development of modern science and technology, and so, too, of the world economy, possesses irreversible consequences for the fate of humankind on this planet. It is far from my intention to suggest that the path along which we have travelled from Greek antiquity through to Christianity will extend, in some mysterious way, into a broad and promising future. Nor do I wish to encourage the hope that everything can once again be brought back into equilibrium. The destructive powers which technology has placed in human hands – weapons technology in general and atomic technology in particular – have, for the first time, made the survival of humankind on this planet into a real issue. What process of critical recovery of the past through social and political education would be required for us to bring about a new equilibrium between nature and culture?

It is not fortuitous that we should raise this question, which possesses such a complex and far-reaching background. The adaptive capacity of the species *Homo sapiens*, although common to all human patterns of life and cultural formations, is not of a uniform nature. If we think, for example, of Far Eastern cultures, such as China and Japan, it is clear that these peoples, along a completely different path from our own, have developed highly prized virtues such as self-discipline, energy and hard work which help enormously in the task of assimilating European science and technology. Down even to the tips of their dextrous fingers, they seem almost predestined for the precision mechanics of the technological world. At the same time, they have long pursued their own independent direction in domains outside of modern industry and technology, resulting in completely different achievements in fields such as architecture and landscape gardening, and in calligraphy and graphics. Moreover, in their own religions they have remained bound to a much greater extent to ancestral tradition and familial structure. This provides the basis for a very different conception of human rights from that which is valid in the West. For example, there is nothing which corresponds to the importance placed on death in European countries.

The participants in this discussion, above all the principal speakers, Vattimo and Derrida, have sought to engage with the problem of religion as it is encountered in the context of the European Enlightenment and from the perspective of our European culture. However, if the undogmatic concern with religious experience which has governed this discussion is to be thought through from a global perspective, it should be possible and indeed necessary to extend this problematic to include other world religions. Whenever it is a question of experience, we should always begin from where we are. None the less, even a cursory glance at the other world religions shows us that there is one thing which seems never to be wholly absent. Namely, the ubiquitous knowledge of one's own death and at the same time the impossibility of the actual experience of death. This is the exemplary characteristic of what it is to be human. The knowledge of one's own limit or end is something which no other living creature possesses.

We need only call to mind the Greek tragedy of Prometheus which is traditionally attributed to Aeschylus. Here, in mythical form, the dramatist seeks to grasp what differentiates human beings from all other living creatures not only in terms of the knowledge of death as such but in the capacity to know in advance the exact day and hour of one's own passing. Prometheus, the divine symbolic figure who represents knowledge of the future as such, is presented in the drama as the person who disguises from human beings the knowledge of the day and hour of their death. He identifies this, rather than the gift of fire, as his principal service to mankind. For man is hereby enabled, through work, enthusiasm and delight in the future, to overcome the inertia and lack of a future which had previously paralysed him. To reinterpret the myth of the theft of fire in this way required an enormous conceptual advance. The possession of fire is now understood not merely as an enrichment of the technological capacity of human beings, but as something which goes far beyond this: it is conceived as the ability to plan and to exercise skill in general. It is clear that this dramatic treatment of the Prometheus myth could only derive from a very advanced stage of enlightenment, and for this reason doubts have repeatedly been raised concerning Aeschylus' authorship. What we learn from the play is that the impenetrable mystery and uncanniness of death accompanies, like a dowry, that capacity to conceive the future which distinguishes human beings from other living creatures, and that this is a dangerous gift. It seems that, in anticipating what is to come, we are irresistibly led to try to think beyond the certain fact of death. Thus it is that human beings are the only living creatures who are known to bury their dead.

In burying the dead we seek to hold on to those who are no longer living and to venerate them through cults as still preserved in memory. Knowledge of all the votive offerings which went into the grave alongside the deceased remains a source of astonishment to anyone who is familiar with the early history of humankind. An entire ship was found in Oslo, and everywhere, as if in preparation for a life beyond, we find the bestowal of gifts without any real intention of future use. Rather, this is a form of symbolic action, like that other undisputed characteristic of humankind, speech. Perhaps the two are inseparable from one another: the attempt to think beyond death and the miracle of language, which can allow something to be brought before us even in its absence. Schelling once observed that 'The anxiety of life drives the creature outside of its own centre.' Human beings are presented with the task of sustaining such an existence, and it is this anxiety before death which Heidegger characterized as anticipation or running towards death <*Vorlaufen zum Tode*>.

Without doubt, the shared background for our discussion of religion here in Capri was provided by the search for God in the thought of Heidegger. The two principal speakers saw themselves confronted by the same task. On the one hand, both recognize that we need to be free of all dogmatism, above all that dogmatism which refuses to see in religion anything other than the deception or self-deception of human beings. Just as decisively, both agree that no matter to what extent we recognize the urgency of religion, there can be no return to the doctrines of the Church. On the other hand, however, the transformation of Greek metaphysics into a form of natural theology no longer appears sustainable in an age of Enlightenment. Both positions clearly have Heidegger's 'overcoming' or extrication from Western metaphysics in view. None the less, we can ask whether the problem which we have characterized in this way has really been resolved. Perhaps we are concerned here with a problem which cannot be solved through human reflection. This is something which Heidegger himself in the end came to recognize: 'Only a God can save us.'

The conspicuous thing about Vattimo's contribution is his particular concern with the problem of return <*Rückkehr*>. Clearly 'return' cannot mean a return to metaphysics or to any sort of ecclesiastical doctrine. In opposition to all hasty proclamations of salvation, both speakers wish to take the non-comprehensibility of death seriously and for this reason will find the answers contained in the promises of religion incompatible with the demands of rationality. Vattimo himself emphasizes that the phenomenon of a return is deeply embedded in religious experience. It is not for nothing that one speaks of a 'conversion' (*Bekehrung*: a turning around). The triumphal appropriation of the world which each of us experiences as a child is preserved through the acquisition of our mother tongue. This is, indeed, an extraordinary experience which we all undergo, but at the same time it is not without risk, since ultimately each of us must encounter the limits of such appropriation or possession. The tremendous encouragement to thought which is elicited through the acquisition of language may well awaken a triumphant feeling of unrestricted possession, but this deluded conception of omnipotence is unavoidably frustrated by the experience of pain and failure and miscarried hopes. The task of avoiding dogmatic hastiness always gets caught up once again in the mystery of death, something which cannot be relieved by any homesickness for the simple faith of childhood. Nobody will ever know the true beginning of their true existence. It must always be a matter of experience, instruction and the investigation of one's own powers, at the end of which there lies an uncrossable border. It would be presumptuous to seek to argue away this original story of one's own childhood and of the formation of one's own experience. This account belongs to what it is to be human, a being whose form of life is not pre-established. Certainly, it makes a difference if someone is introduced into the rituals of religious life when they are in the process of acquiring their first orientation in the world. However, no one is spared confrontation with the claims, and indeed the limits, of the Enlightenment, even if this takes place only with the final emancipation which comes with 'maturity'.

It seems almost unavoidable that our consciousness of our own existence should not only open up new horizons of memory and remembrance – an awareness of where we come from and how we came to be – but that it should also open up a horizon of futurity in which, even towards the end of one's life, expectation or hope strives to win out over faintheartedness. Nature scarcely allows any human being to consent willingly to departure from this life and the struggle against death is sustained as long as strength remains. To this extent, the image of the crucified God, which Christianity opposes to all other representations of the beyond or of a possible future life, appears to impose a demand on us which exceeds what is humanly possible. If there is one thing which characterizes life in all its unwavering vigour, it is the inexhaustibility of the will to live which never ceases to desire a future. Can there be such a thing as acceptance of death? Does this not go beyond our human powers? Here we begin to see what it means that our cultural life is dominated by the Gospel of the sacrificial death of the Son of Man who is also the Son of God, which presents the true redemption, superior to all other promises of salvation.

Vattimo's contribution requires a close study of the literature given in the references. This is something which I am no longer in a position to do. However, in so far as I have been able to derive instruction from the text, things look like this: I understand that he wishes to avoid metaphysics and that theology which continues to make use of metaphysics. I also understand that he considers the work of Levinas, to whom he is otherwise very close, to be insufficient here in so far as Levinas merely seeks to underline the finitude and creatureliness of our consciousness of our own existence. Clearer to me is the way in which Vattimo has presented the idea of incarnation as something unavoidable, situating it within Heidegger's innovative analysis of the metaphysical concept of time (and of its overcoming). Vattimo wishes to free himself from metaphysics by incorporating the turn towards positivity which is found in the work of the later Schelling. On this account, it is necessary to recognize the role of myth, even if, according to Schelling, this role is ultimately to be established through recourse to the message of Christianity. Here, as always with Schelling, it is necessary to relate his position to Hegel's conception of the problem, in particular to Hegel's characterization of the relationship between religion and philosophy as a stage on the way to absolute knowledge. At the end of the *Phenomenology of Spirit* and in the early sketches for the *Encyclopaedia* it gradually becomes clear what form the relationship between religion and art is to take. The transition from the stage of representation to that of the concept cannot be made without art. Here we clearly have to do with the mystery of 'art as beauty'. Hegel identifies the real achievement of religion in its capacity to break free from everything particular, thereby allowing the universal to appear in any content whatsoever. In this way, beautiful art, as 'art', achieves the same thing which philosophy realizes in the universality of the concept. What is intended by both is 'truth'. In paragraph 562 of Hegel's *Encyclopaedia*, we read:

> As regards the close connection between art and the various religions, we can observe that beautiful art is only to be found in those religions in which spirituality has become concrete and free but has not yet been elevated to an absolute principle ... This is connected to the further and higher observation that the introduction of art already signifies the decline of the stage of religion which remains bound to sensible externality ... The sublime divinity which is expressed through the work of art both liberates and satisfies the genius of the artist and the spectator ... the apprehension and the consciousness of spirit's freedom is attained and

preserved. Beautiful art has realized in its own sphere the same as philosophy – the purification of spirit from bondage.

Hegel maintains that true objectivity can only be realized in the medium of thought. But does this represent a limitation on harmonious art? Schelling's further step towards positivity is perhaps a step beyond the absoluteness of reflective spirit.

Derrida's contribution starts out with reference to Kant, and it is clear that Derrida follows the doctrine of the '*parerga*' from Kant's essay on religion. Religious doctrine is indeed beyond our rational comprehension, but it is not incompatible with the concept of freedom which forms the basis of Kant's practical philosophy. Derrida's second point of reference is a repetition of his ingenious play with the concept of the *chora*. In this context, at the risk of being charged with metaphysics, I too can begin to grasp the idea that the *chora*, as that which provides place and space, does not in the least determine what occupies that space. In this way, the concept of *chora* can be applied unproblematically to the neo-Platonic concept of the One and of the divine. The way in which it is used in the *Timaeus* can also appropriately be understood as an expression of the complete indeterminacy which characterizes the relationship between noetic and sensible being. Although this relationship is wholly indeterminate it must, none the less, be unconditionally presupposed. Both numerical calculation and Euclidean geometry are truths which we grasp. At the same time, we cannot grasp how it is that there is a real world and how it is that the world is fashioned in such a way that it corresponds to these truths. The concept of *chora* takes up a Pythagorean heritage. In this it reflects the enormous progress of contemporary mathematics at the time of Plato, which had developed to the point of the Platonic doctrine of regular bodies. At the same time, in this context Plato simply relates a long history of the divine demiurge which established the order of the world and, despite all its evident disorder, regulates all worldly events. Here it is possible to draw upon the structure of the elements, the most recent human science, the geometry of the triangle and the study of stereometry in which, so to speak, one sees once again an approximation to the perfect sphere of being. This is an ingenious game, but in truth nothing more.

Outside of such enthusiastic play with myths, Plato himself

does not provide any definitive statement concerning the relationship between the singular and the universal. The concept of participation, the famed *methexis*, always means the participation of the ideas with one another, as these constitute the *logos*. The participation of the individual in the universal is presupposed as something self-explanatory. For this reason, no more exact account is provided by Plato. This is the case, for example, in the *Phaedrus*. Aristotle was the first to attempt to grasp conceptually – in terms of primary and secondary substances – what Plato presupposed as self-explanatory and as beyond the domain of conceptual thinking. Subsequently, in the age of scholasticism, this led to the dispute over universals and to the establishment of nominalism as the key epistemological concept of the modern period.

To draw our discussion together, both participants are clearly in agreement that neither metaphysics nor theology is able to provide a scientific answer to the fundamental question as to why there is something rather than nothing. But now it is time for the other participants to speak, and I open myself to new reflection.

Translated by Jason Gaiger

Cultural Memory in the Present

Jacques Derrida and Gianni Vattimo, eds., *Religion*

Niklas Luhmann, *Love as Passion: The Codification of Intimacy*

Andrew Baruch Wachtel, *Making a Nation, Breaking a Nation: Literature and Cultural Politics in Yugoslavia*

Jacques Derrida, *Monolingualism of the Other; or, The Prosthesis of Origin*